Today Sardines Are
Not for Sale

Today Sardines Are Not for Sale

A Street Protest in Occupied Paris

Paula Schwartz

OXFORD
UNIVERSITY PRESS

OXFORD
UNIVERSITY PRESS

Oxford University Press is a department of the University of Oxford. It furthers
the University's objective of excellence in research, scholarship, and education
by publishing worldwide. Oxford is a registered trade mark of Oxford University
Press in the UK and certain other countries.

Published in the United States of America by Oxford University Press
198 Madison Avenue, New York, NY 10016, United States of America.

Library of Congress Cataloging-in-Publication Data
Names: Schwartz, Paula L., author.
Title: Today sardines are not for sale : a street protest
in occupied Paris / Paula Schwartz.
Other titles: Street protest in occupied Paris
Description: New York : Oxford University Press, [2020] | Includes index.
Identifiers: LCCN 2019043028 (print) | LCCN 2019043029 (ebook) |
ISBN 9780190681548 (hardback) | ISBN 9780190681562 (epub)
Subjects: LCSH: Paris (France)—History—1940–1944. |
Demonstrations—France—Paris—History—20th century. |
Housewives—Political activity—France—Paris. |
World War, 1939–1945—Food supply—France—Paris. |
World War, 1939–1945—Underground movements—France—Paris. |
Parti communiste français. | Collective memory—France—Paris. |
France—History—German occupation, 1940–1945.
Classification: LCC D762.P3 S388 2020 (print) |
LCC D762.P3 (ebook) | DDC 940.53/44361—dc23
LC record available at https://lccn.loc.gov/2019043028
LC ebook record available at https://lccn.loc.gov/2019043029

1 3 5 7 9 8 6 4 2
Printed by Sheridan Books, Inc., United States of America

CONTENTS

ACKNOWLEDGMENTS

My first debt of gratitude goes to the scholars whom I admire most: Rod Kedward, Dominique Veillon, Laurent Douzou, Arlette Farge, and Jean-Pierre Azéma. They have inspired and supported this project over the long haul. I doubt they are aware of the consequential roles they have played in this project from afar.

The people involved in the Buci affair whose oral testimony is cited in this book are no longer here to see it come to fruition. I hope to have captured their truths and their sentiments. Their legacy far surpasses their presence on these pages.

Miranda Pollard, who gave unsparingly of her time and expertise, is in a class by herself. Her friendship, humor, and wisdom sustained me over the course of this journey. She knew how to dispense just the right doses of encouragement and compassion, discipline and fear.

For their warm home and warm hearts, sparkling minds and sparkling beverages, I thank Anne Boigeol and Jean-Yves Caro, and André Montagne and Pauline Montagne.

Judy Barringer, Marie Bazille, Nancy Coiner, Claudine Ducastel, Rosalie Fisher, Janet Horne, Harriet Jackson, Mary-Claude Morice, Shanny Peer, Gail Radford, Karen Remmler, Danièle Voldman, and Ashley Waddell have been beacons in the long night. Their contributions transcend the scope of this book.

Denis Peschanski, André Tollet, Cécile Lesieur, and Jean-Pierre Vittori, among others, graciously directed me to witnesses and interviewees. I thank them all for their help and their friendship.

Carol Nees and Sally Howland gave valuable feedback at the earliest stage of the manuscript, when they would rather have waited for the movie version.

Gregory T. Woolston drew the expert maps and diagram.

In Vermont, my thanks to Jacob Safari for his technical prowess and to Catharine Wright for her fun and writerly advice. Mary Brevda, for whom hope springs eternal, deserves special mention for her abiding patience and support.

Steve Jensen provided invaluable life-support at the end stage of this process.

Colleagues at the Five College Women's Studies Research Center at Mount Holyoke College in Hadley, Massachusetts, critiqued and encouraged this project in its initial phase. My warmest thanks to them and to then-director Gail Hornstein for her hospitality and support.

The GDT (Danièle Voldman, Fabrice Virgili, François Rouquet, and Luc Capdevila), Henry Rousso, and the entire team at the Institut d'histoire du temps present (IHTP) provided welcome, camaraderie, and a shared sense of purpose throughout my term as a visiting researcher in 1998–1999, and for the many years thereafter.

Funding from various sources made it possible for me to live and work at the same time. My profound gratitude to the Fulbright Foundation, Lois B. Watson, and the Lois B. Watson Endowment for their generous support.

Middlebury College provided invaluable research and travel support over many years. The Ada Howe Kent Foundation and the Middlebury College Rohatyn Center for Global Affairs, directed by Timi Mayer, afforded me the benefit of research assistance on numerous occasions. Irene Estefanía González did a particularly remarkable job of tracking down obscure sources. I also wish to acknowledge my colleagues in the Lois B. '51 and J. Harvey Watson

Department of French and Francophone studies for their friendship and their support, of varying sorts at various times, over the course of our shared adventure.

I thank the archivists and staffs at the institutions named in the bibliography, especially Chantal Tourtier de Bonazzi and Patricia Gillet of the Archives nationales, with whom I worked the most closely at the beginning of this project. Pascal Raimbault, also of the Archives nationales, deserves special thanks for his extraordinary help at the conclusion of this project. I also wish to acknowledge the contributions of CG1 Étienne Chaillet of the Dépôt centrale d'archives de la justice militaire, Leblanc, France; and Madame Christine Diatta, archivist of the Délégation à la mémoire et à l'information historique at the Ministère de la défense. Finally, my appreciation extends to the directors, past and present, of the archives of the Préfecture de police in Paris, where this project began and ended. They acted tough but always found a workaround. I owe a special debt of gratitude to Nathalie Minart of the Service de la mémoire et des affaires culturelles, Cabinet du préfet de police, for her generous assistance at the newly transformed and user-friendly archives of the Paris police.

My deep thanks go to Nancy Toff of Oxford University Press for her guidance of this project, and to the anonymous readers of the proposal and manuscript for suggestions that saved me from myself and helped me to improve the final product.

Finally, it is my hope that this book will benefit new generations of students and readers. May the story in these pages also serve as a reminder to stay informed and to remain vigilant.

INTRODUCTION

This is a book about a short-lived event. An epiphenomenon. A human interest story. Or so it appeared at the time.

On Mother's Day, May 31, 1942, a group of women stormed a small grocery store at the intersection of the rue de Buci and the rue de Seine, the heart of a central Parisian marketplace.[1] It was a Sunday morning, the busiest shopping time of the week. When a woman emerged from the crowd urging shoppers to serve themselves, several others followed her lead, snatching cans of sardines that were stacked on display inside a shop and throwing them to the crowd. A skirmish ensued when the grocer and his assistant intervened, grabbing several of the women, who became trapped inside. As members of the crowd rushed to the aid of the women, neighborhood police responded to the melee. It was then that shots rang out from the crowd. Several police officers were hit. One died on the spot and another would later succumb to his wounds. From the moment of assembly to the conclusion of the chase, the entire incident had lasted some twenty minutes.

For the Vichy authorities, the shooting deaths qualified the incident as a crime against the state; for the German occupiers, it was an act of terrorist violence. The result was a wave of arrests, imprisonments, trials, and deaths that followed over the coming weeks and months. For the Communist underground, which had organized the event to protest food shortages, "the women's demonstration of the rue de Buci," as it came to be known, was a heroic act of people's justice. Within minutes of the incident, a legend

André Fougeron's *Les Parisiennes au marché* (Parisian Women at the Market) (1948) is a stunning example of socialist realism, which first emerged in the Soviet Union in the interwar period. Fougeron, who joined the French Communist Party in 1939, was known for his commitment to art with a conscience (*engagé*) featuring scenes of everyday life and work. Specialty shops and market stalls like the one represented here were not the target of organized food protests such as the one on the rue de Buci. The PCF avoided antagonizing small shopkeepers, whom they hoped to mobilize into profession- or trade-specific popular committees under the umbrella of the Front national, a broad-based Communist party movement. Not surprisingly, the project appears to have been unsuccessful. Small independent merchants were more likely recruits for the right, as the politics of the 1950s would show.

In 1948, the year *Les Parisiennes au marché* was shown, shortages remained but French markets were slowly rebounding from the dire scarcity of the war years. Fish was once again on the menu.

Photo credit: Yves Bresson / Musée d'art moderne et contemporain de Saint-Etienne Métropole. Author credit: ADAGP.

began to take shape that would survive, in various forms, in French Communist memory.

The demonstration at the Buci marketplace had no lasting impact on the war in Europe, in France, or even in Paris. It had neither the strategic impact of the battle of Stalingrad, the moral clout of de Gaulle's call to arms, nor the popular exuberance of the insurrection of Paris. In fact, for the public authorities and citizens who deplored the unrest, the looting, and the violence, it had the opposite effect. Had it not been for the death of two policemen at the time of the incident, few would have taken note of the event in the short term. Had it not been for the wave of repression that followed, the demonstration might have been no more than a human interest story, soon consigned to oblivion. Nor was this particular demonstration unique; other market disturbances and similar demonstrations took place in occupied Paris, like the one on the avenue Ledru-Rollin, for example, about which little is known, or the one on the rue Daguerre that followed one month later. Even the human toll of the incident was sadly banal at a time when imprisonment, executions, and deportations, if never ordinary, were not uncommon. "A brief scuffle of no importance" was how a self-described "ear-witness" characterized the demonstration. He had been tending his cheese shop on the nearby rue de Seine when the violence erupted. And the cheese merchant seemed to have a point—although it must be noted that forty years later, he remembered it just the same.

For all its apparent banality, the demonstration on the rue de Buci turns out to be hugely important—if not necessarily in all the ways its organizers intended. As a protest action emblematic of its time and of its type, the Buci affair presents an extraordinary opportunity to understand some signal features of everyday life in Paris under German occupation. It also reveals the inner workings of the underground Communist movement, from the coordination of its political and paramilitary wings to the deft deployment of illusion and symbol, words and images, by party propagandists. We can see, too, the roles of the Vichy government, the French police, and the German occupation authorities in the elaboration of a system of repression that had its own procedures and its own courts. Yet the Buci affair was as exceptional as it was emblematic. It marked a turning point in the escalation of public protest and

The Buci-Seine market in January 1996. *Photos by Megan Tully Maddern.*

The rue de Buci on May 31, 2016. A series of different shops occupied the site after the closure of the original Eco supermarket. *Photo by author.*

The corner of the rue de Buci and the rue de Seine on May 31, 2018. A chain bakery-café now occupies the former site of the Eco supermarket. *Photo by author.*

the repression of protest, the very moment when the authorities began to recognize the political potential of women. Throughout the story, gender emerges as the fundamental organizing principle: activists and planners considered gender in the formulation of political strategies and the division of political labor between men and women; French and German authorities practiced a gendered politics of repression. From the staging of the demonstration and the prosecution of the offenders to the recuperation of its meaning, gender was deployed by all parties in unusual and surprising ways. For all their emblematic quality, then, the incident and its repercussions were nonetheless extraordinary. But perhaps the single most extraordinary thing about the Buci affair is the very fact that it is knowable in the first place.

The "women's demonstration of the rue de Buci" caught my attention early on: it is referenced in the oral and written testimony of resisters, in the underground and "legal" or state-censored press, and in postwar accounts of women and the Resistance that I had been working on for years. Yet despite the frequent allusions to the story, it remained elusive in the official record. Because I was interested in learning how women and gender functioned in the underground, I was led inexorably to the clandestine organizations of the French Communist Party, the only political group to mobilize women around so-called "women's" issues during the war years. Through the women's popular committees, party activists sought to harness the political potential of women, and of housewives and mothers in particular, by way of their empty shopping baskets. A key method they employed was the staging of demonstrations in markets and market streets such as the rue de Buci in central Paris. My searches converged on this single event because it lay at the very heart of my central research question: What was specific to the role of women in the French Resistance?

By the time I was ensconced in the contemporary section of the Archives nationales in Paris, the demonstration of the rue de Buci had yet to surface in any of the documents I had consulted, there or elsewhere. It was the mid-1980s and access to the papers of the war years was still strictly controlled. Academic specialists had to produce compelling reasons to justify a request for permission to access classified documents. Well-established French historians had to vouch for such requests. The archives of the Vichy government and the German occupying authorities were by law closed to the public for fifty years after the events. Documents that revealed names or personal information—that is, most of them—were sealed for a hundred years to allow for the easing of fratricidal tensions and the demise of principals and survivors whose lives could be affected by the release of sensitive information. The century-long black hole of history also protected the perpetrators, of course: moles, bureaucrats, police, judges, and ordinary citizens who had denounced their neighbors as "terrorists" or Jews. At the time, many archival series from 1940 to 1944 had not even been dusted off and properly inventoried. Existing guides and registers, themselves also closed to researchers, were insufficiently detailed or incomplete. Yet for the persistent and well-credentialed scholar, special dispensations to view sensitive material from the war years, the precious *dérogations*, could be accorded on a case-by-case basis.

I presented my case in person to the *conservatrice en chef* (chief archivist), Madame de Bonazzi. In those years, it was the archivist and not the researcher who consulted the classified registers to locate the series or files that pertained to a researcher's subject. Seated in her office in the Hôtel de Rohan, a former eighteenth-century estate turned property of the Republic, I recounted as much as I knew about the demonstration, but it was not enough. Madame de Bonazzi could not locate any relevant materials in the moldy entrails of the building. In order to do so, she needed more. She needed names. It was a vicious circle, a catch-22. In order to unearth the documents, I needed to supply the names of participants who had been arrested in the demonstration, but in order to supply their names, I needed the documents. The vicious circle had to be broken, which is how I landed at the Préfecture de police.

Once again I found myself seated before the keeper of the archives, this time a high-ranking police official. He presided behind a big desk in an imposing office at central police headquarters that was very different from Madame de Bonazzi's modest sanctuary at the dilapidated but charming Hôtel de Rohan. Monsieur le Commissaire heard my case and then, to my surprise, made his own. Why should such papers be released? What good would it do? Why were Americans exhuming long-buried cadavers in France? In any event, he said, it was unlikely that there were any police records of the event in question. Were such papers to exist, then they were not for me to see. Who was to say how the police conducted themselves in such an instance? he continued. Who was to say that those same police were not also resisters themselves? It was then that I espied the tiny red lapel pin, the discreet but telling Légion d'honneur, the most prestigious order of merit awarded for service to the nation. The *commissaire* went on. It had been a painful period; like many of his countrymen, he explained in a fleeting moment of self-revelation, he had lost his brother during the war years.

My prospects appeared rather bleak. As I leaned forward to press a point, my hand grazed the edge of his desk. M. le Commissaire recoiled in horror; unknowingly I had transgressed the invisible barrier that separated the power of the state from a lowly scholar of another gender, another generation, another country. I took my cue from his movement and drew back my hand. As for his musings about the role of the French police, I could only renew my initial plea: let the documents speak for themselves.

The bureaucratic hazing process left me thinking that I would have to take another tack. But to my surprise, Monsieur le Commissaire had been all bluster; permission to view the police file was granted shortly after our meeting. The report was slim, but it named names. Finding a roster of individuals who had been arrested in connection with the affair from May 31 to June 4, 1942, made it possible, at long last, to locate the complete and voluminous documentary record at the Archives nationales, of which the original police file was but a tiny part. I had waited nearly five years, but it was worth the wait. Thanks to this extraordinary record, the Buci affair is now knowable to an unprecedented extent for an underground resistance operation in this period.

Knowable, but not transparent. Who were the people who got away? What did the incident look like from the perspective of the grocer's assistant who intercepted one of the protesters inside the shop? What did the bystanders say and do? Who was the mysterious woman in a Basque beret reported by an onlooker? *Was* there a woman in a beret? Some elements of the story can be elucidated. Others remain unknowable, or unknowable to me now.

Having such sources is an incomparable joy to the researcher. But the delight of discovery is mitigated by the knowledge that every remaining trace of the underground movement exists because something went terribly wrong. A clandestine movement, by its very definition and in the interests of its own survival, leaves no paper trail. For security reasons, membership rolls, instructions, messages, organizational charts, and position papers generated by underground activists were to be destroyed—if and when such documents ever existed in the first place. In some instances, papers have survived because they were seized by the police in raids, searches, and arrests. In this instance as in others, it was the authorities themselves who generated the written record, one comprising police reports, interrogations, testimony, and official correspondence. Thus the existence of any documentary record at all stands as eloquent testimony to the risks, dangers, and fragility of the resistance enterprise. And when those records emanate from the authorities, in their words alone, under conditions that they alone controlled, the testimony of witnesses and survivors is all the more critical. Living memories, however, are also contingent. They can be as fragile as the crumbling documents in a crusty old file.

When I met the people who had experienced the event firsthand—Madeleine Marzin, Maté Houet, the Berthelet sisters, and Félix Barthélemy, the cheese merchant—they made the Buci affair truly palpable to someone who had been born into a postwar world on another continent. For me, it was history. For activists and bystanders, it was past experience that was still powerfully present because it had been life-altering. Their testimonies shed light on aspects of the case that the official record leaves obscure. This brings me to another, unique aspect of doing historical work on the Resistance and Occupation in the century that followed. The version of the story you are about to read has been shaped by the extant record at the moment of collection. It occupies the confluence of two eminently mutable repositories: the official archival record, once sealed, then restricted, and now accessible to researchers; and the oral testimony of surviving participants and witnesses collected in the 1980s and 1990s. It is—or was—a brief and transient moment when both the papers and the principals could speak to the past. That the papers and the people could finally converge suggested the possibility of a conversation. It would be possible to confront the records of the case with the memories of surviving participants, to tease out the unsaid or the understated, to corroborate or correct; in short, to foster a dialogue.

That dialogue, however, could only be indirect or mediated by the researcher. At the time, I had taken an oath of confidentiality that barred me from sharing information from the files or revealing identities, so my questioning of interviewees had to be careful. I also had a commitment to honor the confidences accorded me by the living, who might reveal a detail or an impression or a sentiment that I was asked not to share. The convergence of those archives and those memories is this story, a representation born of a particular moment in time when both the papers and the people could enter into conversation, if only on the page.

In the future there will be more papers rescued from attics and basements, recovered from the personal effects of passing witnesses, liberated from the imposed silence of the fifty- or hundred-year moratoria. At the same time there are fewer and fewer survivors of the period. The most precious, most perishable sources diminish with time. No product can be isolated from the conditions of its production, and this version of the Buci story is no exception. That ephemeral moment offered a unique opportunity to bring the written and oral fragments together, to craft a certain version of the story at a given time and place.

The sheer volume and minute details of the written and oral record lend themselves handily to the genre of microhistory, the examination and interpretation of a single, emblematic event. A tiny nugget of experience, the event encapsules in miniature many features of the larger story of which it is an integral part. Exploding the event produces a kaleidoscopic effect, enabling us to view it from the inside out and from many different angles. Once recombined, the resulting fragments produce a new narrative, one that can be every bit as instructive as the grand sweep of "history from above." That microhistory has proven fruitful is evidenced by an impressive corpus of impeccably executed studies of the small. A case of mistaken identity and an abandoned wife in sixteenth-century France, a medieval cheesemaker's idiosyncratic view of the cosmos, a mass movement to kill cats in an eighteenth-century Parisian community: eminent historians of Europe have adopted the microhistorical approach to tell us stories larger than the stories themselves.[2] For many years, microhistory was the province of medievalists and historians of early modern Europe, for whom the history of everyday life proved most elusive. Ordinary people left few traces in the grand narrative of the archival record.

Ironically, the fragmentary documentary record of the war years has much in common with that of earlier historical periods. It is not so much that the French and German authorities took little interest in the population; on the contrary, police reports, court records, and prison registries abound. Departmental prefects monitored the disposition of their populations and filed monthly reports about it. But a generation of postwar researchers came and went before the archives fully opened their doors to them. Newspaper collections survived the war, but the legal press was censored. Moreover, resisters committed very little to paper at the time for their own security. It stands to reason, of course, that a disciplined underground whose very modus operandi was invisibility would leave no traces. That leaves people, the bearers of their own stories. Some resisters and survivors, overwhelmingly men, began to record their experiences at war's end. It was not until the 1980s that women picked up the pen in increasing numbers. Then there are the permanent silences. Alas, many others had paid for their activism with their lives; they did not survive the war to tell us what they could not or did not commit to paper.

That is the half-empty part of the glass. And it is what makes the other half all the more precious. When at long last two towering folders of reports, court records, and witness testimony were delivered to my desk at the Archives nationales, I was thunderstruck but ecstatic. It would take many weeks and months to make my way through the documents. According to then-prevailing rules, that meant reading the files in a designated room with a monitor sitting across from me at all times. Sensitive files required confidentiality and special handling. No pens, no reference materials, no bags; photocopies were out of the question. Armed with only a pencil, I copied like a medieval scribe, day after day and week after week, under the watchful scrutiny of the archivist's staff.

What I saw toppled all my assumptions about the women's demonstration of the rue de Buci. I gasped in amazement when I discovered that it had not been a women's demonstration at all—in fact, men had played a critical role in the drama. The archival record revealed a spectacle that was in fact a careful orchestration of both men's and women's parts. Political tasks were divided along gender lines in a neatly synchronized interplay of complementary roles. Once exhumed from the archival coffers, the original trove of documents provided clues that led to the discovery of still more files, more court cases, more repression. And so the story expanded from a presumed footnote to a chapter, from a chapter to this book.

By the spring and summer of 1942, public support for the regime was beginning to ebb. Pierre Laval, the prime minister known for his enthusiastic collaboration with the German occupiers, returned to power in February. The following April, Communist paramilitary groups were formally constituted as the FTP. Conflicts between occupiers and occupied were on the rise. People were standing in line for hours on end for very little food, and empty bellies made for a restive populace. It was in this context of heightened tensions that the demonstration on the rue de Buci was conceived and executed.

The terrible consequences of the demonstration ensured its promotion to "affair" status. Initial representations of the event had everything to do with how the demonstration would be prosecuted in French and German courts. Sexual difference infused policies of repression, which in turn accounted for the gender-specific fates of men and women. The itineraries of two protagonists of the affair, a women's organizer and "ringleader" of the demonstration and a high school student turned urban guerrilla, are emblematic of this division of labor.

The afterlife of the Buci affair stretches into the twentieth and twenty-first centuries. Competing versions of the event endured for many years. What became of the demonstrators and how their individual and collective legacies were shaped both informed and reflected subsequent memory of the event. For some it had become a cause célèbre; for others it was a painful reminder of suffering and loss. Ultimately, the demonstration on the rue de Buci served as a template for a future generation of postwar protesters.

We begin with a narrative of the demonstration, pieced together from oral and written testimony, police reports, and court records. A network of families and friends, neighbors and coworkers, men and women provided the cast for the drama. Who they were, how they were connected, and the nature of their respective roles permit us to analyze the event from the inside out. Once this composite picture is complete, it will then be possible to expose the many moving parts that drove the event and shaped its memory in the years that followed.

THE EVENT

The "women's demonstration of the rue de Buci," as it was dubbed
in literature and in memory, was not a demonstration in the sense
we think of today, with big crowds, flashy banners, megaphones,
slogans, and attendance figures disputed by organizers and police. It did not bring the city to a standstill, impede traffic, or cause
services to be suspended. But it did "demonstrate," or exhibit, the
mounting tensions between shoppers and suppliers, citizens and
public authorities. Demonstrations are deeply anchored in French
political culture; they were a distinctive feature of the Popular Front
period, when many resisters got their political education and experience. When the Vichy government came to power in June 1940, republican images and symbols—Marianne, *liberté, égalité, fraternité*,
"La Marseillaise"—were swept away, and with them republican
freedoms. Large gatherings and public displays of discontent were
banned. Public protest in an occupied country with a collaboration
government had to take a different form. The incident on the rue
de Buci was indeed a "demonstration," but a demonstration of a different kind. And while it may share some features with the common
food riot—raison d'être, target, rhetoric—it was anything but spontaneous, as many food riots are said to have been. The organizers
of the demonstration drew their inspiration from the popular food
riots of the *ancien régime*, but the demonstration on the rue de Buci
was no food riot.

Nor was the event a purely women's affair. Male and female
demonstrators occupied different positions in the physical space
of the marketplace, with women occupying center stage and men

largely in the wings. Gender was the central organizing principle of the demonstration from its inception. The attribution of political tasks was based on expectations of women's and men's behavior and the social roles specific to their sex. This in turn affected representations of the event and the manner in which it would be prosecuted. The authorities also pursued a policy of repression based, in part, on the sex of the alleged offender. The division of political labor between women and men later enabled defendants to develop gender-specific defense strategies in their testimony to the police. Gender was thus deployed in different, sometimes surprising, ways by organizers, demonstrators, state officials, and finally, party propagandists. It would have critical ramifications for the crafting of the Buci legend, for repression of the "offenders," and, not least of all, for the postwar memory of the affair.

Despite the dire food shortages—or perhaps because of them—the market streets off the boulevard St.-Germain were bustling on that Sunday morning in May. It is hard to imagine an industrialized Western nation in the grip of hunger in the mid-twentieth century, but this was precisely the case in wartime France. Infantile disease and malnutrition, a rise in stillbirths, and severe nutritional deficiencies in laboring and school-age populations were common. With the exception of those who could afford to buy on the black market or had access to farmers in the countryside, hunger was a common scourge. Food had become a major preoccupation, even an obsession; it was a constant subject of conversation, government reports, and articles in the popular press.

This is precisely the situation that the women's committees of the then-banned French Communist Party sought to use and denounce. Outlawed since September 1939, the party had been functioning underground even before a "resistance" can properly be said to have taken place. Much of the leadership, overwhelmingly male, had been arrested and placed in internment camps after the Hitler-Stalin pact of 1939. This opened a space for women, often the wives, sisters, daughters, and coworkers of Communist activists, who assumed the task of reconstituting the party, now forced underground. As early as the fall of 1940 there had been public stirrings around the problems of provisioning. By the spring of 1942, party organizers were creating networks of locally based women's groups, the *comités populaires féminins*, to mobilize the female "masses" around food and scarcity issues. Their overarching goal was to create a groundswell of opposition to the regime and to recruit activists and sympathizers, especially housewives and mothers, to the movement. A prolific underground press, aimed specifically at a female readership, advocated public protest as one means of obtaining relief from the material hardships suffered in the home.

The demonstration on the rue de Buci was only one of hundreds of such food protests that reportedly took place in France over the course of the war. The food demonstration was not new to France—on the contrary, it was part of a centuries-old tradition in which women played starring (and sometimes the only) roles. This was not lost on party organizers, who based their claims to legitimacy on the example of the October Days of 1789, when market women marched from Paris to Versailles demanding bread. But unlike earlier food protests in the French tradition, this one was not "spontaneous" but meticulously, if imperfectly, planned.

On May 31, 1942, the Eco grocery store located on the corner of the rue de Buci and the rue de Seine was featuring sardines packed in oil, cans of which were stacked inside the shop. It was common for shopkeepers to announce a one-time distribution of a particular foodstuff—potatoes or beans or rice or pasta—in advance of upcoming deliveries. So it was that Sunday morning in May, and special distributions always attracted a crowd. This time the crowd swelled with shoppers from surrounding neighborhoods, in addition to local residents of the Sixth Arrondissement, or district.

In the days preceding the spectacle, the script of the drama had been written and the leading roles cast. Women would occupy center stage; they were to take up position in the long line of shoppers outside the doors of the target store, and once the signal had been given, they would follow the movement of the crowd. Those men who had been convened by the political wing of the underground organization would mingle with members of the "audience": they were the "extras" who would swell the ranks of the crowd. Another group of men was to remain hidden in the wings; they would take their places in clusters opposite the store and along the tiny streets surrounding it. They had been convened by the paramilitary branch of the underground party to constitute the *groupe de protection*, a backup security team that would intervene to protect the demonstrators in the event of conflict. Some of these men, members of underground partisan groups, came armed; most of them did not.

The women were to join the interminable line that had already formed in front of the grocery store, interspersed among the usual Sunday morning market-goers. There they would await their cue, to be given at the stroke of ten o'clock. One of the women "shoppers" had been assigned the task of launching the movement by singing "La Marseillaise." The then-banned former national anthem was in itself a powerful symbol that would lend a patriotic tone to the event and situate it for onlookers as a political act in the republican tradition. Not only would it trigger an act of people's justice, it would effectively "sign" and explain the event even as it was unfolding. The singing of "La Marseillaise" was the signal for the women in line to force their way into the shop, seize the sardines can by can, and throw them into the waiting hands of the hungry crowd. The action was to be announced and accompanied by shouts of "Housewives, serve yourselves!" The operation would take place in a flash, and the demonstrators would disband without delay after the cans of sardines had been "distributed" to the shoppers.

Crafting this scenario required careful advance planning and orchestration. At the heart of the affair was the principal organizer, Madeleine Marzin. An elementary school teacher by training and a member of the rank and file of the French Communist Party (Parti communiste français, PCF) since the 1920s, Marzin was already a seasoned party activist by the time of the Buci affair. During the resistance period, her primary mission was to bring women into the underground movement. She drew on women who were already party activists at the local level with the ultimate aim of politicizing others and bringing them into the fight against the Vichy regime and the German occupation. Her job was not so much to enlighten housewives and mothers about the food shortages; there was already a wellspring of frustration and anger on that score. Rather, she sought to harness that frustration and anger to political purpose. Rumblings, complaints, petitions, and small-scale food protests had escalated by spring 1942. Marzin's task was to build on these stirrings by organizing women into neighborhood committees, which in turn would stage other food demonstrations in the capital. Where, when, and how would her first such demonstration take place?

The first order of business was venue. The Paris of 1942 was a network of small communities, each with its own commercial streets with clusters of food shops, enclosed markets, and open-air spaces where itinerant vendors sold their wares. The rue de Buci and the rue de Seine were lined with bakeries, cafés, butcher shops, a cheese shop, a wine store, and a produce shop, many with stalls outside the shops on the small, primarily pedestrian streets. The Buci-Seine marketplace was central, it was small, and it was situated in a neighborhood. Shoppers were local residents; they came from the surrounding area in the Sixth Arrondissement of Paris. Since the ultimate aim of organizing women was to found a women's committee in as many neighborhoods as possible, staging a demonstration at the Buci marketplace might well serve to motivate the local populace. At the intersection of the rue de Seine and the rue de Buci lay a tiny square, the carrefour Buci, occupied by the Eco grocery store. It was here that the drama would unfold.

The site of choice, the Eco store, was part of a burgeoning chain of retail groceries run by a larger entity, Leclerc, with branches throughout the capital.[1] Targetting it rather than an independent, family-run establishment was a conscious choice on the part of party organizers. The same criteria would apply to the choice of venue for another such demonstration on the rue Daguerre one month later, which took place at the entrance of the Félix Potin grocery store. The women's underground press made much of the fact that small shopkeepers did not bear responsibility for the shortages or high prices; rather, it was the large, faceless capitalist entrepreneurs who stood to profit from the people's hunger. Indeed, at the time, the party had hoped to make inroads among the small shopkeepers, the backbone of the middle classes and pivotal players in the political arena. Ultimately, little if anything would come of those efforts. At very least, the point was to avoid antagonizing small businesses who were squeezed between limited supply and pressing demand, between the rationing system of the French government and the depredations of the Germans. As the interface between suppliers and hungry consumers, the small shopkeepers bore the brunt of people's anger.

Eco's strategic location at the heart of the marketplace, where escape routes were in abundance, made it a suitable location for an illegal public display. Suitable, perhaps, but not entirely safe; the Buci intersection was located a stone's throw from the local police station on the rue de l'Abbaye. Moreover, as the local cheese merchant remarked in his oral testimony many years later, German troops had taken up residence at the Luxembourg Palace at the far end of the rue de Seine. Although they did not respond to the disturbance, their relative proximity to the site made it less than ideal for an illegal operation of a highly public nature.

Organizers appear to have known in advance that Eco would be featuring cans of sardines that Sunday morning. This meant that Marzin or another organizer would have done some reconnaissance on foot, assessing the site and evaluating its suitability. Since deliveries were infrequent and stocks unpredictable, it was customary for vendors to alert their customers to the imminent availability of this or that foodstuff. The anticipated supply of sardines was known in advance, probably by way of signs posted on the shop window. This was sure to attract shoppers foraging for their next meal.

Marzin's second preoccupation was the timing of the operation. Sunday morning in Paris—and, indeed, throughout France—then as now, was prime food-shopping time. Despite the paucity of foodstuffs, people still flocked to the market in the hopes of finding something to cook for the traditional Sunday noon meal. While the predominant patrons of food shops and markets were women, on Sundays men also frequented the area. Some were shoppers, but traditionally, men gathered in cafés while women did the shopping. The larger the audience, the wider the impact of the operation and the greater the chance of drawing bystanders into the movement. Moreover, staging the event when the market was at its busiest would give demonstrators greater anonymity.

These were practical considerations. But for maximum impact, the demonstration had to have symbolic significance as well. For that reason, the demonstration was to be an occasion, and according to word-of-mouth advance publicity, it would be an operation in honor of Mother's Day. It was a perfect fit with the principal leitmotif of the Communist Party's underground press urging women, in their roles as mothers and "keepers of the hearth" to demand bread for their children. Was it not the solemn duty of mothers to feed their families? What better way to acknowledge mothers on their special day than to showcase their dedication, concern, and perseverance in the struggle to put food on the table?

There was another, more blatantly political reason for choosing Mother's Day, however. Mother's Day had fallen out of fashion, but Maréchal Philippe Pétain, the head of state of the Vichy regime, was reviving the tradition. Mother's Day had originally been created after the Great War to honor the widows and mothers of fallen soldiers. Just as the patriotic duty of French men was to give their lives in battle, so were French women to fulfill their duty by making babies for France. For Pétain, it was an opportunity to promote the family, part two of the holy trinity of values—*travail, famille, patrie* (work, family, fatherland)—that undergirded his political program, the Révolution nationale. The Vichy government had promoted

Mother's Day 1941 with posters, radio shows, free distributions of milk, and abundant rhetoric. In 1942, Communist Party organizers resolved to take back the day by touting the occasion in the underground women's press—and by showing that mothers could exercise their own power by helping themselves to what food there was.

Marzin, however, had promoted the event as a commemoration of the Paris Commune. Upon their arrest, some demonstrators told police that they had been invited to participate in a demonstration celebrating the anniversary of the Commune in 1871, when the people of Paris seized city hall and installed their own democratic form of government. It followed the fall of the French emperor, Napoleon III; the defeat of the French army by Prussian troops; and the infamous Siege of Paris, when the Prussians imposed a four-month blockade to starve the city and bring it to heel. The heroic role of the people, the symbolic importance of the capital, the enemy's use of food as a weapon, the historic revolutionary model, the revolt against French and Prussian tyranny: each feature was clearly analogous to the situation at hand.

Participant testimony diverged—some attributed their presence at the market to Mother's Day, others to the Commune. But both Mother's Day and the anniversary of the Commune fit the message that the demonstration was intended to send. Both occasions corresponded to the logic of the operation, whatever the original call to arms. Unlike the Commune, however, Mother's Day had the added value of a specific gender connotation, one that could legitimize the operation and thereby lend some semblance of cover to the demonstrators.

Of the two ostensible occasions, Mother's Day had a unique strategic advantage for two reasons. First, it conveyed the idea that mothers' work was just and necessary, thereby legitimizing an otherwise illegal operation. Second, it could also help exculpate crowd "extras" who were arrested for being at the scene. A celebration in honor of mothers was inclusive, politically neutral, or even *pétainiste*. It had none of the left-wing, "Communistic," or contestatory associations of the revolutionary uprising of 1871 and would have made for a more convincing –or at least less provocative—defense on the part of demonstrators who would later face police questioning. Indeed, a number of the women and men who later found themselves in police custody named the Commune as the reason for their presence at the market that day. They might have done better to plead Mother's Day, celebrated by the regime and billed as universal; commemorating the Commune was politically marked as left-wing. Did such considerations figure in the decision to cite a particular occasion as pretext for the operation? It was more likely a felicitous side effect. Marzin did not expect arrests, but she was astute and experienced enough to know that such an operation was not without risk. Never did she think, however, that the risk would be so high. If the point was to inspire other women to follow in her footsteps, the risk would have to be downplayed or minimized, if not eliminated altogether.

But Marzin was not the only planner; partisan commanders in the paramilitary wing of the underground movement were also involved in preparations for the demonstration. Although the political and paramilitary wings were separate and distinct, their functions and operations could and did overlap, as in this instance. In April 1942, the Francs-tireurs et partisans (FTP) were formally constituted. Formerly known as the Organisation spéciale (OS), the FTP specialized in sabotage, attacks on German troops, and armed combat. Planning on the paramilitary side for the Buci operation was the work of Georges Vallet and Henri Tanguy, partisan commanders of the Paris region. Under their direction, a *groupe de protection*, or security team, was assembled to be on hand in the event any of the protesters came into harm's way. Marzin knew that there would be men posted for protection in the "shadow crowd," outsiders who had been convened to demonstrate rather than shop for food. What she did not know is that some of those men would come armed.

Once the site and the timing of the operation had been established, it remained for Marzin to recruit the actors of the drama and to plan the unfolding of the event. To this end, she did what other party organizers and resisters did at the time: she mobilized the networks of people at her disposal, people she knew as friends, friends of friends, acquaintances, or fellow party members or sympathizers. Her objective was to assemble a crowd that had been briefed ahead of time and who knew what to do and how to act. The women would play active roles; a few men would round out the crowd and act as sympathetic bystanders. In the week prior to the demonstration, Marzin and several other party organizers had rounded up a critical mass of people, members of an extended party "family" to constitute a crowd (*faire foule*, in the political lingo of the time). Some forty people eventually ended up in the hands of the police. Other demonstrators and members of the shadow crowd eluded capture, so it is impossible to know how many people actually turned out for the event. Police estimates put the crowd at some fifty to one hundred people, but those figures do not distinguish between regular shoppers and members of the shadow crowd. Some recruits were full-time activists in the underground Communist organization. Others had some connection to the party, even if that connection was tenuous, unofficial, part-time, or casual.

For security reasons, participants did not arrive at the scene en masse, but surreptitiously in couples or small groups emerging from different directions. They convened first at approximately nine-thirty, a half hour before the demonstration was to begin, at various metro stations in the area. A group that originated in the Fifth Arrondissement a few metro stations away convened at Odéon; those coming from the Fifteenth Arrondissement, Marzin's home turf, assembled at the Mabillon and St.-Germain stations before setting off for the Buci-Seine intersection. A group of young male partisans came from the direction of the Palais-Royal. They traversed the Seine and arrived at the marketplace on foot. Others arrived individually. The actual site of the demonstration and the details of the plan had remained secret until the last minute. Each group was met en route, usually at a metro station, by a party delegate who issued the final instructions. A street map of the area shows the Buci-Seine intersection as a hub, surrounded by a constellation of metro stations.

By ten o'clock the women had joined the line of shoppers in front of the Eco grocery store; the men who had accompanied them to the market merged with the crowd on the sidewalk and around the stalls. On the perimeter and along the side streets leading to the Buci-Seine intersection, members of the security team stood at the ready. Everyone was in position. The demonstrators had only to await their cue: "Allons enfants de la patrie," the first words of the national anthem.

Up to this point, everything had gone according to plan.

Alas, the operation was cruelly thwarted by a series of flaws. The first one was the critical signal to launch the operation. Members of the shadow crowd awaited their cue . . . but there was no "La Marseillaise." The woman charged with triggering the action was either overcome by stage fright or failed to show. Minutes ticked by and the silence grew worrisome. Her understudy failed to come to the rescue. People grew restless and looked questioningly to their neighbors. It was at this point that Madeleine Marzin, fearing the moment would be lost, rushed to the front of the line herself, crying, "Housewives, serve yourselves!" She stormed the shop, leading the group of women who were to aid in the "free distribution" of sardines. A shop hand barred her passage. "Your tickets?" he demanded, to which she replied, "Today is without tickets!"[2]

Sardines were not for sale that day, implied Marzin, whether with ration tickets or without; they were there for the taking. Once inside, Marzin and others seized the cans of sardines and tossed them through the opening of the shop, which was framed by an iron grate. Some demonstrators measured their success by the reaction of the other shoppers, who, they reported, scrambled to obtain their share of the booty.

Meanwhile, a scuffle had erupted within the shop as the proprietor, Alexandre Chasseau, and his shop assistants came running to

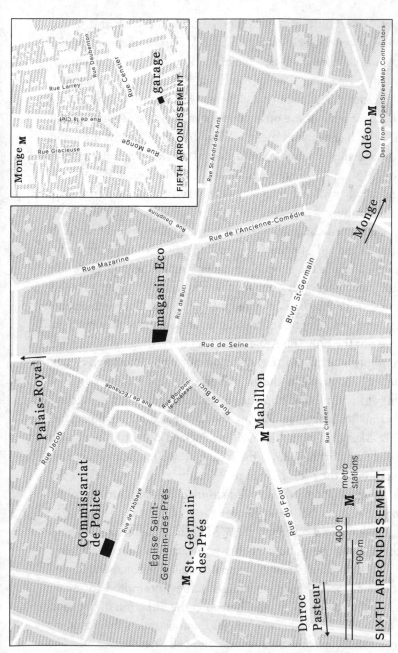

The Buci-Seine neighborhood in the Sixth Arrondissement and the metro stations from which demonstrators converged upon the site. The inset shows the location of the garage in the contiguous Fifth Arrondissement, where some demonstrators were later arrested. *Map by Gregory T. Woolston.*

investigate. The house butcher emerged from the back and seized Madeleine Marzin. Seeing Marzin in his grip, a member of the backup group, André Dalmas, a twenty-nine-year-old postal worker, intervened to free her. "One of the doors had already been closed. Just as the other was about to close as well, Dalmas, who in the melee had lost sight of me on account of my small size . . . punched the man who had grabbed me. He let go but then caught me again by the other arm. A young *camarade* seized my free arm with Ida and Yvonne's help. . . . I don't remember how I landed outside."[3] Marzin fled into the crowd and into the entryway of a nearby building, where she removed her beige rain cape to change her appearance.

At the same time, another member of the backup group, Elie Gras, had come to the aid of other women, including Maté Houet, who were trapped inside the shop by the lowering of the iron grate. He lifted the grate just high enough for them to wriggle to safety. By this time, the disturbance had attracted a large crowd, and participants mingled with onlookers, local residents, and vendors. But partisan men were not the only "invisible" agents in the crowd that morning. The commotion attracted the attention of plainclothes police, off-duty police who lived in the neighborhood and happened to be shopping at the time, and uniformed officers on duty at the market.

A second hitch occurred during the scuffle inside the shop. After liberating Marzin, Dalmas himself was seized by the police, who proceeded to escort him amid the raging crowd to the neighboring police station on the rue de l'Abbaye. According to two witnesses, the men in the shadow crowd appeared stunned and failed to mobilize. A woman called out "are you just going to let them take him away?," at which point crowd members stepped up and tried to free Dalmas from the grip of the police. At this point, the violence escalated. Members of the security team carried out their mission. Men posted along the side streets fired on police as they attempted to escort Dalmas up the rue Bourbon-le-Chateau in the direction of the local police station. The crowd scattered, the demonstrators fleeing down side streets leading from the intersection in all directions, several of the armed men with them. When the smoke cleared, five policemen had been shot, one fatally; another died shortly thereafter.

A third snag in the operation had critical consequences for the participants. In the course of the melee, a demonstrator's pocketbook had fallen to the floor. By the time she reached her home, several plainclothes detectives were already waiting for her. After initially denying her involvement, she was forced to back down in the face of the evidence. The roundup of other demonstrators began after she was forced to give police the names of her co-conspirators. Based on her testimony and on leads from other sources, some forty people said to have been involved in the operation were arrested, interrogated, and incarcerated over the course of the next several months.

The shootings had not been part of the original plan. In this sense, the demonstration can be said to have gone awry. Yet provisions had been made for some of the men to protect the demonstrators in the event of conflict. Thanks to them, a number of demonstrators were able to elude the police. For that reason alone, the operation was at the very least a partial success. It was not until the massive waves of arrests that followed that the human costs of the demonstration could be seen to far outweigh the gains. In view of this, playing up the operation for its symbolic value, as the party later did, would in some measure serve to redeem it.

The ensuing disaster is a stark demonstration of the risks incurred by resisters. In an ideal world, they observed the practice of *cloisonnement*, or compartmentalization, according to which each individual activist knew as little as possible about the big picture, other operations, and the identities of her coworkers. Resisters adopted noms de guerre to protect themselves not only from the French and German authorities but also from each other. In the best of cases, a hierarchical triangle structure was the rule: each activist knew only the two other members of her triangle. It was expressly forbidden for full-time underground operatives who were married to each other to remain in contact, and it was out of the question that they live together (although this rule was broken time and time again). Limiting each person's access to information and identities preserved the integrity of the mission and the lives of the activists. It was well known that friends and family members were often used as bait by the French and German police to coax "perpetrators" out of hiding. In this way, were one stone to be removed from the edifice, the whole structure would not be compromised.

In principle, compartmentalization certainly made sense, but in practice it was often impossible to implement. Working conditions were far from ideal: the ranks of the activists were thin and arrests culled their numbers still more. Moreover, recruitment was based on preexisting networks of friends, family, and coworkers. Resisters were people, and people needed the support and comfort of spouses, friends, and family all the more when their daily lives were in peril. Few if any underground operatives were fully prepared to function under such conditions. All such rules and practices had been hard won by experience in the field. Experienced operatives were a minority. With amateurism there came a heavy cost. But there was no other option.

The problem was that some demonstrators *did* know each other, and by their real names. When the terrified Marguerite Bronner was discovered by way of her lost pocketbook, she gave those names to the police when they threatened to take her child. A threat to resisters' families was a commonly used interrogation tactic, and those threats were not empty. Time and again family members were arrested as hostages.

However, compartmentalization did play a vital role in isolating the protesting women from the partisan men. The two branches of the underground party functioned separately—up to a point. The political wing was responsible for aboveground street actions like this one, for propaganda, and for the underground press. The paramilitary branch was charged with "direct action" operations: sabotage, assassination, and armed combat. Both wings included men and women, but men heavily predominated in the partisan groups, just as women predominated among the demonstrators. As a general rule the branches functioned independently, each hermetically separate from the other.

It is rare to catch a glimpse of the internal workings of the two branches in collaboration with one another; the Buci affair provides such a vantage point. Here they joined forces, working together to stage an illegal aboveground (or public) protest and to protect the protesters. It is not clear what the paramilitary or "direct action" leadership knew about the demonstration side of the plan. All we know for sure is that Marzin herself was aware that party *camarades* would be in attendance for the purpose of protecting the demonstrators, should that become necessary. In accordance with the practice of compartmentalization, however, she did not know who they were.

The disturbance at the Buci-Seine marketplace may not have come as a complete surprise to locals. There is an intriguing indication in the police files that Chasseau had requested an enhanced police presence at his shop the day before the events. Did Chasseau catch wind of the impending demonstration, and if so, how? The supply of sardines at the Eco market, a rare occurrence, may also have been advertised to local shoppers in advance. In any case, the shop's proprietor might well have anticipated a bigger crowd than usual on a Sunday morning that was also Mother's Day. Some witnesses told police that they had seen flyers on Saturday announcing a "free distribution" the following day. This is unlikely, however, since even the principals themselves knew neither the location of the demonstration nor the nature of their assigned tasks until the last minute.

It was customary for there to be a uniformed police presence at markets or wherever there were concentrations of people. Since scarcity and hunger had made markets a frequent site of contestation, it had become a matter of routine to post plainclothesmen at the Buci-Seine marketplace. While the local plainclothes patrols might be known to shopkeepers and other regulars, they would have been invisible to shoppers coming from other areas. Such is the downside of anonymity. Being outsiders, as our demonstrators were, was a form of protection, but it also came with being in unfamiliar territory.

It was not until the demonstrators were assembled and awaiting their cue that Marzin's attention was drawn to the presence of plainclothes police in the crowd. "Some *camarades* . . . pointed out that the market was full of plainclothes police. Moreover, one of our groups en route to the rue de Buci had some trouble losing a tail at the Grenelle metro stop," recalled Marzin. The authorities were clearly on high alert. "A few steps away from us a passer-by carrying a little package was stopped by a policeman who made him open his package. In it was just tobacco."[4] The mood was tense.

Audience response to the spectacle had not been left to chance. Operational planning also included the *travail d'explication*, the drafting and printing of a flyer to be thrown into the crowd or onto the street at the time of the demonstration. Such "distributions" were often the work of liaison agents speeding by on bicycles. Marzin or another party organizer, most likely an activist involved with the underground press, had prepared packets of a one-page document. Like a program note for a live performance, the flyer would explain or decode the event for the public even as it unfolded. Without it, the demonstration might appear to surprised or fearful onlookers as no more than a momentary disturbance by unruly elements.

The entire operation was itself an act of propaganda; party organizers had staged the event not so much to distribute a few cans of sardines but rather to send a message, ciphers of which were the movements and gestures of participating activists. Decoding this message for the public and making explicit the purpose, rationale, and meaning of the demonstration was every bit a part of the larger operation as storming the shop or protecting the demonstrators.

Some of the protesters present on the rue de Buci and the rue de Seine had been charged with propaganda properly speaking: it was their job to circulate the flyers that had been prepared in advance by throwing them into the air. From the testimony of Edgar Lefébure, who told police that he was responsible for overseeing the work of a propaganda team, it appears that at least several people at different levels in the party hierarchy were onsite to distribute the flyers. The material was brought to the scene in separate packets by different individuals. In the confusion of the ensuing melee, the flyers were emptied onto the street for witnesses, shoppers, and later passersby to collect. When questioned by police, several of them mentioned finding the flyer.

What became of these flyers? Did shoppers scramble to pick them up as they did the sardines? In his memoir of the war years, Maurice Garçon, a lawyer, chronicler, and resident of the Sixth Arrondissement, reports a discussion with a neighbor who lived "two steps" away from the rue de Buci: "His maid returned [from shopping] with flyers addressed 'to the housewives of the Sixth Arrondissement' that were distributed at the very moment shots rang out."[5] This passing comment adds more uncertainty to the actual timing of the "distribution": some testified that the flyers were thrown into the air before the women stormed the shop, others said during, and another witness claimed it was the preceding day.

The single extant copy of this text, torn and crumbling, was appended to the first police report summarizing the incident and its consequences in the hours after it occurred. The flyer is undated and makes no specific reference to the rue de Buci marketplace, but the scenario is unmistakable. This lone document is stunningly typical of the entire body of the underground women's press that has come down to us. Every principal theme of an elaborate and prolific clandestine press aimed at mobilizing women for the resistance effort is included in the space of a single, tightly packed page. Mimeographed on cheap, flimsy paper, the flyer reads like a statement from concerned and politically committed women addressed to friends and neighbors—ordinary women, like their interlocutors. They could have been standing in line outside a bakery or butcher shop, speaking to the other shoppers around them. In tone the language is not militant but determined, not grandiloquent but practical and matter-of-fact.

Like hundreds of flyers and underground newspapers of the period, it is signed by a collective, "Un groupe de ménagères du 6e arrondissement" (a group of housewives from the Sixth Arrondissement)." Félix Barthélémy, the owner of the dairy shop on the rue de Seine, said that the demonstrators were regular neighborhood shoppers, members of the local Communist cell. According to his testimony in 1985, the "troublemakers" were regular customers. But there is no evidence that any residents of the Sixth Arrondissement were in the shadow crowd that day, with the exception of Lucie Pucheux and her husband, both party activists who lived on the nearby rue Monsieur-le-Prince. Indeed, Madeleine Marzin said that neither she nor other organizers had been able to make inroads in the Sixth Arrondissement.

The main protagonists were residents of the Fifth and Fifteenth Arrondissement, and this was precisely because they did *not* live in the neighborhood of the Buci market. The signature on such papers was meant to conceal, not identify, their authors. Underground broadsheets, newspapers, and flyers of this sort were produced to incite women to create such groups themselves by suggesting that a groundswell of activity was already under way. Time and again we see that the purpose of the underground press was primarily to inspire and mobilize, and only secondarily to inform. In this one might say that such "signatures," while false and misleading, were actually signatures of another sort: they personalized the message, indicated that it was the work of a group and not just one person, and protected its authors, all at the same time. In short, "a group of housewives from the Sixth Arrondissement" was a nom de guerre like any other.

This text is addressed to women by women; clearly the demonstration on the rue de Buci was defined exclusively as women's business, just as feeding one's family devolved upon the woman of the house. The challenge of fulfilling this role, according to the flyer, threatened the very survival of the family and took aim at women's special mission. The argument was based on a certain notion of

The flyer distributed at the scene maximizes the use of valuable space. The prose is densely packed; margins and print are tiny. The same concern for economy extends to the generic message and lack of specifics regarding place and time. A nearly identical flyer could be used for any food protest action.

In our age of perpetual solicitation for products, a flyer intended to capture the reader's attention would feature images, colors, and varied font sizes for maximum eye appeal. The underground press had no such luxury. Paper was scarce, equipment was invaluable, and people were risking their lives to produce and distribute this material. Organizers had to make the most of their resources. Moreover, they had not only a message to convey but also an argument.

Archives nationales, Pierrefitte, France.

women's role. It appealed to what they had in common: husbands, children, families, dependents, all of them hungry. References to conversations in the food lines resonated with everyone. Citing the laments commonly exchanged among shoppers was intended to establish an insider's complicity among women.

In accordance with the PCF's broad-based Front national agenda,[6] the "group of housewives" carefully avoided making invidious distinctions among different elements of the population, all of whom shared the same set of problems, whatever their status. Shopkeepers and peasants, whom shoppers often criticized for their nefarious practices (trading on the black market, showing favoritism for preferred clients) were represented as partners in the struggle to feed France. The problem as represented here was not so much about production: peasants reaped the bounty of France's rich earth, food supplies were stocked in warehouses, Germans served themselves first and whatever was left "nous passe par le nez" (passes under our noses).

Instead, distribution was identified as the real issue. Neither food-producing peasants in the countryside nor the shopkeepers were to blame for the shortages. The enemies of the people and the small shopkeepers both were the large-scale distributors, the grocery store chains or *grands magasins d'alimentation*, who were guilty of hoarding and holding back supplies. And here the flyer bore another extremely important signature feature. "Les Potin, les Damoy, *les Eco*" are at fault—not just a particular store, not just a particular chain, but an entire category, the *grands magasins*.[7] Thus it was that the Eco market at 77 rue de Seine was designated the scene of the operation on May 31. The Félix Potin grocery store was the chosen site of another such incident, the demonstration of the rue Daguerre, which took place in the Fourteenth Arrondissement on August 1 later that same summer.

The *travail d'explication* not only interpreted the scene that was about to unfold or had just unfolded. It was also a prescription for action that urged women to take matters into their own hands and to "serve themselves" in the name of their children. Appropriating food that was hoarded in warehouses or large retail chain stores, awaiting shipment to Germany, was not only a solemn duty toward her family; it was a patriotic act in the tradition of the courageous Frenchwomen who marched for bread in October 1789. The "group of housewives" exhorted women to cease complaining and start demanding, for the authorities were fearful of angry women who raise their voices. When women intervene aggressively, stated the authors of the flyer, their demands are often met: "a kilo of potatoes here, some pasta there, dried vegetables another day." Such claims are difficult to verify, although the underground women's newspapers that flourished in this period made frequent reference to authorities acceding to women's demands by releasing foodstuffs stored and reserved for other purposes. While the possible gains of such actions were enumerated, the possible risks to demonstrators were left unsaid.

Not only were women to make noise and raise their voices, they were invited to serve themselves by invading grocery stores like the one on the corner of the rue de Seine and the rue de Buci: "Our children are hungry, and that counts above all else." The permanent solution to the hunger problem was to rid France of the Germans. That such actions defied the law and were subject to sanctions is elided here. Protests like the one in the Eco supermarket were deemed a fully legitimate form of people's justice, one that recognized a higher law based on fundamental human rights, including the right to eat and to feed one's family.

The flyers that party operatives distributed on the rue de Buci and the rue de Seine described and interpreted a future action as it was supposed to happen. Never was there mention of the presence of men or the threat of male violence, although Madeleine Marzin was aware that male *camarades* would be scattered in the crowd. Indeed, she had recruited some of them herself for the purpose of swelling the ranks of the onlookers. The flyer did not instruct the women to "invade" shops and to "loot" goods, but rather to join together to "take deliberately anything that can be used to feed the kids." Collective action had to be loud and aggressive, but women were to be armed only with their bodies and voices, not with guns. Nor was there any allusion to the French Communist Party, whose members had scripted the event and authored the text that explained it to the public. Demonstrating for food was not only for converts and *camarades;* on the contrary, it was open to all. The reasons for these omissions were strategic and political, as we will see. The *travail d'explication* was only the first stage of what would become a contentious battle of interpretation, memory making, and legend building.

The Commune, which "occurred this very month of May," was also cited in the flyer collected at the site. This reference effectively dated the otherwise undated, one-size-fits-all flyer, which had presumably been composed for different situations. By changing only a reference and the signature, the same template could be used for other actions.

The ambiguity surrounding the occasion the demonstration was meant to commemorate is highly significant, for it underscores the essentially symbolic nature of the demonstration, regardless of whether the event was meant to honor mothers or pay homage to the Communards. The symbolic allusion was what counted the most; the event to which it alluded was secondary. Both were equally valid; both did the job of assigning meaning. Mother's Day and the Commune, two markers in the month of May, were pretexts rather than reasons for the demonstration. Both occasions could give the demonstration meaning. They anchored the event in a national tradition, one in which French women took center stage. Framing the demonstration as part of a commemorative process was part of shaping its meaning, both before and after the fact. Imparting special meaning to its location in time was to deploy the full symbolic potential of the event. Not only did the event hold a place in the historic tradition, it also *demonstrated* the evident disparity between Vichy's discourse in praise of the French family (the larger the better) and the realities of the food crisis. It prevented women from being good mothers—and this on the special day created to honor them, so vigorously promoted by the Vichy regime.

How the Buci incident was defined would have everything to do with how it would be prosecuted. Looting, petty thievery, disturbing the peace, unlawful assembly, "Bolshevik subversion," and even demonstrating were punishable offenses in the Vichy period, but they did not carry the death penalty. The presence of armed men and the killing of the police officers qualified the event as a crime against the state. The stakes were high and the repression was merciless. The French court sentenced five of the six women arrested in connection with the events to prison for periods ranging from five years to life. What this meant in the terms of the day was deportation to Ravensbrück, the concentration camp for women east of Berlin. Of the twelve men found to be directly implicated in the operation, eight were condemned to death. The first three were executed in the courtyard of the Santé prison in central Paris: on July 23, 1942, they were guillotined at dawn. After an initial sentencing by French courts, some male prisoners were turned over to the Germans, who judged them again, this time before a military tribunal. The following February, a group of five high school students, who had been members of the security team, were shot by firing squad.

Thus were separate fates reserved for men and women. Repression, too, then was gendered, and two exceptions confirm the rule. The first exception is that of Mayer Kaliski, a thirty-one-year-old Polish-born unemployed metalworker. He faced neither the executioner's blade nor the firing squad. Despite his acquittal in the Buci affair, Kaliski was detained by French authorities. He had two marks against him. First, he knew some of the other demonstrators, which alone made him suspect. Second, he was thought to be Jewish, though one document in his police file expressly identifies him as being "of Aryan race." Mayer Kaliski was shipped to Auschwitz in July 1942 in one of the first transports to leave Paris.[8] He never returned.

The second exception is that of Madeleine Marzin, whose story is remarkable in more ways than one. Marzin's role on the women's side of the operation also qualified her as a full-fledged "terrorist." In an extraordinary move, Marzin was condemned to death along with the men. She was quite possibly the first woman to receive the death penalty for political crimes under Vichy. Her sentence, however, was never carried out. In a bizarre and unprecedented series of events, Marzin escaped both capital punishment and deportation.

The story does not end here; there is also the story of the story. From the moment of its inception, the demonstration on the rue de Buci began to acquire the status of legend. Some found it inspirational, others menacing; some inflated its impact, others diminished it. What is clear is that the story itself became a site of contest. World war, foreign occupation, collaboration government: a unique set of conditions set the stage for confrontation. Foremost among them was hunger.

HUNGER AND SCARCITY

Today the rue de Buci is an animated hub with trendy cafés, expensive hotels, and high-end specialty food shops. The carrefour de Buci, where the rue de Buci meets the rue de Seine, is in the very heart of Paris, though once it lay on the periphery of the medieval city. In character, physiognomy, and relative location, the market has evolved over time, but the rue Buci and the rue de Seine have been a commercial crossroads since the fourteenth century. The original Buci passage dates from 1351. It got its name in 1388 from Simon de Buci, who purchased the St.-Germain gate, later the Porte de Buci, when the medieval city was surrounded by walls. Simon de Buci (sometimes written "de Bussy," as the name is pronounced) amassed his fortune collecting tariffs on goods and people that passed through his gate. The intersecting rue de Seine, so named in 1489, dates from the thirteenth century.[1] The convergence of the two passageways was a natural locus of commercial activity long before the demonstration was staged on this site in 1942. Then as now, crowds and commerce mandated a police presence; in 1621 a police station was erected here. It was the predecessor to the one on the rue de l'Abbaye where André Dalmas, one of the few demonstrators apprehended at the scene, was taken upon his arrest.

Tucked behind the boulevard St.-Germain, the Buci-Seine crossroads is just a few steps away from the celebrated St.-Germain church and abbey. Across from the church are two famous cafés, the Deux Magots and the Flore, frequented by Sartre, Beauvoir, and a host of other artists and writers, including Jacques Prévert, who devoted a poem to his favorite marketplace in 1942, the very year of the food demonstration. Before and after the war, this was one of the nerve centers of intellectual and literary life in Paris. In the opposite direction lies a tangle of tiny streets all the way to the banks of the Seine. A cluster of universities, bookstores, and cafés stretches from the adjacent Latin Quarter. The Buci market and surrounding shops supplies the area, which was more densely populated than it is today.[2]

Although the total population of Paris has more than doubled since the end of the Second World War, both the population and population density of the Sixth Arrondissement have fallen by half. According to the 1936 census, the last one before the war, there were 90,000 people living in the Sixth Arrondissement. By 1946, the population had dropped to some 84,000.[3] Yet despite the fact that many Parisians had abandoned the capital in the summer of 1940, there still remained many mouths to feed in the summer of 1942.

In April 1939, the carrefour Buci was a thriving marketplace. This photograph shows the rue de Seine, with the Eco supermarket on the right. *Coll. Pavillon de l'Arsenal / cliché DAUCVP.*

The nature of these demographic shifts was described by Félix Barthélemy, the owner of the cheese shop on the rue de Seine for decades, who was deeply attached to the neighborhood and knew it well. In order to convey the bustling, lively character of the Buci-Seine marketplace that had been his home and workplace before, during, and after the Second World War, he emphasized the volume and composition of the neighborhood's inhabitants.

> Before the war, in 1939, the neighborhood was much more populated than it is today. There was an extraordinary concentration of people living there. It was a neighborhood of schools and universities. At the time there was no student housing. There was an enormous number of older people, people of retirement age, only at the time there was no guaranteed retirement as there is now. They had big apartments on the boulevard St.-Germain, the rue Bonaparte, the rue de Tournon. In the interwar period, older people made some extra income by renting rooms out to students; some lodgers even provided daily meals. These people were very good customers, they shopped every day, they had to feed young people who had ravenous appetites! The war turned all of that upside down.[4]

The poet Jacques Prévert was also well positioned to chronicle the transformation of the once-prosperous neighborhood market. He had grown up in the Sixth Arrondissement and spent a good part of his adult life there. Like many residents of the capital, he fled Paris for the south of France when the Germans invaded in June 1940. Upon his return in 1942, the ambience, character, and physiognomy of his familiar market street had undergone a profound change.

Prévert depicts the rue de Buci as a lugubrious place, steeped in silence and fringed by shuttered shops. "La rue de Buci maintenant..." (The rue de Buci now...) is among the few poems in his collection *Paroles* that bears a date. Whether Prévert wrote his elegy about the marketplace before or after the demonstration of May 31 is unclear;

there is no explicit reference to political upheaval or violence, only a meditation on absence and loss. After two years of deprivation, the familiar, well-appointed, and robust market is now "mismatched and malnourished," disfigured by the scourge of want and despair. The lively Sunday morning crowd of peacetime days has vanished. Gone, too, are the displays of sunny oranges and lemons that summoned dreams of distant places. By 1942, a heavy curtain of dust and iron has descended on the somber corridor that runs from one dead end to another.[5]

Prévert represents the street itself, like the demonstration of May 31 that unfolded there, as female. Gone are the merchants, all women, who once sold their wares: the old hag ("vieille cloche"), the fruit and vegetable cart vendors ("filles des quatre saisons"), the itinerant hawkers ("les marchandes à la sauvette"). Only a few pro- duce vendors remain, but all they have to sell are weeds. There is no sign of the girl in the diaphanous summer dress who sashayed on Sunday mornings, dog in tow and loaf of bread on her arm. Her provocative youthfulness has disappeared, her pride and freedom along with it. Bread has been taken from her mouth, the grass has been cut from under her feet, and song has been stifled in her throat. Most striking of all is the sexualized image of her mutilated female body: the ovaries have been ripped from her gut. The street, like its female protagonists, has been ravaged and starved by war, and war is male. In "La rue de Buci maintenant . . ." the girl has been replaced by a wounded veteran of the Great War, once fat and now thin, whose legless torso ambles on a rolling platform. His infirmity and emasculation are legacies of the earlier war; the diminishment of his wounded body a legacy of the new one. As the street and the war are gendered in this poem, so too are their respective mutilations. In the first case, the result is sterility; in the second, impotence.

It is hard to imagine a vibrant neighborhood hub in the grip of hunger, but Prévert's dramatization is not far from the mark. The scarcity of all goods—textiles, rubber, leather, paper, fuel—and es- pecially food—was taking a toll on Parisians by the spring of 1942.

People were scrounging, recycling, making do, and most of all waiting in long lines for a few raw materials from which to craft a meal. The Germans had first pick, leaving little behind for the French population. Production was poor, distribution was faulty, and the rationing system left much to be desired. Peasants hoarded part of the goods they produced or sold directly to consumers. An underground traffic in food and other commodities, the black market, emerged to fill the void.

In the division of labor between French and Germans, it was the French authorities who had control of provisioning the cities and towns. The rationing system that became effective in the spring of 1940 was never sufficient to meet the needs of the population. In short, the food system was profoundly altered, and with it the relationships between urban and rural areas, regions with diversified agriculture and regions specializing in particular crops, shopkeepers and patrons, and among shoppers themselves. By 1942, a new culture of scarcity had taken root, one that pervaded economic, social, and political life.

The demonstration on the rue de Buci was a response to those conditions. For the French Communist Party, food shortages created an opportunity to mobilize women against the regime and the occupiers. Efforts to bring women into the underground movement had begun as early as the autumn of 1940. The *comités populaires féminins* were formed at the neighborhood level to recruit women by appealing to their traditional roles as mothers and housewives. Their purpose was to exert pressure on the authorities and to channel private frustrations into meaningful public action. A prolific women's underground press was an integral part of this activity.

Memoirs and testimony from just about anyone who lived through the war years are replete with talk of food, the lack of food, the quest for food. A Vichy bureaucrat, a nursing mother, a prominent novelist, a housekeeper, a bistro owner, a postal worker: all were beset by hunger, complained about it, and fantasized about unrestricted prewar meals.[6] Scarcity was the ultimate preoccupation for

Henri Meunier, incarcerated for his involvement in the Buci demonstration. One of the last letters he wrote while awaiting his execution by guillotine was addressed to his friend Marcel Leclerc, asking him to make sure his soon-to-be widow got enough food to eat and coal to keep warm.[7] Alas, Leclerc was in no position to look after Meunier's wife. Meunier did not know that Leclerc, who was later deported to Buchenwald, had also been arrested in the roundup of demonstrators.

For some the experience of hunger was not so new. Cécile Borras, a working-class woman who endured French prisons and then Auschwitz, Ravensbrück, and Neuengamme for more than two years, attributed her survival under harsh conditions to the fact that she had been accustomed to hunger all her life. By her account, her fellow resisters and co-detainees from more prosperous backgrounds suffered even more miserably. Hunger was no more pleasant for her, of course, but it was certainly more familiar. Hunger, she said, had armed her for the underground struggle and consequent detention in prisons and camps.[8]

The fact of hunger even came to define existence for many French people. Marie-Louise Claudé, a prisoner-of-war's wife who hid a German soldier after his defection from the Wehrmacht, summarized her experience of the war years in two words: hunger and fear.[9] Hunger and fear, fear of hunger: they dogged everyone, though not equally. Even those who were spared total deprivation— food-producing farmers and their customers; the wealthy and privileged, who could buy on the black market—were preoccupied with food and eating.

The authorities also feared hunger, but for different reasons. Hunger was the fuel of protest, and food protests were the stuff of historical tradition. The prospect of civil strife haunted public officials: the police who were charged with maintaining public order, civil servants responsible for rationing and distribution, high-ranking Vichy officials whose impotence was exposed and legitimacy undermined, German occupying troops and authorities who feared the explosive anger of the crowd or the random violence of the lone partisan. Sympathetic prefects, compassionate mayors, and other civil servants with obligations to the regime but also a keenly felt duty to their constituents were caught in the middle. They were constantly confronted with complaints of food scarcity. Some were pained by their inability to ensure their fellow citizens access to the very basics required for human survival.

It took little time for the police to recognize that queues, tightly packed like powder kegs, could be readily combusted by the spark of frustrations and resentments great and small. As a result, *gardiens de la paix* were routinely assigned to areas of urban affluence, particularly markets and market streets. None were more alert to the political import of social interaction in the marketplace than the agents who were charged with patrolling market crowds, reporting on them, and transmitting comments overheard in lines. When possible, extra police protection was provided for shopkeepers who felt vulnerable or threatened at the prospect of having to manage hungry crowds. The observations of regular police patrols, both uniformed officers and plainclothesmen, were meticulously recorded; their field notes became the basis for extensive, regular reporting on food supply problems, public disturbances, and the evolution of public opinion.

Even the newly appointed Minister of Agriculture and Food Supply, Jacques Le Roy Ladurie, slipped incognito into food lines during his lunch hour or after work in order to hear firsthand what had been reported all along: the food system was in crisis.

> Toward late morning, I left my office to hang around the neighborhood markets, slipping into lines of housewives and overhearing their recriminations against the bloodsuckers [the Ministry of Food Supply] who grew fatter as the misery of the people got worse. Soon it was clear: people were not getting enough to eat, they were suffering. Obvious, one might say. But I wanted to take stock of the sinister reality with my own eyes.[10]

From the first months of the occupation through the post-Liberation period, police viewed markets, shops, and food lines as potentially—even inevitably—explosive urban spaces. Their worries were not unfounded. Incidents were frequent in Paris proper and in the surrounding areas. As early as December 1940, the police commissioner of the Sixth Arrondissement reported tensions on the rue de Buci. Even before formal reports of market-place disturbances had become routine, the local commissioner alerted central headquarters to the menacing "physiognomy of the Buci market":

> At 5:00 a.m. an enormous crowd began gathering near the various shops. By 9:00 a.m. streets and sidewalks were overrun. Almost all butcher shops were closed because they had nothing to sell.
>
> In a space of 300 meters at most, it took twenty policemen to control and handle the crowd, which was more than agitated on account of the cold temperatures and the dwindling food on display.
>
> By way of example, the sum total of available merchandise at the large Eco market amounted to only 150 rabbits in halved portions. Although they had been apprised of the situation, a line of approximately two thousand people formed nearby. . . . After the market closed, I gathered together the police officers and plainclothesmen who had been on duty. Our unanimous opinion: if this situation continues, hunger and cold will lead to unrest.
>
> I have no reservation in saying that I consider the situation very serious, based on what I saw this morning at the Buci market alone.[11]

Throughout the occupation, police described the situation in terms ranging from merely agitated to outright incendiary. In the town of Drancy, for example, there was an emergency distribution of extra tickets on February 2, 1941 for numerous residents who had already exhausted their monthly rations. In a telegram to central police intelligence services, the commissioner of Pantin warned that local police "expect[ed] a large crowd and fear[ed] possible demonstrations."[12] By June, "anxiety and tension ha[d] increased considerably."[13] Crowds were "effervescent," situations remained "critical," "queues appear[ed] tense." In reports, memoranda, and communiqués issued throughout the course of the war, the political consequences of urban hunger was a major preoccupation. In December 1944, months after the liberation of Paris, police still dreaded the consequences of food shortages: "[Some claim that] it is no longer a question of scarcity," reported one officer, "but of staving off famine."[14]

The day after the demonstration at the Buci-Seine marketplace, lawyer Maurice Garçon, a resident of the quarter, inquired about the incident.

> I was unable to establish . . . [whether] we should see this as an expression of local exasperation or the beginnings of a larger movement. I questioned two neighboring merchants who have no doubt that Communists were behind it. Passers-by are less sure. What is certain is that the masses are restless.[15]

Restless they were. Hunger was chronic and relentless and powerful. Slowly but surely it poisoned public opinion and weakened popular support for the Vichy regime. Hunger aroused opposition and helped to manufacture active resistance to the regime. It gave credence to claims that the enemy was out to starve the people. In short, hunger made the authorities look bad. Popular opinion attributed primary responsibility for the food shortages to German requisitions. Among the many powers ceded to the German occupiers by the armistice of June 1940 was the authority to requisition any and all food, supplies, or lodgings for their own use. Much of French agricultural production was being diverted to Germany, not so much to provision soldiers as to feed civilians. Feeding tens of thousands of German troops and administrative personnel stationed in France was an additional drain on scarce resources.[16] Soldiers were known to raid farms, warehouses, and storerooms. In anticipation of the plundering, some farmers buried their wine as their forebears had done during the Franco-Prussian War in 1870. Others were inclined to drink it.

Provisioning was also hindered by lack of access to trains and control of railroad traffic. Some policies related to food scarcity, such as the ban on imports from the French colonies in North Africa, could be directly and explicitly linked to the occupiers. Other food supply problems caused by lack of human and material resources were implicitly related to German occupation policy. For one, there were too few people to work the land since the capture of French troops in 1940: some 1.8 million men were prisoners of war in Germany. The requisitioning of horses from farms by the Wehrmacht deprived farms of necessary work animals. Fertilizer was in short supply. Popular responses to the shortages—peasants holding back production for personal use, hoarding, the black market—only made matters worse.

Scholars have long assumed that food scarcity in occupied France was merely a by-product of broader German economic policies and military aims. The agricultural production of occupied countries all over Europe, not just France, was diverted to feed Germans civilians and, by the winter of 1941–42, to support the beleaguered Wehrmacht in its Russian campaign. As it happens, however, popular opinions about Germany's role in food scarcity were well founded: starving France was part of a conscious German policy of humiliation and oppression.[17]

The everyday face of the food crisis, however, was French. Vichy's Ministère du ravitaillement (Ministry of Food Supply) was in charge of rationing and distribution, which were administered by French civil servants on the departmental and local levels. Consumers dealt directly with prefects, mayors, and town clerks to retrieve their monthly ration cards and tickets. In exchange for rationed goods, shoppers surrendered tickets (and money) to vendors, who in turn recorded purchases on the card.

Rations diminished in wartime, but the caloric needs of people did not. Not eating enough and not eating well were responsible for a rise in stillbirths and infant mortality; low birth weights; slow growth rates and underweight children; diseases, such as rickets, caused by malnutrition; a fatigued and physically diminished laboring population; and general weight loss and fragile health. French children who grew up during the war years were smaller, shorter, and less robust as adults than those of the preceding generation.

Rations were assessed according to the projected caloric needs of an individual profile based on sex, age, and occupation. There were six categories in October 1940 when rationing began; additional categories and subcategories were added over time.[18] At the top of the list were workers performing hard labor and pregnant women; the elderly were at the bottom. In June 1940, when the system was first put in place, the daily bread ration for adults, the most numerous category of the population, was 350 grams; by May 31, 1942, in Paris, it had already dwindled to 275 grams. Some goods were attributed solely on the basis of sex: men had ration cards for cigarettes but women did not.

Resisters who operated fully underground using false identities were particularly hard hit by the rationing system, which required everyone to be registered with the local town hall in order to receive ration tickets. Living under a different name—and often a series of false names over the course of one's activism—necessitated not only a fake ID card but also a ration card and tickets under the same false name. Fabricating false identification for resisters was an underground operation all its own. After Madeleine Marzin's arrest, the police lost no time searching her residence. They found there incriminating evidence such as illicit Communist Party flyers calling the French to arms, and a cache of "real" false papers, including ration cards. Unlike amateur renderings, "real" false papers like the ones in Marzin's possession were made with official blanks and seals stolen from town halls and prefects' offices. These materials were to be funneled to the forgers of the underground organization. This was a critical support apparatus without which many resisters, whether full-time and fully underground or threshold activists who straddled both worlds, would have been even more exposed and vulnerable.

Eugénie Dietrich, the oldest member of the women's committee organized by Marzin, was deeply implicated in the struggle for food even before she was arrested in the wake of the demonstration. When the police raided her home, they found scores of receipts for provisions that bore the names of her customers, some of whom were arrested in the roundup of presumed demonstrators. Dietrich was a retired teacher who, unlike many, had the time and freedom to make regular trips to the Breton countryside for food. She regularly supplied friends and neighbors. Dietrich told police that her activities were motivated by a desire to help those in her entourage who were unable to make shopping trips to distant farms. She did not try to conceal her activities and maintained careful records, but it was those same records that revealed the identities of her customers and presumed co-conspirators. Swiss chocolate-maker Julien Baudois and his French wife, Georgette Duperray Baudois, stopped by on the morning of June 2 bearing a box of chocolates to thank her for supplying them with a food package. Dietrich's apartment was under police surveillance. They were swept into the dragnet.

On the immediate level, it was French shopkeepers who stood between hungry shoppers and diminishing stock. As the intermediaries between wholesalers and consumers, merchants were thought to have control, however modest, over who got what. Shopkeepers had their favorite or long-standing clients, and were often suspected of holding back or reserving supplies for special customers. In a 1947 anthropological study of French culture, one informant stated that during the war regular customers who frequented the same supplier banded together to protect their shared access to food.[19] The ambiguous role of shopkeepers was aptly captured in a wartime memoir by Gertrude Stein, who situated them "on the border between friend and enemy."[20]

Getting enough to eat often depended on cultivating favoritism from suppliers. Wealth was no longer measured in francs but in contacts. Economic capital was necessary to pay high prices, but social capital was also important for getting access to anything to buy in the first place. In his classic cookbook published in 1940, food scientist Edouard de Pomiane gave his recipe for brown sauce. The first step: "Get in the good graces of your butcher."[21] His recipe for leg of lamb is even more succinct: "There isn't any. Therefore, when you to go a restaurant, never fail to order a slice of leg of lamb so as not to forget what it tastes like."[22]

If sellers once curried favor with potential buyers, now customers had to ingratiate themselves with food providers, be they farmers or merchants, in order to earn the privilege of buying. The roles of shopkeeper and customer were now reversed. Gertrude Stein cites the words of her neighbor:

> As Madame Pierlot said, you do not buy now-a-days only with money you buy with your personality.... [N]ow it is not a question of selling [by personality] it is a question of buying by personality. Nothing is sadder these days than people who never make friends, the poor dears have nothing to eat, neither do the indiscreet.[23]

The market was more than an impersonal crossroads of buyers and sellers; it was a community of shoppers, merchants, residents, and passers-by. Public interactions over a grocer's stall, however superficial or informal, could spill over into private complicities. Such relationships formed a dense web, visible to regulars but unseen by outsiders. Given the conditions of the day, it is small wonder that party organizers staged the demonstration on a Sunday morning, the busiest time, at a site where members of the "shadow crowd" could not be identified by local shoppers or merchants. Félix Barthélemy painted a colorful tableau of the denizens of the Buci-Seine market:

> A market is a big village, everyone gets to know each other over time. . . . People knew each other with regard to what was going on, that is, at street level. . . . You know the merchant across the

way, you know this one and that one. . . . On a market street, when the shopkeepers know what is happening at ground level, when they are in contact with the streets and the sidewalks, you understand, they know what is going on. They know each other . . . and they talk and people talk to them. And, you understand, you have no idea how much people, housewives, the women who shop for food every day, how much they talk. They are happy to chat and one day there is a word about this and another day there is a word about that, and little by little one ends up taking in the whole picture and news gets around. That can only exist at street level! And especially—*especially*—in a food shop; it is not the same for other types of stores, people are more closed.[24]

The intimacy of the market, and the Buci marketplace in particular, is borne out by the testimony of locksmith Gaston Lucas. When Lucas returned to his old workshop in the Buci-Seine neighborhood after five years in a prisoner-of-war camp in Germany, he was surprised to discover that butter and meat were scarce, even with ration tickets. The nest egg he had left behind was gone; his wife had "eaten" their savings in order to buy on the black market to feed their young family. People were different, attitudes had changed, and the solidarity of the old days had vanished. His one fond memory of those days was the kindness of two merchants on the rue de Buci, one of whom contrived to supply him with extras.

On the rue de Buci near where I worked and where I knew all the shopkeepers, there was a *charcutier* who knew I had just returned [from a pow camp] and that we had little to eat at home. From time to time he came to the workshop and pretended that he had a job for me. He took me back to the shop and made me a snack and gave me a sausage to take home and the butcher did the same. 'Do you want meat for stew, a piece of roast beef?' On the rue de Buci there were some good people.[25]

If the more familiar face of the food crisis was French, many attributed the food shortages to the German occupiers. Police patrolling the rue de Buci in December 1940 predicted that anger against the German occupiers was likely to escalate. "The nature and violence of the outburst will be all the more intense because the crowd maintains that they are being *bullied on purpose* by the occupying authorities, who, according to the crowd, will continue to diminish the food supply."[26] The telling language of this police report reveals that shoppers resented the Germans not only for taking their food but also for taking their dignity.

Public displays of consumption by occupying forces fueled popular resentments. In his diary of the war years, German officer Ernst Jünger commented on the gulf between hungry Parisians and the wealthy patrons of one of Paris's most celebrated restaurants, the Tour d'Argent, located then as now in a three-story building overlooking the Seine. He likened the dining room to a flying ship (*aéronef*) soaring above the city. In this description, the restaurant was a spatial expression of social relations, with diners literally on top.

> As they consume the sole and the famous ducks [that are the specialties of the restaurant], the diners at the Tour d'Argent seem like gargoyles, peering down below with diabolical satisfaction at the gray ocean of roofs where the hungry people live, eking out a meager existence. *In such times, eating, eating well and eating a lot, gives one a sense of power.*[27]

The Tour d'Argent and luxury restaurants of its class were the near-exclusive preserve of the German elite. High-level officers and administrators, together with highly privileged French people, enjoyed lavish meals in what resembled a prewar world without restrictions. This did not go unremarked by the populace. Resentments were patent. Jünger also noted:

Lines growing longer in front of offices open to the public and in front of shops. When I pass by in uniform, I see furtive glances marked by the deepest aversion, combined with the wish to kill. One sees on these faces what a joy it would be if we [the German occupiers] disappeared into thin air and vanished like a dream.[28]

That food was seen as a weapon in the war against the French is also demonstrated by this report of an incident in Lyon. In her diary entry of February 10, 1941, Léonie Villard, a fifty-year-old professor at the University of Lyon, wrote:

> The cost of living has more than trebled in six months.... The other day, a German officer seated in a tram beside Lili tried to speak to her. As she would not listen, he began to say as if to himself in very good French: "What a pity this pretty girl and so many others will soon be starving to death." The Stuttgart radio recently boasted that the French would be driven to grubbing for food in dustbins. They think this will frighten us into submission.[29]

Food scarcity was far from the only humiliation inflicted on the defeated and occupied nation. But in a country where food is a privileged vector of national identity, it carried added symbolic weight. Food was seen as a gauge of national character and cultural superiority, both physical and moral. Gertrude Stein recounted a conversation with a neighbor in the Ain (the home of Brillat-Savarin and a region famous for its wine and cuisine), where she lived with Alice B. Toklas after 1943. In her memoir of the war years, written in her characteristic literary style, she reported this comment: "[M. Labadie] said of course the Germans cannot win, which is natural enough because their country is so poor they know nothing about cooking and eating, people who know nothing about cooking and eating naturally cannot win."[30]

The way the French think about themselves, their values, and their culture has everything to do with food: producing it, cooking it, presenting it artfully, talking and writing about it. Food was (and remains) so much more than mere sustenance. For this reason, too, hunger at the hand of the Germans hit all the harder. The impact was not only on bellies but also on minds. Scarcity affected relationships and public institutions, *haute politique* and street politics. It transformed the urban face of the capital, turned markets into sites of perpetual conflict and frustration, and pitted French against Germans and French against French.

An inalienable feature of the cityscape of the occupied capital was a new locus of sociability, the food line, or queue.[31] Food lines primarily comprised women, housewives or others, who were not employed outside the home. Indeed, the salaried population, overwhelmingly male, was at a distinct disadvantage because they had to shop in the narrow window of time before or after work. Shops might open as early as 7:00 a.m. and close at 8:00 p.m., but none stayed open continuously, serving clients for only several hours at a stretch. Teamwork was necessary for the operation of the household; families formed relays, where children took turns standing in line. Single people had to stand in line for themselves unless they hired stand-ins. Like the market itself, the food line was a women's space. The exception here confirms the rule: a young man who stood in line among women reported feeling out of place, though he noted the brighter side—it afforded him the opportunity to meet girls.[32]

The mood in line could be restless and prickly, or somber and resigned. Everyone was frustrated at having to stand in line for so little, and furious after standing in line for hours only to find that there was nothing left to be had when it was their turn to be served. A ration card entitled a person to a specific allotment of a given item per month. For every purchase, a shopper surrendered a ration ticket, but having a ticket did not guarantee that goods would be available or sufficient. Cards and tickets were necessary in addition to money. And ration tickets became a kind of currency under the circumstances: people sold them, stole them, used them for restaurant meals, and sometimes presented them as their contribution to a shared meal. Guests even offered ration tickets to their hosts in lieu of contributing a bottle of wine. But supplies could run out long before a person ran out of tickets. So, too, could patience.

The food line could also be a site of complicities. Conversations were wide-ranging, but the main focus was the shared difficulty of getting enough to eat. It was something everyone could talk about, and did. Preoccupation with food and eating were universal, and so talking about these topics could be perfectly banal, like talking about the weather. Eliciting such discussion could also be a discreet way of assessing the political disposition of one's interlocutor at a time when public opinion was intensely divided. In his diary of the war years, writer Jean Galtier-Boissière reports a "true story": a destitute woman was offered sixty francs a day by German authorities in exchange for reporting anti-German sentiment overheard in food lines.[33] Food talk was the perfect subject for sizing up a person, for assessing who might be inclined to protest and who would not. The subject of food might appear apolitical or neutral, but it had very profound political implications.

Given these changes in the food system, the gendered nature of food shopping and food preparation, and the gendered constitution of the food line, it is not surprising that the French Communist Party found in food scarcity the perfect issue around which to mobilize the population, particularly women. Women were thought to be the opening wedge into the wider population. Provisioning and cooking were quintessential women's work, but everyone had to eat. Food was the perfect one-size-fits-all mobilizing issue.

The first mention of women's food protests to appear in the underground press and police reports dates from the fall of 1940. Such protests took place in cities and towns throughout France. Those in the occupied or northern zone, including the Paris region, were overwhelmingly if not exclusively the work of the underground Communist Party, which targeted "housewives," "mothers," "women." These are broad categories that cross-cut social class, profession, and locality, but activity remained heavily concentrated in working-class neighborhoods and towns, where organizers had the greatest successes forming popular committees to spearhead local initiatives.

Demonstrations, marches, and petitions continued until well into 1945, with timing and frequency more a question of human resources and working conditions than cycles of scarcity and food supply. Delegations of women marched to town halls, prefects' offices, or warehouses, where they demanded better provisions and the release of stockpiled foodstuffs. Groups of women representing larger constituencies presented petitions to local French officials. Sometimes their demands were met with limited, short-lived, but nonetheless satisfying success: the release of potatoes, rice, or lentils. The propaganda value of this activity was twofold: there was the spectacle itself, and there was the report of a favorable outcome in the women's underground press.

What constituted a "demonstration" in occupied Paris was most often a brief display of righteous anger, peaceful if noisy. It might involve as few as ten women or as many as several dozen. A speaker would sometimes address the crowd, flyers would be distributed, and the group would quickly disband. Police were wary, but arrests and physical violence were rare. An example of this is a lesser-known women's demonstration at the open-air market on the avenue Ledru-Rollin in the Twelfth Arrondissement. It occurred on June 27, 1942, a month after the demonstration on the rue de Buci. The entire affair lasted some five to ten minutes.

The absence of conflict and the discretion of the organizer, Georgette Wallé, who did little to publicize the event after the end of the war, contributed to the relative silence surrounding the incident. Wallé said that she had been involved in women's organizing since late 1940 or early 1941, when party leadership assigned her the task of "motivating" women for protest actions.[34] She filed a report of the demonstration with her supervisor, Lise London Ricol, who, a month later, would lead the demonstration on the rue Daguerre. In one of the rare such written traces that have come down to us, Wallé describes crowd response and details the attendance of her women recruits.

> At exactly 3:00, when the *camarade* who was supposed to shout the instructions, gather the women and begin, did not see the team that was supposed to sing, [she] sang a refrain of "La Marseillaise." Afterward all of the women threw flyers that they had made by hand into the air.
> The reaction of passers-by was curious to see, their faces beamed with delight. They all scrambled to collect the flyers, read them right then and there on the street, without worrying about whether it would get them in trouble.[35]

The modus operandi is familiar: "La Marseillaise" launches the event and identifies it for the crowd as a patriotic, republican act. More familiar still is the last-minute deviation from the original plan: as in the demonstration on the rue de Buci, no one showed up to sing it.

None of the demonstrators was native to the Twelfth Arrondissement. Organizer Georgette Wallé lived across town, in the Sixteenth Arrondissement. All of her women recruits had traveled into Paris from their homes in the "red belt" suburbs of Paris: nine from Argenteuil, three each from Poissy and Sèvres, four each from Vélizy, Vaucresson, and Conflans, and one each from Brévannes, Villeneuve St.-Georges, Dourdan, and Arpajon, in addition to three *chefs de file*, or leaders.[36] Wallé had covered a wide swath of territory well beyond Paris, and it must have taken her a good deal of time and legwork. She accounted for thirty-four demonstrators in all. It was a very good turnout.

The demonstration on the avenue Ledru-Rollin was exactly as billed: it was a public protest to denounce food scarcity, and it consisted exclusively of women. According to Wallé's testimony, there was no seizure of foodstuffs, no security team on site to protect the demonstrators, and no eruption of violence. There were no arrests in connection with the incident, nor is there any trace of it in the police files. In these ways, the event diverged significantly from the demonstrations on the rue de Buci and the rue Daguerre.

There was another, more salient difference. At the avenue Ledru-Rollin market stood a statue, which in this time of penury would soon be melted down for its bronze. But the statue served one last purpose before meeting its demise: Wallé used it to string up a hand-made effigy of Laval, which she then set aflame. This unusual feature of the demonstration, a clear denunciation of the Vichy authorities in the person of the prime minister, was her own personal touch.[37]

The only documentary evidence of the event was generated by Wallé herself immediately after the demonstration. Her oral testimony some forty-three years later adds the critical detail of the immolation of Laval's effigy. Why is there no mention of this in the report she made to her supervisor? Was Wallé loath to call attention to acting off-script? Was it an oversight? If Wallé's oral testimony is correct, then all of this leaves the researcher wondering what is missing from the records, both those of the authorities and those of the opposition. It is maddeningly suggestive of a larger picture that remains out of reach.[38]

The PCF's mobilization of women was successful according to some supporters, disappointing in the estimation of others. But mobilization against whom? The signing of the Nazi-Soviet nonaggression pact in August 1939 isolated the PCF and formally prohibited it from opposing the Germans. The Third Republic had responded quickly to the treasonous pact by outlawing the PCF on September 1, 1939, nine months before the invasion. Although nonaggression was official party policy, Communist-led protest activities did not cease—on the contrary. Because food supply was in French hands, the PCF could organize underground groups around food issues without violating the nonaggression treaty. Then, on June 22, 1941, in blatant violation of the pact, Germany invaded the Soviet Union. The invasion signaled a momentous reversal, nullifying the nonaggression pact and releasing party activists from previous constraints.

There was no longer any formal prohibition against targeting the German occupiers in addition to the Vichy regime. Hitler's about-face relieved the ambivalence of Party members who had been loath to contravene official party policy by participating in resistance activities. The result was an escalation of partisan strikes and the redoubling of underground activity. The emperor had been naked all along, but after June 22, 1941, it was acceptable to say so and to act accordingly.

June 22, 1941, however, did not mark a significant uptick in the frequency of food protests, nor was there a noticeable shift in the nature or espoused purpose of protest activity. The chronology of women's underground work does not fit the pattern of other Communist-led activity. Housewives and mothers continued to level their accusations against the Vichy regime as they had since 1940, sometimes—but not always—blaming the Germans as well. A case in point is the June 1942 demonstration on the avenue Ledru-Rollin. By fashioning her effigy in the image of prime minister Laval, Georgette Wallé focused her denunciation on the French alone.

By the spring of 1942, the pro-German aims of the Vichy regime had come into fuller view. April marked the return of Laval, Pétain's prime minister, and with him the further radicalization of Vichy policy. That June, Laval uttered his infamous statement: "I wish for Germany's victory, for without it, Bolshevism will soon triumph everywhere." The Vichy regime implemented its anti-Semitic policy with increasing severity in the spring and summer of 1942, culminating in the first massive roundups and deportations of Jews, initially those who were foreign-born and then those who were native French. As a result of the very public raids and roundups of Jews, in Paris and elsewhere, public opinion was shifting, with increasing sympathy, if not support, for victims of the regime.

Communist resistance activities had also moved into a new register by 1942. Partisan attacks had been on the rise since August 1941, when Colonel Fabien felled a German officer on the platform of the Barbès-Rochechouart metro station in broad daylight. An upsurge in illegal political activity crowded jails, prisons, and court dockets. The Brigades spéciales, elite police units specialized in tracking down "Bolsheviks" and "terrorists," moved into high gear. New "exceptional" French courts were created to expedite a growing "terrorist" caseload. The Germans formed their firing squads. Tensions were coming to a head.

It was against this backdrop that the food protest on the rue de Buci unfolded on the morning of May 31. Party organizers billed it as a demonstration for food by "honest housewives" in honor of Mother's Day; for others it was "a free distribution of sardines"; for one witness, it was no more than "a derisory affair of no importance." However qualified and by whom, the event that Sunday morning would become a cause célèbre for the party and a capital case for public authorities.

PROTESTING WOMEN,
PARTISAN MEN

A nurse and a postman, teachers and metalworkers, high school students and retirees, women and men: the protagonists of the Buci affair were a diverse lot. The "shadow crowd" that converged for the distribution of free sardines that Sunday morning in May spanned three generations, plied different trades, and had different interests. Among them were newcomers to politics and old party hands. Although some would survive the war and others would not, their trajectories would forever be linked to the events of that day. Who were the protagonists, the walk-ons, and the extras? What led them from their homes, factories, schools, and workshops on that Sunday morning in May?

The incident at the Buci marketplace kicked off a manhunt that continued for many weeks. Police rounded up some eighteen individuals in the immediate aftermath of the demonstration, and preparing background reports on each arrestee was the first item of business. Police inspectors were dispatched to their homes, neighborhoods, and workplaces to gather personal information. They interviewed neighbors, family members, and associates in an effort to assess the character and standing of each individual. By June 13, two weeks after the event, police had created a profile on each of the people they had identified. Of this first batch of suspects, only Pierre Benoit, a seventeen-year-old runaway, had yet to be apprehended; he would remain on the run until the end of August.

All told, more than forty people were ultimately arrested in connection with the demonstration: one-third of them were women and two-thirds were men.[1] In some cases their connection to the incident was indisputable, while in others it was tenuous; in others still it was based on guilt by association rather than direct involvement itself. Some crowd members escaped detection altogether.

On the morning of May 31, the "shadow crowd"—demonstrators from neighboring arrondissements who did not typically frequent the Buci-Seine market—threaded themselves among the regulars and took up their positions according to the tasks assigned to them. Protesting women joined the other shoppers in line. Partisan men folded themselves into the usual Sunday crowd along the pavement and side streets. Women and men played complementary roles, had different levels of visibility, and faced different consequences.

As the event unfolded, women occupied center stage: they entered the shop, seized cans of sardines, and threw them into the crowd. Men of the shadow crowd intervened to protect the women when they met with resistance from shop hands. Sézille de Mazancourt testified that he had been directed to alert others in the event that a police van came into view. He was unarmed but no less charged with security. Some members of the security team, such as Edgar Lefébure and Lucien Legros, had guns. Others, like André Dalmas, would intervene to protect the women demonstrators with their fists and bodies. Protesting women and partisan men thus occupied the two extremes of the gender spectrum: the feminine "keeper of the hearth" and protester on one end, and the masculine soldier and protector on the other.

In principle, the two branches of the underground Communist organization—the political branch and the military branch—functioned separately. The demonstration on the rue de Buci is a rare instance in which the two branches converged to stage a joint aboveground operation. The political branch was responsible for a range of activities: the underground press (writing, printing, distribution), intelligence collection, support services (false papers, food, supplies), the establishment of popular committees, and public protest. It was the political leadership that conceived the demonstration, directed Marzin to organize it, and prepared the flyers that were thrown into the air on the day of the operation. It fell to Marzin to recruit the demonstrators, members of the women's group, and some of the unarmed men of the shadow crowd.[2]

Guerrilla actions, attacks, sabotage, and other paramilitary functions came under the purview of the military branch, which included the Francs-tireurs et partisans. The FTP was still tiny but active. The unrelenting pace of sabotage, attacks on German installations, and attacks on German officers was intended to make the authorities think the movement was more heavily manned than it really was. The FTP would assume greater importance over the course of the war as the underground fight shifted increasingly from symbolic and political actions to outright urban and rural guerrilla warfare.

On the rue de Buci, a group of both women and men constituted a middle ground of crowd "extras" or *figurants*—propagandists, couriers, observers—and blended into a crowd of real neighborhood shoppers who were oblivious to the plan. They would witness the spectacle as members of the audience and comment upon it for the benefit of their fellow spectators. Some of them had come from far-flung arrondissements and suburban areas to *faire foule*, or swell the ranks of the public. The crowd was not merely part of the stage set; it was at once subject and object of the action, sender and receiver of the message.

The local dairy shop owner, Félix Barthélemy, maintained that the demonstrators were regular customers of the Buci-Seine market from the surrounding neighborhood. In reality, organizers recruited the shadow crowd from other parts of the city, precisely because locals would have been known to other shoppers and storekeepers. According to Madeleine Marzin, the Communist rank-and-file population of the Sixth Arrondissement was nonexistent. When questioned by police, André Dalmas commented:

I suppose that the organizers of this demonstration intended to create a minor scene and, not wanting to compromise people of the neighborhood where the demonstration took place, chose demonstrators like me who lived at a distance from the incident. I lived in Maisons-Lafitte [a Parisian suburb], in fact, where I am not involved in political activity.[3]

Despite his statement to police, Dalmas had been involved in the illegal underground movement for some time.[4]

Police files and participant testimony accord with Dalmas' assertion, which also happens to fit with the logic of above-ground activity. Moreover, even those shadow crowd members who escaped detection altogether did not belong to the usual clientele who patronized the shops on the rue de Buci and the rue de Seine.

Although some witness testimony indicates that demonstrators arrived from points throughout the capital city, most of those who were known to the police came primarily from two distinct neighborhoods: the Fifth and Fifteenth Arrondissements. A third group, comprising members of the security team, was based at the partisan camp in the forest near the town of Moret-sur-Loing in the Seine-et-Marne, an area to the southeast of Paris. They converged on the market from metro stations at Odéon, Mabillon, and Port-Royal.

Under police questioning, demonstrators explained how they arrived at the site, what they had been instructed to do, and where they had been asked to stand. As previously noted, women demonstrators positioned themselves in the food line outside the Eco grocery store, while male members of the security team were positioned on the sidewalks and streets. Thus were the physical spaces of the market also gendered.

The topography of the demonstrators' places of residence also cleaves roughly along gender lines. Family, work, and friendship connections all overlap with two neighborhoods: the Fifteenth Arrondissement, the area of Madeleine Marzin's primary activity, and the Fifth Arrondissement, where there lived another cluster of people, mostly men, arrested in connection with the affair. Both

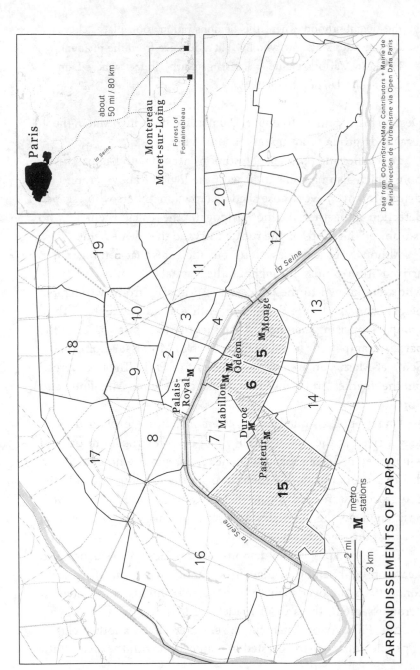

ARRONDISSEMENTS OF PARIS

M métro stations

2 mi
3 km

The twenty arrondissements of Paris. The demonstrators' arrondissements of origin are shaded. The inset shows the location of the Fontainebleau forest and the partisan base camp in the towns of Moret-sur-Loing and Montereau. *Map by Gregory T. Woolston.*

Data from ©OpenStreetMap Contributors + Mairie de Paris/Direction de l'Urbanisme via Open Data Paris arrondissements are adjacent to the Sixth, where the Buci-Seine market is located.

Public protest, while prohibited by law, was by definition aboveground activity; thus most female demonstrators were "legals," living under their real names in their own homes and working at their regular jobs. These were the so-called threshold resisters, men and women, who functioned both aboveground and underground at once, or moved from one plane to another in the course of their resistance careers.

Partisan operations, on the other hand, required that activists be unseen, or underground. Activists whose real identities had already been compromised (including several male students and some members of the security team) lived completely underground. They were full-timers who operated under noms de guerre, sometimes changed their physical appearance, severed ties to friends and family, used forged papers, and left their homes and jobs.

The collective portrait of the shadow crowd that emerges from the police investigation is strikingly emblematic of the underground movement. The links among them reveal a web of interrelated itineraries, family connections, coworkers, and local Communist cells. The party was not only a family in the figurative sense; political opinion, affinities, and activism were a family affair, sometimes "inherited" from parents or other family members, shared between couples, or extending to in-laws and other relatives. Some activists worked together or had done so previously; their connections were forged on the factory floor, in the sorting area of the post office, in the schoolyard, or in laundries. In turn, family and work dovetailed with neighborhood: most of these people lived in close proximity to one another in the Fifteenth or Fifth Arrondissement.

Equally striking is the social plurality of the group, a long-vaunted aspect of resistance in general. This modest, forty-person sample is diverse: men and women; new recruits to the party and old-timers; high school students and retirees; manual laborers, employees, artisans, and intellectuals; members of the working

RELATIONSHIPS

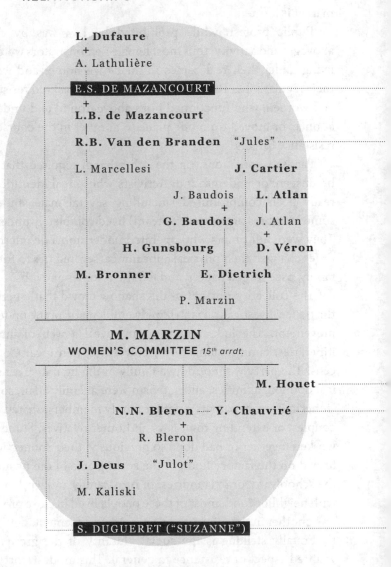

L. Dufaure
+
A. Lathulière

E.S. DE MAZANCOURT
+
L.B. de Mazancourt
|
R.B. Van den Branden   "Jules"

L. Marcellesi   J. Cartier

              J. Baudois   L. Atlan
                  + |
              G. Baudois   J. Atlan
                                +
          H. Gunsbourg   D. Véron
                                |
M. Bronner   E. Dietrich

                 P. Marzin
                      |

M. MARZIN
WOMEN'S COMMITTEE *15ʰ arrdt.*

                          M. Houet

          N.N. Bleron ---- Y. Chauviré
                  +
             R. Bleron

J. Deus   "Julot"

M. Kaliski

S. DUGUERET ("SUZANNE")

This diagram depicts the demonstrators' principal points of origin and the dense web of familial and associational ties connecting them to each other. *Diagram by Gregory T. Woolston.*

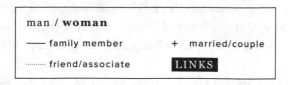

man / **woman**
—— family member + married/couple
········· friend/associate ▮LINKS▮

A. Cousin
▮E. LEFEBURE▮

E. Blanchon   R. Desvignes
    R. Pluvinet   A. Martin

GARAGE *5th arrdt.*

▮R. ESTRADE▮   M. Leclerc   L. Menut
    H. Meunier

A. Dalmas   J. Arthus   P. Grelot

FTP   **LYCÉE BUFFON** *15th arrdt.*

E. Gras   ▮P. BENOIT▮   L. Legros

G. Vallet ("Louis," "Ludovic," "Raoul"), *FTP commander*
PARTISAN CAMP *Moret-sur-Loing*
+
S. Rousseau   A. Barrachi   G. Gauthier
L. Chapiro ("Labadie")   M. Le Berre
+

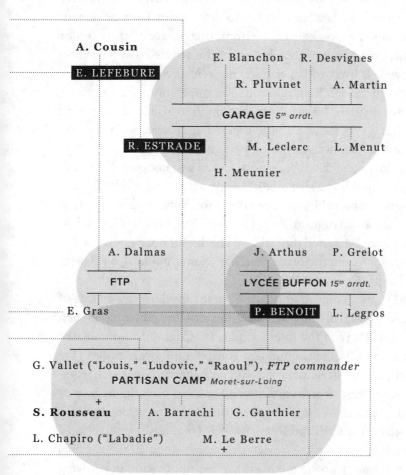

class and bourgeois *de bonne famille*; single, married, and divorced. What unites them above all is left-wing political orientation— or, in the curious words of one investigator, "advanced political opinions."

The critical mass of demonstrators, both women and men, were working people in their late twenties to early forties. For a movement meant to mobilize housewives, it is ironic that only one demonstrator was a full-time housewife. All but six of the arrested demonstrators were married, lived with partners, or were divorced. Many were mothers and fathers. Their subsequent incarcerations, deportations, and deaths deprived some twenty-two children of at least one parent for the duration of the war. The youngest demonstrators of the group left behind at least twelve grieving parents and siblings.

Participation in the Buci demonstration was not only a response to a call to arms. It was also predicated on a dense network of family ties, work relationships, residential proximity, shared political sensibilities, and past histories. Of all these variables, it was past history that most interested the police. Whether or not a given suspect had played a role in the Buci affair, her former political allegiances sufficed to justify an arrest.

Most of the demonstrators had been involved in one or more of the broad-based, left-wing organizations dominated by the French Communist Party in the interwar period: Communist-dominated unions, local cells, the Communist-run veterans' organization (the Association républicaine des anciens combattants, or ARAC), workshop committees, women's groups, and youth groups. In the heavily charged language of the time, their political sympathies lay with "the doctrines of the Third International" (that is, the international organization, based in the Soviet Union, of which all the national Communist parties were members). Their implication in left-wing political activity ranged from allegation of opinion ("maintains his/her sympathy for Muscovite theories," "has left-wing sympathies without engaging in political activism") to impressive, decades-long records of political work.

Women's organizations of the interwar period are well represented among the protesting women. Eugénie Dietrich dated her first foray into leftist politics to 1916. She had been a member of the Groupes des femmes socialistes before the PCF even existed. In the 1920s she became a member of the *commission féminine* of the Confédération générale du travail unitaire (CGTU), the PCF labor union. She subscribed to the women's newspaper *La Voix des femmes*, along with an array of other left-wing publications such as the PCF daily *L'Humanité* and *L'Enseignement laïque*, which promoted secular Republican ideals in education. Fellow demonstrator Marguerite Bronner had been a member of the Comité mondial des femmes contre la guerre et le fascisme (World Committee of Women Against War and Fascism) as well as the Confédération générale du travail (CGT).[5]

On the other hand, the youngest demonstrators were new recruits to politics. They were the high school students of the security team: Jean Arthus, Pierre Benoit, Pierre Grelot, and Lucien Legros. They had been politicized—some say radicalized—by the extinction of democratic institutions and the concomitant creation of an anti-Semitic and repressive state. The four teenagers, who were already known as "the students of the Lycée Buffon," had previous experience with political protest.[6] They were (and remain) famous for organizing a large demonstration of high school students to protest the arrest of their literature teacher, Raymond Burgard, a founder of the underground newspaper *Valmy*. After Lucien Legros was arrested for his participation in the Buci affair, an appeal for clemency from his lawyer claimed that young Legros had been "seduced [by] unscrupulous elements" who had sought to exploit his "utter despair about the French defeat."[7] But the young partisans were exceptions. The majority of demonstrators at the rue de Buci had been shaped by the antifascist, popular front politics of the preceding decade.

Past experience alone does not explain how or why these individuals joined the demonstration, or even the underground movement. Involvement was also predicated on preexisting relationships. The identities of the participants reveal another characteristic feature of resistance organization in general: the critical importance of social and familial networks. It is precisely such relationships that account for the mobilization of many resisters in this period, particularly women. Resistance was a family affair. The path to the underground was very often by way of a sibling, a parent, or a spouse. In much resistance work, men, women, and children were coequal members of family teams.

French and German authorities were aware of this. They had made it clear that family members would be arrested and held as hostages if a suspect could not be found. This was not only to coax a suspect out of hiding but also because the authorities were well aware of such complicities. To protect party operations, resisters themselves, and their family members, the party leadership instructed full-time underground activists to sever family ties, as previously noted. But oftentimes this rule was not respected, either because it was impractical (if not impossible) or because it was unbearably taxing to relationships.

In the summer of 1942, it was simply not possible to stage an illegal aboveground action that required a crowd without relying on family and associational ties. Crowd members who had been recruited for the Buci protest included couples and family members. This increased the protestors' vulnerability, but it also gave them cover. A couple strolling together attracted less attention than a lone individual. A solitary man, especially a younger one, fit the image of a "terrorist." A man accompanied by a woman—a real couple or two resisters masquerading as a couple—were less suspect, at least for a time.

Then as ever, Communist Party sympathies and membership ran in families. The PCF of the 1930s had been not only a subculture or universe unto itself but also, in a very literal sense, an extended family.[8] Numerous couples, married or unmarried, either attended the demonstration together or were arrested in connection with the Buci affair: Émile Sézille de Mazancourt, Marzin's own liaison agent, and his wife, Louise; Roger Bléron and Norma Nicoletti; Jean Atlan and Denise Véron; Julien Baudois and Georgette Duperray; Edgar Lefébure and Angèle Cousin; Jeanne Deus and Mayer Kaliski; Arthur Lathulière and Lucienne Dufaure; and Georges Vallet and a woman noted only as "la femme Rousseau." She was Simone Rousseau, Vallet's partner.

Other family members were linked to the demonstration as well. Louise Berthelet Sézille de Mazancourt, wife of Émile, recruited her widowed sister, Raymonde Berthelet Van den Branden. They worked together at a laundry. Denise Véron was the daughter of Eugénie Dietrich, whose home was an epicenter of political activity. Véron's partner, Jean Atlan, was swept into the raid along with the others. As a result, Atlan's mother, Laure, was also arrested. Émile Blanchon and Raymond Pluvinet, who shared a garage where illegal propaganda was stored, were brothers-in-law. Pierre Marzin, brother of the ring-leader, Madeleine, was arrested in his sister's wake. A long list of subversive activities was attributed to him, although he denied having anything to do with the demonstration and he insisted (falsely) that he had broken ties with his sister over political disagreements.

Of the women arrested in the immediate aftermath of May 31, three were married to men who were already behind bars for underground Communist activity: Julia Cartier's husband had been arrested in February 1942, Angèle Cousin's husband had been arrested in February 1941 and handed over to the Germans in January 1942, and Henriette Gunsbourg's husband had been condemned in 1941 for "Communist propaganda." That politics was a family affair is amply demonstrated by the Baudois family. "The whole family was identified as Communist propagandists," said a police report. One of two grown sons had been found guilty of association with a "notorious terrorist" in 1941.

Then there were friends and friends of friends. Gunsbourg testified that Dietrich was an old friend of her mother's. Léonard Marcellesi's son attended the Lycée Buffon along with Legros,

Benoit, Grelot, and Arthus, all members of the security team. On the night of May 31, Raymond Estrade had spent the night at the home of his friend Marcel Leclerc. Madeleine Marzin stayed frequently at the apartment of her friend Eugénie Dietrich and had lived with her for years prior. At the time of the Buci affair, Maté Houet, who was fully underground at the time, was rooming with Madeleine Marzin in Plessis-Robinson, a small suburb to the south of Paris.

Other demonstrators and associates shared professional ties. Teachers were overrepresented among the women involved in the Buci affair, no doubt because Madeleine Marzin was one herself. A teacher at the primary level, Marzin knew other teachers on whom she could rely and who shared her beliefs. It is not unlikely that her political network derived from the union organizing she did in the 1930s. All of these teachers lived in the Fifteenth Arrondissement: Jeanne Deus, a twenty-nine-year-old primary schoolteacher; Julia Cartier, a retired German teacher who gave private lessons; and Eugénie Dietrich, another retired schoolteacher. Dietrich's daughter Denise Véron and her companion, Jean Atlan, both taught at the secondary level.

When questioned by police, Marzin proudly identified herself as a *public* schoolteacher. This mattered to Marzin; the public school system was both testament to and guarantor of the egalitarian French Republic. The public sector was further represented by André Dalmas and Léonard Marcellesi, both of whom worked for the PTT (post and telegraph services); Robert Desvignes, a street cleaner employed by the city of Paris; André Martin, a gatekeeper at the Préfecture de police; Raymond Pluvinet, a transporter at the Ministry of Youth; and Henri Meunier, an "errand boy" (*garçon de bureau*, despite his forty-four years) at the Préfecture de la Seine.

Several of the men in the Mouffetard area of the Fifth Arrondissement were or had been autoworkers at the Renault factory in Boulogne-Billancourt. Here again, party activism, workplace, and union membership overlap with neighborhood. Two of them had been in the same local party cell and were employed in the same workshop. Five of them shared space in a garage on the rue de la Clef, which had been rented under Henri Meunier's name. They used it to store bicycles, equipment, and illicit clandestine newspapers and flyers. When police gained access to the garage, they found a veritable warehouse of incriminating material.

While this tangle of intersecting relationships promoted recruitment, it also facilitated discovery and arrest. Under ideal clandestine circumstances, activists did not know each other by their real names. But such conditions did not obtain for aboveground actors like the demonstrators on the rue de Buci. Not only did many know each other by their real names, but their lives were often deeply entwined. By pulling on single threads, the police were able to unravel large pieces of the whole.

While the shadow crowd was crisscrossed by common political affinities, kinship ties, friendships, shared workplaces, and residential proximity, in other ways it was a motley collection of individuals and life stories. There were important differences in background, profession, and age.

The profiles of the people arrested by police stipulate that all but two were "of Aryan race." With the exception of the Polish-born Mayer Kaliski and the Swiss chocolatier Julien Baudois and his wife, Georgette Duperray (French by birth, Swiss by marriage), all were French citizens (Italian-born Norma Nicoletti had acquired French nationality when she married Roger Bléron).

Two of the alleged demonstrators were Jewish men whose situation had become increasingly dire in the wake of Vichy's anti-Semitic legislation. Mayer Kaliski was rounded up with the first batch of demonstrators. There is very little information on him in the files, no doubt because his case was handled with dispatch. Kaliski had three strikes against him: he was Polish-born, Jewish, and, like many east European refugees, assumed to be of "Bolshevik" persuasion. When questioned by French police, he claimed not to know whether or not he was of "Aryan race." Kaliski was handed over to the Germans on

July 26 and left France on the next train to Auschwitz the following day. He never returned.[9]

Jean Atlan, of Algerian descent, had taken the name of his partner, Denise Véron, in an attempt to conceal his Jewish identity. He had been fired from his teaching position at the prestigious Lycée Condorcet after the Vichy legislation of October 1940, which barred Jews from the civil service and teaching professions. A philosopher by training, Atlan described himself as a "man of letters." His fifty-nine-year-old mother, Laure, a former nurse, was rounded up as well. "Given her frequentations," states one report, "it seems certain that her sympathies lie with communism." Her "frequentations" included the home of Eugénie Dietrich, where she was scooped up by police. It is not clear whether Jean or his mother played a role in the Buci affair. They moved in suspect circles, and that alone sufficed. Laure Atlan was subsequently interned at Pithiviers, a holding camp for Jews.

Atlan's political sympathies are cited in his file: "Since 1933, he has openly participated in the Union fédérale des étudiants [Federal Union of Students], a communist organization, and has been a dogged propagator of muscovite theories." Atlan's pleas for clemency and release were increasingly desperate throughout his incarceration. French authorities considered him more suited to St. Anne's, the Parisian institution for the mentally disturbed, than to prison. From what we know of the living conditions in institutional settings of the period, Atlan was fortunate not to die of starvation.[10] That said, confinement to St. Anne's may have saved his life; Atlan escaped deportation to a concentration camp for Jews. In the end he survived his detention, but his request for postwar reparations accorded political detainees was denied.[11]

Whether Atlan's alleged disturbance was real or feigned, we do not know. Based on the content of a letter he wrote from his prison cell condemning his unjust detention in the strongest possible terms, he appears to have been rather lucid:

After all, Monsieur le Directeur de la Police Judiciaire, there was a time when Communist activity was legal, in France. . . . Can you imagine a "terrorist" addressing an audience for two hours on the mysteries of Sainte-Thérèse or a Tibetan yogi? . . . I can assure you, my fiancée and I live in a world that has nothing to do with the one that seems to interest your police. I do not think that poetry and music are now considered a threat to state security. It is my misfortune to be "of Jewish race." I know full well that you have every right to throw me in a camp where, like my young brother or my mother, I would have a choice between tuberculosis and insanity.[12]

Atlan's letter lacks the apologetic, even obsequious tone of Marguerite Bronner's correspondence with authorities from her prison cell, but his points are well taken. No doubt the vehemence of his expression, not to mention his mockery of the police, did little to ingratiate him with his captors.

The majority of demonstrators, both women and men, were civil servants (teachers and other state employees) and manual laborers. Among the latter were a warehouse worker, a maid or housecleaner, factory workers, and a street cleaner. Important exceptions were the midlevel workers and artisans: nurses, a head chocolate maker, a necktie maker, a printer, and a carpenter. The high school students were of *bonne famille*, so-called good families—the term has nothing to do with virtue and everything to do with social class. Their fathers included a high civil servant in the Ministry of Finance, an engineer in the PTT, a police administrator, and a military doctor.

Finally, the ages of the demonstrators ranged from seventeen to sixty-four.[13] The center of gravity was men and women in their thirties. On average, the women were slightly older than the men; the youngest members of the group were the four lycée students, which accounts for the age discrepancy by sex. The oldest demonstrators were born in the nineteenth century, between 1878 and 1900. Garage-renters Blanchon and Pluvinet were veterans of the First World War. One of the demonstrators, Angèle Cousin, was a war orphan herself, having lost her father at the age of five.

At sixty-four, Eugénie Dietrich was the doyenne of the group. Dietrich's home on the rue Léon-Dierx in the Fifteenth Arrondissement was a veritable crossroads of activity. A police stakeout of her apartment over several days yielded some eight arrests. The Dietrich residence was very likely the center of the local women's committee (organized by Marzin), from which most of the women demonstrators were recruited.

Dietrich was a twentieth-century *pétroleuse* (incendiary), the sobriquet for the unruly women of the Paris Commune who were said to use arson as a political weapon. Associates questioned by the police described her as stubborn, opinionated, and strong-willed. Her police record appears to confirm this. In 1926, Dietrich had been arrested for insulting a police officer (*outrage à agent*).

In 1942, among Dietrich's offenses was giving shelter to Madeleine Marzin, who had in fact stayed at her apartment on the night of May 30–31. Dietrich was also found to be in possession of compromising materials: ration tickets in the names of various people and fake ID cards, including that of Madeleine Marzin. She denied any knowledge of the demonstration and, in her characteristically provocative fashion, asserted, "No doubt I was not informed because of my age but I would have gone had I known about it."[14]

Indeed, police investigators were unable to establish Dietrich's participation in the demonstration: she was acquitted in a court judgment on June 25. Despite her acquittal, however, she remained in custody, damned by her network of associates—not to mention her impudence. Dietrich was judged a second time, along with the next round of arrestees, and was acquitted once again, but she was still not released. Deemed a "menace to public order," she spent the rest of the war in an internment camp.

On the opposite end of the age spectrum was Lucien Legros. In age, he was similar to other young partisan recruits who were drawn to direct action. Unlike many of their fellow demonstrators who were seasoned union and party members, they were too young to have been forged in the political hothouse that was France in the 1930s. Legros' baptism by fire had taken place in late 1941, when he became involved in some early partisan operations. Legros was seventeen years old at the time of his arrest. A month after his eighteenth birthday, he was executed by a German firing squad.

What about the ones who got away? Those who escaped capture remain absent from the story and from the memory of the story. Some members of the shadow crowd will remain forever in the shadows. Only participant or second-hand testimony can fill the gaps in the archival record, but points of intersection between the written and spoken records are rare. Moreover, there are contradictions between the official record and oral testimony, between witnesses themselves, between a demonstrator who testified in 1942 and others who testified forty or fifty years later, and between a self-described "earwitness" who was hostile to the protest and crowd members who were there to support it. All of this is a powerful—and humbling—reminder that much about the incident is unknowable. Parts of the story have been lost, eclipsed, or suppressed. From these miscellaneous written and oral fragments we can only limn the uncertain contours of a collective portrait— more a Picasso than a Rembrandt.

Madeleine Marzin's accomplice, Berthe Houet, known as Maté, was one of the lucky demonstrators who escaped capture. Her name was neither Maté nor Houet at the time. She was born Berthe Barot and acquired the surname Houet from her second husband, whom she married after the war. Madeleine Marzin's affectionate nickname for her was "Totoche," and this is how Houet is referenced in some of Marzin's testimony. At the time of the demonstration she was known as Léna. Another of her other noms de guerre was Marie-Thérèse, which she shortened to Maté. Like many other resisters, she carried her adopted name for the rest of her life as a proud reminder of her wartime experience. Houet managed to continue her work without mishap until the end of the war. However, were one to search for her in the documentary record using the name she bore in the postwar period, Maté Houet would be invisible. This is the case for many women resisters, whose clandestine monikers differed from their given names, and whose given names were not the same as their married ones. As a result, many underground operatives like Maté Houet have been doubly invisible.

Marzin and Houet met through Eugénie Dietrich. Although Houet was fully underground in May 1942, Marzin insisted that she attend the demonstration. Despite the risk, Marzin needed to assemble as many people as possible.[15] Houet managed to "pass between the raindrops," in the words of Roger Arnould, a Communist resister like Maté, who also eluded arrest and detention over the course of the war after many a close call.[16]

Thanks to Maté Houet, whose oral testimony is critical to the reconstruction of events, we know the identity of Elie Gras. Maté was about to be trapped inside the shop when Gras, who had been charged with protecting the demonstrators, lifted the iron grate to free her just as it was being slammed shut. Thanks to him, she was able to wriggle underneath to safety. Both Maté and Gras were lucky enough to evade capture that day. Gras, however, was arrested several months later in connection with another operation. He died under torture.[17]

Other demonstrators who do not figure in the official record of the Buci affair may include Jean Pottier and Lucette Pécheux. According to one source, Pottier, a member of the FTP, was part of the security team charged with protecting the demonstrations at the Buci market.[18] If that is indeed true, then it is not unlikely that his partner, Lucette, was also among the protesting women. Couples often worked in tandem even though it was a serious breach of security. Moreover, Pécheux and Pottier lived together in the immediate vicinity of the Buci market, on the rue de l'Odéon. These suggestive tidbits leave us wanting to know more. Was Lucette Pécheux among the anonymous members of the shadow crowd who got away?

If so, it was not for long. The couple was arrested by the Brigades spéciales at their home on June 18, 1942, for other illegal activities. On August 11, a mere three weeks after his arrest, Jean Pottier was executed by firing squad on Mont-Valérien. Lucette Pécheux was deported to Auschwitz on January 24, 1943. She was in the convoy of women prisoners known as "the 31,000," many of whom worked in the Communist underground.[19] It was the closest thing to a death sentence short of execution. According to a biographical profile written by her fellow prisoner Charlotte Delbo, Lucette Pécheux died a month after her arrival in Auschwitz. Her story died with her.[20]

It also happens that demonstrators from the Fifteenth and Fifth Arrondissements of Paris were joined by contingents from the Thirteenth and Fourteenth Arrondissements. In 1951 Marzin recalled the Buci case in an extraordinary fifteen-page report entitled "What I know about the demonstration of June 1, 1942 (*sic*), on the rue de Buci."[21] She was responding to a request to supply an account of the event from a high-ranking member of the PCF leadership André Marty, who also represented the Thirteenth Arrondissement in the National Assembly. In an internal PCF report summarizing the wartime activities in his district, there was mention of local FTP participation in the demonstrations of the rue de Buci and the rue Daguerre.[22] Marty wanted to know more, so he asked Marzin to fill in the blanks.

Marzin reconstituted, to the best of her memory, the names of people who had been present at the Buci-Seine marketplace on May 31, 1942. Her testimony reveals the identities of some previously unidentified women and men of the shadow crowd. This is precious information she withheld from the police; it appears nowhere in her interrogations or other official accounts of the event. Compartmentalization protected the ones who got away; even Marzin herself did not know their names, or in some cases their real names.

In addition to the twenty or so people from her own sector, the Saint-Lambert district of the Fifteenth Arrondissement, Marzin remembered Julie Mailloux of the Plaisance area of the Fourteenth Arrondissement. Mailloux was accompanied by several others from her neighborhood, including an unnamed young man. A certain Ginette was also among the women who stormed the shop, according to Marzin's 1951 version of the affair. But Ginette appears nowhere else in written or oral accounts of the demonstration. Who was she?

Among heretofore unidentified members of the security team, Marzin also mentioned Roger Mathieu. The unnamed local *responsable politique* was on-site as well. He introduced Marzin and Dalmas, telling Dalmas, "This is the *camarade* you will be watching over." She also reported speaking with two individuals from the section in charge of organization on the rue de Buci. They were new to their posts, and Marzin recalled "neither their faces nor their noms de guerre."[23]

Who else passed between the raindrops? According to André Tollet, a high-ranking member of the Communist party leadership during the war, the shadow crowd included Jeanne Fanonnel.[24] Like Tollet, Fanonnel was an important figure in the Communist labor movement, a member of the Comité parisien de Libération in 1945, and a life-long activist from the prewar period until her death in 1982. However, her participation in the demonstration on the rue de Buci has never been confirmed. The trail of the anonymous shadow members of the shadow crowd ends here—at least for now.

The partisan counterpart to Madeleine Marzin was Georges Vallet, aka "Raoul" or "Ludovic," who commanded the security team on-site. He was most likely the elusive "man in the trenchcoat" whom witnesses and participants noticed at the scene. For Pierre Benoit, he was "the boss." Vallet was allegedly overheard identifying himself to a group of men, saying: "I am the commander here" (*C'est moi qui commande*). He was captured by French police in the spring of 1943, then tried and executed by the Germans. The Buci affair was but a detail in his lengthy resumé of partisan activities.[25]

Vallet reported to Henri Tanguy, later known as "Colonel Rol," the commander in chief of partisan operations in the Ile-de-France. Based on Vallet's assessment of the demonstration, Rol designed a new strategy in the interest of limiting, if not preventing, further partisan losses. The participants responsible for security were divided into three-man teams, and each member of the team would have a specific role: one to protect the demonstrators, another to protect the protector, and a third to cover their getaway. This revised practice was put into practice a month later, when the party staged another demonstration at the central Parisian market on the rue Daguerre.[26] Alas, the human toll was equally grave: a policemen and a passerby lost their lives in the scuffle. However, there were no arrests on-site. It was not until the following days that several demonstrators were rounded up by police. The ringleader of the operation, Lise London Ricol, was arrested several days later, but in connection with another case.[27]

Thus the demonstration on the rue de Buci marked a significant turning point in the waging of urban guerrilla warfare. It also inaugurated a new level of state repression, as French authorities were keen to make examples of the demonstrators.

ACTS OF WAR

"Association with evildoers," "sympathies for principles espoused by the Third International," "use of force in an act of pillage as part of a gang," "attempted murder," "murder," "act of war": this is how a public protest for food that ended in violence was defined in legal terms, listed in order of increasing severity, in occupied Paris.[1]

More than forty people with ties to the demonstration on the rue de Buci were rounded up and stood trial before four different jurisdictions, both French and German. Some activists who had played key roles in the affair were in fact arrested in the course of other investigations that had nothing to do with the Buci affair. Thus the list of suspects grew, even after what would be only the first of several trials. The courts rendered verdicts ranging from acquittal to the death penalty. A handful of people were tried more than once in different courts, either for the same offense or for related offenses uncovered in the course of the investigation. The roundups began on the day of the incident and continued for many months. The last person with known ties to the Buci affair was arrested in April 1943.

The demonstration on the rue de Buci was a joint operation of the political and paramilitary branches of the underground Communist Party, which in turn correlated with the respective roles of protesting women and partisan men. The demonstration was also closely imbricated with two other important cases, or "affairs": that of the students of the Lycée Buffon, a public high school in the Fifteenth Arrondissement, where many of the demonstrators lived, and another case that involved the partisan camp at Moret-sur-Loing in the forest of Fontainebleau outside of Paris. Both of these cases are well known individually, but their deep connection to the Buci affair has gone undetected until now. All three cases share key protagonists with ties to multiple operations in the Paris region.

The investigation began on the morning of May 31 at the scene of the incident. The police of the local commissariat on the rue de l'Abbaye collected the first set of evidence, but the case was quickly turned over to higher authorities in the interior and justice ministries. The matter eventually landed on the desk of the head of state, Maréchal Pétain.

Captured at the scene of the demonstration *in flagrante delicto* were André Dalmas and Henri Meunier, who were immediately escorted to the local police station. Edgar Lefébure, also arrested that same day, was identified by a policeman who said that he saw him give the order to open fire. He attempted to flee the scene but was apprehended. Police also recovered the pocket book of one demonstrator, Marguerite Bronner, who had dropped it in the scuffle inside the shop. By the end of the day, police had some six demonstrators (or supposed demonstrators) in custody: Dalmas; Meunier; Lefébure; Meunier's associate Raymond Estrade; Bronner; and Bronner's mother, Elisabeth Bonnier, who lived with Bronner and her son.

When the thirty-nine-year-old machine operator Marguerite Bronner realized, with horror, that she had lost her pocketbook, she hurried to her local *commissariat de police* in the Fifteenth Arrondissement to report the loss, claiming to have been at her local market on the rue de la Convention when her purse went missing. Bronner had had the right impulse: to cover her tracks and establish an alibi. Her efforts proved fruitless, however. The three detectives assigned to stake out her apartment were already waiting for her by the time she got home. She was arrested on the spot.

Twenty-eight-year-old postal worker André Dalmas was arrested after he intervened to protect the women demonstrators inside the Eco market. When the salesperson in charge of sardines, André Delcros, seized Marzin, Dalmas freed her by punching him

Police photos were taken immediately after the incident. They show the tiny rue Bourbon-le-Château where it intersects with the rue de Buci from two different angles. The shops are shuttered and the streets have been cleared. Police were taking André Dalmas along this street en route to the local police station on the rue de l'Abbaye when shots rang out. (The rue de l'Abbaye is the extension of the rue Bourbon-le-Château that runs along the north side of the church of Saint-Germain-des-Prés.)

The white patch on the middle left side of the second photo is a hole where the originals were strung together with a piece of twine. Government offices also suffered from the penury of paper and office supplies. *Archives nationales, Pierrefitte, France.*

Here we see the section of the rue de Buci that stretches from the rue Bourbon-le-Château. Police are standing at the opening of the rue Bourbon-le-Château on the left. The Eco supermarket is in the background, situated to the right of the tiny intersection of the rue de Buci and the rue de Seine. *Archives nationales, Pierrefitte, France.*

in the face. Dalmas himself was then seized by police. Members of the crowd were unsuccessful in their attempts to free him as police escorted him down the rue Bourbon-le-Château en route to the local police station. According to one police report, a crowd of some one hundred people teemed around Dalmas as the agent led him away.

An armed member of the security team, forty-four-year-old civil servant Henri Meunier, who worked as an "office boy" at the Préfecture de la Seine, was seen fleeing the scene by an off-duty policeman. He had crossed the boulevard Saint-Germain and was racing down one of the tiny side streets, the rue Clément, where he entered a garage to dispose of his firearm. He was captured upon emerging from the garage, and the police retrieved the smoking revolver he had flung there. Later that same evening, Meunier's associate Raymond Estrade was arrested at his home.

The arrest of Meunier led police to the garage he had rented in the Fifth Arrondissement, which was placed under surveillance. Police also uncovered a duplicating machine for printing illegal underground newspapers in a civil defense shelter on the nearby rue Blainville, where Meunier had stored it for safekeeping.

A third member of the security team, thirty-two-year-old metalworker Edgar Lefébure, was likewise taken into custody. A plainclothes detective testified that he had seen Lefébure give the order to open fire. He, too, was seized on-site at the time of the demonstration. The same detective also testified that he had seen two men escaping over the roofs at 28 rue de Buci. Their identities were unknown at the time, but they escaped capture, at least in the short term.

If the response from police was swift, it is because there was as a matter of course a police presence at pressure points in the capital, including—or especially—near markets and market streets. Two uniformed police officers were on regular patrol when the trouble erupted. Others arrived from the local station on the rue de l'Abbaye. Tucked away in the shadow crowd was a shadow policeman, a plainclothesman who also walked the Buci-Seine beat. He was invisible to demonstrators but known to merchants and regulars. In addition to the usual police presence, an off-duty policeman who lived on the neighboring rue Clément was also in the area. It so happened that he was accompanying his wife on her Sunday morning shopping rounds at the time of the incident. Later, police vans from the Fifth, Sixth, and Seventh Arrondissements responded to a call for backup, but there was no massive roundup of demonstrators. By then the crowd had scattered.

Gardien de la paix Camille Morbois, who made his rounds on a bicycle, died from a bullet wound on the scene. His colleague Brigadier Eugène Vaudrey succumbed to his injuries shortly thereafter. Three other policemen, François Metzinger, Jean-Baptiste

Thomas, and René Massnet, were wounded in the struggle. It was abundantly clear that the affair had far-reaching consequences that exceeded the competence of the local commissariat. On June 1 the case was turned over to the Brigades spéciales I, an elite police unit that specialized in the repression of subversive Communist activities. It was soon determined, however, that the nature and severity of the crimes transcended the realm of illegal political activity. The Brigades spéciales II, whose charge was the hunt for terrorists, took over the investigation from there.

From May 31 on, the arrests multiplied. The police set up stakeouts at various locations, starting with the residences of the first people arrested. Some suspects were arrested at their homes; others, like Émile Sézille de Mazancourt, were arrested at work. Many more demonstrators or suspected demonstrators were ensnared when they showed up at the homes of those already in custody. Considerable resources had been devoted to this surveillance, with three detectives at the most promising sites. The most fruitful stakeouts proved to be Eugénie Dietrich's apartment in the Fifteenth Arrondissement, the garage on the rue de la Clef in the Fifth Arrondissement, the (false) address Marzin gave as her home, and Marzin's actual residence in Plessy-Robinson.

Eugénie Dietrich's apartment on the rue Léon-Dierx was the epicenter of the women's committee. She was taken into custody the day after the demonstration. Her apartment was under surveillance when Norma Nicoletti appeared. This in turn led police to Nicoletti's husband, Roger Bléron, who was arrested at their home the next day. A number of other demonstrators were subsequently apprehended there, including Yvonne Chauviré, Mayer Kaliski, Léonard Marcellesi, Jean Atlan and his mother, Laure, Georgette Duperray Baudois and her husband, Julien Baudois, Julia Cartier, and Henriette Gunsbourg.

The many comings and goings reported by Dietrich's neighbors cast plenty of suspicion. In fact, Dietrich told police that she made regular visits to Brittany to bring packages of foodstuffs back to

Paris, where she made distributions from her apartment. Receipts for these packages bearing names were found in her possession, which in turn led police to more suspects.

Marzin was arrested on June 1. She gave as her address an empty apartment that was used to store illicit clandestine literature. She did this to buy time because she knew that others who frequented her home were in danger of being caught. However, when police arrived at the false address, her brother Pierre, who was living fully underground, happened to be there. He was arrested on the spot. He had not played a role in the demonstration but had committed a number of other offenses, including having escaped from an internment camp where he had been held for "reconstitution of a disbanded league."[2]

Police also uncovered a veritable arsenal of illegal propaganda, false ration cards and ID cards, several guns, and cash. This implicated Madeleine Marzin as more than just the organizer of a women's demonstration for food. Ration cards in the names of Mayer Kaliski and Denise Véron were in Marzin's possession. Véron was also Dietrich's daughter; she was one of many people linking Marzin and Dietrich. All of these people were pursued by police or arrested when they appeared at one of the sites under surveillance.

The surveillance of the garage on the rue de la Clef in the Fifth Arrondissement yielded yet more suspects. Raymond Pluvinet was arrested there when he showed up to store his bicycle. Émile Blanchon, Marcel Leclerc, and André Martin also fell into the net.

The police amassed a great deal of witness and participant testimony as part of their investigation. They interviewed the employees of the Eco market who had been on duty the morning of May 31, including the store manager and proprietor, Alexandre Chasseau; the house butcher, Émilien Boudaut; and the shop assistant, André Delcros. They reconstructed the events of that day, established the putative role of each player, and traced the relationships among them in an effort to uncover more of the underground network.

The most valuable sources of information, however, were the suspects themselves. Between May 31 and June 6, some twenty-three people were interrogated approximately fifty times. Most were questioned repeatedly. Within twenty-four hours of her arrest, Madeleine Marzin was interrogated seven times. There is no mention in the police record of how information was extracted, but it is well known that interrogators inflicted both physical and emotional pain on the accused.

Unsolicited input might also be added to a suspect's file, for better or for worse. Baudois's employer wrote to the court saying that he needed his skilled worker back at the chocolate factory. Likewise, the magistrate in charge of Marzin's case received a letter addressed to Marzin from her students. It was never communicated to the addressee herself. The forwarding message to the magistrate and the postscript, clearly written by an adult, indicate that the declaration was as much intended for the magistrate as for Marzin herself. The letter was typewritten and mailed from the Gare Montparnasse for the sake of anonymity.

Monsieur le Juge d'Instruction,
We appeal to your goodness to convey this open letter to Mademoiselle Marzin from her former and current students. Thank you in advance.

Dear Mademoiselle,
We are too young to judge the grave events that have made you a prisoner, and that is why we are writing.

We cannot believe that you could knowingly have brought harm to anyone, and if this can bring you any comfort, know that your students big or small, reserve for you their affection and their gratitude.

People should know that in your often thankless role, you are the most devoted, the most humane and the most understanding of teachers, and all we can do for you today is to thank you and to share with you, with all our children's hearts, the tragic times that you and your family must now be living through.

A former student of Class A,
School of Plessy-Robinson

PS: This letter comes from a student whose future you shaped and who is assuming the role of interpreter for all her schoolmates. We hope that M. le Juge d'Instruction will find it in his heart to convey this letter to you.

It should also be known that you have scrupulously kept your personal opinions to yourself and that everyone was shocked to learn of your arrest. No one can accuse you of having influenced the young minds in your charge in any way.[3]

Not all the unsolicited input was positive, however. One of the more sickening features of everyday life under the Vichy regime and the German occupation was the practice of denunciation. Police files contain anonymous letters alerting the authorities to a Jew in hiding, a household with suspicious comings and goings, a prisoner of war's wife and her dubious boarder, and so on. Many an arrest was made during the war on the basis of information supplied by anonymous sources. Both Meunier and Lefébure had in fact been the victims of such denunciations. In August 1941 Meunier's residence had been searched—unsuccessfully—on a tip from an informer. As for Lefébure, on June 19, 1942, after he had been arrested, the state prosecutor received a tiny, handwritten note on a slip of paper smaller than a postcard.

Lefébure . . . a postal employee arrested in the rue de Buci case, steals letters and packages. Last winter he was seen carrying bags over his shoulder at nightfall.

Apéritifs, good wine and women can't be bought on the income of a postal worker. . . .

By doing a careful search and investigation, you will be successful.

Excuse me for remaining anonymous but there is reason to fear reprisals from an anarchist.

Respectfully yours.[4]

Based on the yield from interrogations, investigators chased down leads and surveilled the residences of the people they had taken into custody. Police attempted to cross-check and verify information, some of it conflicting, that had been extracted from arrestees through interrogation. They did this, in part, by conducting a series of confrontations. Suspects were confronted with witnesses and with each other. Confrontations gave rise to new rounds of interrogations. Pierre Menut was identified by police officer Lajoie as the man who had boasted to him that he had been at the rue de Buci when the action took place, a fact Menut adamantly denied when confronted with Lajoie. The same detective who arrested Lefébure identified Marguerite Bronner as the woman who had struck him repeatedly with an umbrella. André Dalmas and André Delcros, the man in charge of the sardine display who had grabbed Marzin, were brought face-to-face. Delcros could not identify Dalmas as the man who had punched him, but Dalmas identified Delcros as the man he had assaulted.

Meanwhile, on June 3, an unrelated search for the authors of a series of partisan attacks turned up three men who had been members of the armed security team on the rue de Buci. Jean Arthus, a seventeen-year-old student, claimed that he never fired a shot even though he was found to be in possession of two firearms. When police searched his parents' home, they found a briefcase containing a gun under his bed. Arthus alleged that he had been asked to convey the briefcase to a person whose identity was unknown to him, and that he had been told that it contained laundry.

Two other students, Pierre Grelot and Lucien Legros, both associates of Arthus, were apprehended shortly thereafter. They were wanted for the attempt on the life of another student who was reputed to be a collaborator. In the course of his interrogation, Grelot told police that he and Arthus had been recruited to the underground movement by Pierre Benoit. Together with Benoit, who commanded the group, they had taken part in the protection of demonstrators at the Buci marketplace. Arthus, Grelot, Legros, and Benoit were four of the five legendary students of the Lycée Buffon. They would become Resistance legends in their own right, but not for their role in the demonstration on the rue de Buci.

By the end of June, police had rounded up more than thirty people who were suspected of involvement in the demonstration of May 31. However, the investigation was far from over. More suspects would be arrested over the course of the following months.

The original batch of nineteen demonstrators was tried on June 23, less than a month after the incident. The first jurisdiction to deal with this group was the Tribunal de première instance of the Department of the Seine, a criminal court that typically dealt with thefts, public disturbances, and the like. But in the summer of 1942, in occupied Paris, flinging cans of sardines to the crowd was no ordinary theft, rushing a shop was no ordinary trespass, and a market protest was no ordinary disturbance.

News of the Buci affair traveled as far as the highest reaches of the Vichy government. The Conseil de ministres, or cabinet, decided to refer the case to the Tribunal d'état, a so-called exceptional jurisdiction that was mandated in September 1941 for the express purpose of prosecuting serious political crimes.

On June 23, the state prosecutor brought the case to the Tribunal d'état. The charges were association with evildoers and attempted assassination and assassination. Thus were all demonstrators—women and men, protesters and security team members—thought to bear responsibility for the ultimate and fatal consequences of the incident.

French authorities had previously asked the German occupation authorities whether they would have any objection to capital sentencing. As long as the condemned were neither German nor

Italian citizens, the Germans responded, the French were free to rule as they saw fit. In such cases, they were happy to leave policing to the French Ministère de l'intérieur (Ministry of Interior), and trials and sentencing to the French Ministère de la justice (Ministry of Justice). That French courts condemned French citizens was an internal matter as far as the occupiers were concerned.

Two days later, on June 25, the Tribunal d'état rendered its judgment. The participation of Eugénie Dietrich, Mayer Kaliski, and Léonard Marcellesi in the demonstration could not be established. They were acquitted but not released. Those whose presence at or participation in the demonstration were shown to be indisputable received sentences ranging from five years to life imprisonment. Three women, Raymonde Van den Branden, Norma Nicoletti Bléron, and Yvonne Chauviré, were sentenced to five years of hard labor (*travaux forcés*). Arthur Lathulière and Roger Bléron were sentenced to twenty years of hard labor, and Louise Sézille de Mazancourt got ten. Life sentences were meted out to Émile Sézille de Mazancourt, Raymond Estrade, Jean Arthus, Lucien Legros, Pierre Grelot, and one woman, Marguerite Bronner. Another suspect, Pierre Benoit, was still on the run but sentenced to life imprisonment in absentia. (He was finally arrested on August 28.) Lefébure, Meunier, and Dalmas were sentenced to death. Madeleine Marzin had not been armed, but as ringleader of the operation, she too got the death penalty.

Dalmas reportedly had this to say about their day in court: "When the verdict was pronounced, only one person shuddered: President Devise [the ruling magistrate]. We remained expressionless. At no time did I cry, but tears come to my eyes whenever I think of Madeleine Marzin's magnificent and unforgettable smile after the verdict."[5]

The sentencing reveals a striking cleavage along gender lines, with most women getting lighter sentences than most men. This was a direct consequence of the gender-specific roles accorded male and female demonstrators in the first place, a policy that had ripple effects throughout the affair.

The two notable exceptions were Marguerite Bronner and Madeleine Marzin. Like the men, both women were implicated in the violence. In addition to recruiting the demonstrators, Marzin had been responsible for organizing *groupes de choc*, men who would intervene to protect the demonstrators but who were not armed. Marguerite Bronner was not a member of the security team, but she beat a policeman with her umbrella. One of the men condemned to death, André Dalmas, was also unarmed. He had punched a shop employee in the face. These acts of violence, while not lethal, had called for stiffer sentences.

The defendants were represented by state-appointed lawyers. The lawyers did not call witnesses or lead investigations of their own. Then as now, the role of the lawyer was limited to arguing in favor of the accused based on the evidence presented by the prosecutor. After the sentencing, the lawyers of the four people condemned to death appealed to the head of state, Maréchal Pétain, to spare the lives of their clients. They asked that the death sentences be commuted to mere life imprisonment.

The commissaire du gouvernement près le Tribunal d'état, or state prosecutor, Colonel Paul Farge, forwarded the lawyers' requests for commutations of the four death sentences to the Minister of Justice. In an eight-page cover letter, he summarized the case and argued against a commutation of these sentences.

> Members of the court, in full knowledge of the facts of the case and the role of each of the condemned, convinced of the seriousness of the acts and the indisputable guilt of the condemned individuals, pronounced the death penalty for each of them.
>
> I believe, based on the facts of the case and their consequences (public order seriously disrupted, the attempt to provoke a mass uprising regarding food supply, which is a particularly sensitive issue at the moment, two policemen killed, three others severely wounded) that the sentence handed down is the only appropriate one, that there can be no room for pity or even indulgence for any of

the condemned, all of whom are Communist Party sympathizers, and that justice should take its course as swiftly and as soon as possible, and this in the interest of setting an example.

Therefore I can only recommend in the strongest terms that the requests for clemency be refused.[6]

But some governmental officials actually wanted to avoid issuing a death sentence. They feared the public would interpret a capital sentence as an example of the wrong kind: that of the perfidy and ruthlessness of the regime. Multiple executions, including that of a woman, were sure to antagonize public opinion. Moreover, the incident had shown that the authorities' fear of public disorder was well founded, that a few disgruntled voices could ignite the crowd, and that hunger and anger had dangerously explosive potential.

In his argument contesting the appeal, Colonel Farge, the prosecutor, made no distinction among the condemned on the basis of sex. His superiors in the Ministère de justice, however, saw things differently. Madeleine Marzin alone was singled out for a reprieve. In a providential stroke of the pen on July 17, Marzin's sentence was commuted to life imprisonment, or "hard labor in perpetuity," by the head of state himself, Maréchal Pétain.

The appeal to save Lefébure, Meunier, and Dalmas had fallen on deaf ears. Preparations were made to carry out the death sentences without delay. On July 22, eleven witnesses, including a doctor, a priest, and the lawyers of the condemned men, were ordered to be at the Santé prison in the Fourteenth Arrondissement of Paris no later than 5:15 the next morning. The executioner was summoned from Liancourt (Oise) to Paris, where he would spend the night before performing his official duties at dawn the next day. Gravediggers at the cemetery in Ivry, a suburb of Paris, were instructed to prepare three gravesites in the Carré des suppliciés, an area reserved for the victims of state executions.

At first light on the morning of July 23, at 5:58, 5:59, and 6:00, Lefébure, Meunier, and Dalmas were guillotined, in that order, one after the other. Within the hour, the police commissioner confirmed that a horse-drawn hearse was bringing the bodies to the cemetery, where they would be placed in coffins and buried. He warned the gravediggers that the bodies had been decapitated.

This swift response from the French authorities showed the Germans that the evildoers had been rounded up and brought to justice with dispatch. Although nineteen defendants were tried a mere three weeks after the incident, the investigation did not come to a close. The *juge d'instruction*, the magistrate responsible for overseeing the investigation, directed police to continue their search for anyone connected to the demonstration, whatever their apparent role. They were to cast a wide net. "Involvement" in the demonstration was to be interpreted in very broad terms.

Guilt by association was not an incorrect assumption on the part of the police. Some of the people arrested by police had been recruited by other participants, often at the last minute. Other suspects had lent support to the operation indirectly, by helping demonstrators elude the police after the fact, or through their participation in a larger network of communication and support (transmitting messages, providing food or shelter). In their aggressive hunt for the demonstrators, police also discovered that some participants in the demonstration were involved in other "terrorist" activities that dwarfed their roles in the Buci affair.

A second batch of seventeen people was referred to a lower court, the Tribunal de première instance, for Communist activity. They were accused of offenses that did not meet the conditions for prosecution by the Tribunal d'état under whose auspices the investigation had been conducted. To the same docket were added the cases of three people who had already been acquitted by the Tribunal d'état for their alleged involvement in the affair. In all, eleven men and nine women stood trial in January 1943.

On January 7, the state prosecutor delivered the results of the investigations and his recommendations for sentencing. The charges against the overwhelming majority of defendants, fifteen of the twenty, were considered insufficient to justify further prosecution (*non-lieu*). The prosecutor asked for their release, but the accused remained in detention.

Two of the defendants, Jeanne Deus and Pierre Marzin, had worse crimes on their records. Deus had been arrested while attempting to blow up a building that housed German troops. According to police, she was accompanied by a child accomplice. It so happened that she was also Kaliski's partner, which is why she was implicated in the Buci demonstration and Communist activities more generally. It is likely that Deus was handed over to the Germans. In any event, her trail in the Buci affair ends here.

So, too, that of Pierre Marzin. Marzin was a full-time clandestine operator at the time of his arrest. Before the PCF was outlawed, he had been the party functionary in charge of five Breton departments. But when the party was declared illegal in 1939, Marzin was subjected to "administrative internment," meaning that he was put in an internment camp as a preventative measure. In 1940, he escaped and returned to his former activities. Pierre Marzin was a big fish whose capture was for police a fortuitous side effect of the hunt for the demonstrators.

The cases of Léonard Marcellesi, Eugénie Dietrich, Mayer Kaliski, Marcel Leclerc, and Robert Desvignes were handled differently. Marcellesi, Dietrich, and Kaliski had already been tried twice, first before the Tribunal d'état, and then the Tribunal de première instance. Soon they would be tried before a *third* jurisdiction.

Those three cases, along with those of Leclerc and Desvignes, were recommended for referral to another court, the infamous Section spéciale, which had been created in August 1941 for the express purpose of prosecuting Communists and anarchists. The charges against these individuals were deemed less relevant to the Buci affair in particular than to subversive Communist activities in general. The Section spéciale was therefore determined to be the proper purview for this discrete set of cases.

The trial before the Section spéciale on February 26, 1943, was closed to the public: "In view of the fact that debating this case in public could present a danger for public order, the Court ordains that the trial be conducted in secret."[7] This was typically the case for trials before the Section spéciale. On March 10, 1943, the Section spéciale acquitted Marcellesi and Dietrich for lack of sufficient evidence. The cases of Kaliski, Leclerc, and Desvignes were postponed because elements of the file had not been communicated to the defense in time for the trial. Their cases were presented again on March 26, 1943, and all charges against Leclerc and Desvignes were dropped. However, they were not released from prison.

It is at this point that Kaliski's name disappears from the record. Mayer Kaliski, who was detained at the Tourelles prison in the Twentieth Arrondissement after his arrest, had already been handed over to the Germans on July 23, 1942. The French had proceeded with his case just the same, but what they did not know in March 1943 was that Kaliski was already long gone. At the last minute, his name had been appended to the prisoner manifest of Transport no. 11, a train that left France for Auschwitz on July 27. Like Kaliski, who had been born in Lodz, most of the prisoners were of Polish origin. Eleven of the one thousand people in Kaliski's convoy returned to France in 1945. Kaliski was not among them.

Up to this point in our story, the German occupiers have lurked offstage. Some demonstrators, including Madeleine Marzin, testified that planners designated the Eco market because it was always well provisioned for its German clients. However, there was no reported German presence at the market or its environs that Sunday morning in May. The dairy shop owner, Félix Barthélémy, also remarked that German troops were billeted not far from the Buci-Seine neighborhood on the rue Bonaparte, but again, none intervened in the demonstration. The German occupiers pressured the French to step up their prosecution of terrorist activity, and as we have seen, the French sought their input on the imposition of capital punishment. Mayer Kaliski had been turned over to the Germans despite having been tried and acquitted; while he was found innocent of participation in the demonstration, he was guilty of being Jewish. But to this point the Germans had not played a direct role in sentencing the protagonists of the Buci demonstration.

However, political offenses that rose to the level of "acts of war" were the province of the occupying authorities. They were especially keen on hunting down and killing "Bolshevik elements" involved in attacks on German installations or German troops. They had an extensive repressive apparatus of their own in both the political police (Gestapo) and the German military police. Captured "terrorists" were tried by the Tribunal Commandant de Grand Paris, as well as the various military tribunals, one for each branch of the military.

On June 27, 1942, two days after being sentenced to hard labor in perpetuity, French authorities handed Arthus, Grelot, and Legros over to the Germans, along with their associate Jacques Baudry, and transferred them to the Santé prison. Baudry had been arrested in a roundup of partisans that had taken place on June 4. Pierre Benoit, who in absentia had been sentenced to life by the Tribunal d'état along with Arthus, Grelot, and Legros, was finally captured on August 28. All five of them had been implicated in other "terrorist" activity, including the attempted assassination of a German air force officer on May 19, 1942.

Although four of the five young men had already been sentenced to hard labor for life by the Tribunal d'état on June 25, 1942, they were tried again by the military tribunal of the Luftwaffe on October 15 of that same year. This time, all five were sentenced to death.

The French ambassador to the German occupation authorities, Fernand de Brinon, intervened on their behalf. His first plea on August 12 had been on behalf of Lucien Legros.[8] On October 20, he asked for clemency for all five of the condemned on account of their age. He also argued that the execution of five young men would have a negative impact on public opinion. The German authorities did not respond to Brinon's letters.

On February 8, 1943, Arthus, Baudry, Benoit, Grelot, and Legros faced a German firing squad—what Albert Camus referred to as "the twelve little black eyes of German destiny."[9] The French authorities were not notified; they learned of the executions two weeks after the fact from the families, and only later from the Germans themselves.

The young men were buried side by side in unmarked graves in the Ivry cemetery. On February 25, 1943, French authorities intervened one last time on behalf of the families, asking that individual grave sites be identified as a small concession to the grieving, who did not know which grave belonged to whom. It is doubtful that the Germans acceded to the families' wishes. After the war, the bodies of the five were exhumed and cremated. In 1952, an urn containing their ashes was placed in the crypt of the Sorbonne. Had the individual bodies been identified at the time of burial or shortly thereafter, it is unlikely that their remains would have been combined.

Ten months after the Buci demonstration, Georges Vallet, who had commanded the security teams on the rue de Buci and the rue Daguerre, was finally arrested by French police. Vallet had been actively hunted by both French and German authorities but remained on the loose until April 1, 1943. By then he had added a number of impressive partisan strikes to his record. After French police turned Vallet over to the Germans, he was held at the infamous headquarters of the Gestapo on the rue de Saussaies, a site synonymous with torture and killing. On May 27, he was condemned to death by the Tribunal Commandant de Grand Paris. On July 9, Georges Vallet was executed by a German firing squad.

Of the partisan men said to have been under Vallet's direction, eight had been members of the security team on the rue de Buci. They included four of the five boys from the Lycée Buffon who had been executed the preceding February. The other four were Maurice Le Berre, Jean Barrachi, Guy Gauthier ("André," according to investigators), and Latapie or Labadie, whose identity was uncertain and who remained at large. All were alleged to have been on the rue de Buci.

The death toll of the Buci affair was staggering: three people were beheaded, five were shot by firing squad for their actions at the Buci market, at least two more men who participated in the demonstration were executed on the basis of additional charges that extended beyond the Buci affair, and two policemen lost their lives at the scene.

The side effects rippled out into families—children, parents, and spouses. The mother of Jean Arthus committed suicide following her son's arrest. Aimée Dalmas, the wife of André, had a mental breakdown after hearing her husband being tortured in an adjacent room at the headquarters of the Brigades spéciales. Meunier's wife reportedly committed suicide.

How did people account for their actions on May 31, 1942? How did they shape their own narratives, and under what conditions? Faced with intensive questioning that was often accompanied by threats, violence, and even torture, the accused women and men made every effort to save themselves. They responded with various stories in their own defense, seeking to weaken or deflect the serious charges against them. What they said to police, how their remarks were heard, and how they were interpreted, would determine their futures. Their stories were critical to the history of the rue de Buci demonstration. In them we hear the voices of moral and legal self-defense, but, even more poignant, the struggle of self-conscious resisters facing implacable repression.

What did the people who were apprehended tell police about their roles in the Sunday morning melee? What was the range of narrative options, and how did those narratives stack up against the facts established by the police in their investigation of the affair? How did participant testimony evolve over the course of repeated interrogations, from the first series of interrogations through the second and third waves?

Whatever they may have said in their interrogations, the people being questioned shared a primary goal at the outset: exculpation. In attempting to explain away their involvement in the demonstration or their association with other *malfaiteurs*, or evildoers, or to justify their presence at the scene when evidence of that presence could not be plausibly denied, they told stories.

Some defense strategies were common to both protesting women and partisan men. A first line of defense was to deny having been present at the demonstration site in the first place. In separate instances, two demonstrators, both residents of the Fifteenth Arrondissement, claimed that they were shopping at their own neighborhood market several metro stops away when the Buci incident occurred. Moreover, each of them had attempted to establish an alibi to this effect.

Raymond Estrade had foreseen the possibility of trouble. Before reporting to duty at the Buci-Seine marketplace, he had taken a stroll through the Convention market in the hope of running into someone he knew who could vouch for him later. He had no luck, and therefore this alibi, while not untrue, did not absolve him of suspicion.

When it was no longer possible or plausible to deny their presence at the site, the next line of defense was to deny involvement in the demonstration. Roger Bléron initially denied foreknowledge of the event but not his presence in the vicinity, which he attributed to mere coincidence. Others who conceded their presence claimed to have been onlookers; in point of fact, they had been recruited as "onlookers" who were to orient crowd response by voicing their support of the demonstrators. In this sense, their claims were true. However, none of them could reasonably explain why they happened to be shopping on the rue de Buci on that particular day when comparable or larger markets, like the one on the rue de la Convention, were closer to their home. This was the case of the Sézille de Mazancourt couple and Raymonde Van den Branden, who lived in two apartments at the same address in the Fifteenth Arrondissement.

When can participant testimony be characterized as defense strategy, and when were participants telling the truth about their prior knowledge and intent? In some cases, they are the same: the truth *is* the defense strategy. Madeleine Marzin, however, denied neither her presence nor her agency. From the very outset Marzin assumed responsibility for her leadership role in the affair. She told the truth about her own involvement, her objectives, and her movements on the days before and after the event. In this sense, her posture was an affirmation rather than a defense. Her only "lie" was one of omission in refusing to disclose the names of her "co-conspirators."

Moreover, Marzin's testimony did not change over time; even her version of the Buci demonstration in oral and written accounts published long after the war remains all of a piece with her initial declaration to the police. Though it is well known that long-term memory tends to conform to early narratives of experience when those narratives are repeatedly articulated, this was not the case with other participants, whose postwar representations were not always identical to earlier police and court testimony.

Marzin's history of activism had prepared her for eventual arrest. This is not to say that she was resigned to the inevitability of getting caught or that she necessarily expected it, but she accepted the consequences of her actions as she accepted the choice she had freely made when she committed to illicit political activity. This was the disposition of a seasoned, fully committed activist with a long experience of political militancy.

Some participants lied through omission. They formulated responses that were not untrue but were certainly incomplete. Others devised stories that were artful admixtures of truth and lies, where indisputable facts were laced with misleading, even fanciful information.

In early interrogations, Lefébure and Meunier confessed to their support roles as propagandists. Edgar Lefébure told police that he met a friend at a café on the neighboring rue des Arts before going to the Buci-Seine market to distribute flyers to the public. This was also the claim made by Meunier, whose role, at least in part, consisted of "oral propaganda" in defense of the demonstrators:

> An individual whom I do not know and whose first and last names I do not know, told me to go to a demonstration on the rue de Buci to "make some noise." . . . I had told Estrade to come with me to participate in a demonstration concerning food supply. . . . The man in the black slicker gave me instructions to "make noise" as soon as the food demonstration got under way.[10]

Participants who had in fact been recruited as onlookers, shoppers, and crowd members were able to speak honestly about their own roles. Many demonstrators had received their instructions en route to the event only moments before it was slated to begin. For participants' own protection and for the protection of the operation, organizers told recruits as little as possible about the big picture, and told them only at the last minute. These men and women could legitimately confess to having played minor roles.

Even mid-level organizers remained unaware of the full scope of what their supervisors had in mind. Madeleine Marzin, for example, had been unaware of the full extent of the plans made by her counterpart Georges Vallet, the leader of the security team. What participants did not know could not hurt them or the larger movement of which they were a part. This was for their own protection and that of the movement as a whole.

When suspects could deny neither presence nor involvement, some found ways to deny their own responsibility. They claimed to have been misled, or to have been unaware of the full extent of the plan or of the likelihood of other illegal activity, such as looting. Pleading ignorance was a defense strategy adopted by both protesting women and partisan men. Arthur Lathulière told investigators that his coworker at the Renault factory, Émile Sézille de Mazancourt, had come to his home on Saturday, the day before the demonstration, to ask if he wanted to participate in a distribution of canned goods without tickets. "It [was] the first time I had heard about such a distribution. I did not think I had to get in line and I went to take a look at the nearby stalls. I was thinking that there might be a trick for getting some canned goods without standing in line."[11]

Sézille de Mazancourt had recruited his sister-in-law, Raymonde Berthelet Van den Branden, who pleaded ignorance: "The circumstances of this business did not seem strange to me at the beginning and it was not until I was on-site that I realized that a demonstration was planned."[12]

Two members of the security team emphasized the innocuous food-related character of the event. They claimed to have had no expectation of conflict. Said Raymond Estrade: "Meunier told me that the next day, there was a demonstration, without saying anything about what kind of demonstration it would be. In my mind, I thought it was a demonstration having to do with food. . . . I did not think that the demonstration would be serious."[13]

Young Grelot's testimony also minimizes the expectation of conflict, but his statement stretches credulity. "[I expected] a demonstration organized near the Latin Quarter that would be a protest against food supply. . . . I thought it would be insignificant; however, when Benoit gave us a revolver, I found that strange."[14] And his schoolmate Lucien Legros claimed to have discovered a revolver in his pocket only upon running from the scene.

Likewise, Edgar Lefébure, who apparently arrived at the scene with a revolver, made the improbable statement that he assumed he had been recruited to distribute flyers: " 'René' did not give me the slightest indication of the purpose of our meeting. I thought that it was about distributing flyers."[15] Distributing political material was no more legal than demonstrating, but it did not require a gun.

Some of the claims may have been sincere, while others may have been partially sincere but woven together with purposely misleading, incomplete, or fabricated elements. A false statement can be more convincing, more seamlessly delivered, when intertwined with snippets of truth.

There is one thing common to much of the testimony: few if any demonstrators admitted to having heard the shots. One demonstrator said he was nearby at the time but was hard of hearing; others said they learned about the violence on the radio or in the papers the next day. A woman said she learned about the shots fired when she was at the Odéon metro station, from a child who had been separated from its mother. Others reported running from the scene after the scuffle began but before the shots rang out. In this way, they could claim ignorance of the killings, by far the most damning aspect of the illegal operation. However, in some instances their testimony was contradicted by that of other witnesses.

Few participants had full or even partial knowledge of the plan to stage a protest when they were recruited by organizers. Was it wrong or exploitative to deny details of the operation to recruits under the circumstances? We now know that some participants were putting their very lives at risk. Organizers, too, were aware of the risk, although in the summer of 1942 it would not have seemed likely to anyone that a street protest by housewives would call for the full deployment of Vichy's repressive apparatus.

In top-down underground organizations operating in defiance of authoritarian rule, failure to disclose was a form of protection. *Cloisonnement,* or compartmentalization, was a collective survival strategy, a necessity for any underground organization that does not want to see its membership decimated. "The woman in the Basque beret," "the man in the black slicker": these are descriptions of key players given by participants in testimony to the police. "René," "Ludovic," "Suzanne": many contacts were known only by their noms de guerre. Ignorance was the best protection. But the security rules were often contravened. At this level and at this time, underground activists had neither the professionalism, the experience, nor the resources to craft a more perfect protection.

What accounts for the range of responses? Degree of responsibility or involvement, the political experience of the detainee, personal stakes, risks to family members: these are some of the knowable variables that account for different postures vis-à-vis police interrogators. To some extent, directly or indirectly, many of these variables share a gender component. As gender structured the attribution of roles in the demonstration, so too did it affect the varieties of participant testimony.

Men and women could and did adopt different, gender-inflected defense strategies in their testimony to the police. Women attempted to justify their presence at the demonstration by invoking their nurturing roles as mothers and keepers of the hearth. Many of them may have attended the demonstration with the expectation of getting something to eat. The best evidence of that—cans of sardines in a shopping basket or pantry—would also have been the most damning. But police reports of the searches and seizures conducted at suspects' homes make no mention of cans of sardines packed in oil..

Protesting women cited Mother's Day as the reason for their presence at the site. Louise Sézille de Mazancourt testified that she had learned about the demonstration from her husband. She pleaded ignorance of the details or the possibility of nefarious activity, allowing her husband to appear in the acceptable role as the head of household, or *chef de famille*:

> My husband told me that for Mother's Day, there was a demonstration, after which there would be a distribution of canned goods. I did not know how he found out about it; I did not know what kind of demonstration it would be, I did not know where the demonstration was supposed to take place. Nor did I know who was going to do the distributing. Moreover, it was the first time I had heard about a free distribution of canned goods. . . . I did not bother to see who was doing the distributing, nor how I might be eligible for a free distribution in the Sixth Arrondissement when I lived in the Fifteenth.[16]

Mother's Day, the occasion the demonstration was ostensibly meant to celebrate, reappeared in the testimony of Norma

Nicoletti Bléron, who accompanied the Berthelet sisters, Louise and Raymonde. She invoked the most innocent-sounding justification for her presence on the rue de Buci: "At the Odéon metro stop, we were told to go stand in front of a food shop at the corner of the rue de Seine and the rue de Buci to participate in a distribution of canned goods without tickets . . . for Mother's Day."[17]

Because men and women peeled off in different directions in accordance with assigned roles—women in line and men on the sidelines—they could also tell police that they lost track of each other. It was another built-in protection. That men and women occupied different spaces at the marketplace allowed them plausible deniability of the others' movements.

The prospect of heterosexual romantic entanglements provided yet another level of deniability. One illicit affair could be used to hide another. Male and female operatives working together could plead guilty to a lesser offense, that of forbidden romantic or sexual activity. Posing as couples, either real or feigned, served to cover other, more serious complicities.

The reluctance to divulge compromising information about one's intimacies could be proffered as a justification either for having been at the scene or for originally having made a false statement to police. Lucien Menut claimed to have been in the Buci environs that day because he was going to visit a woman, whose name he refused to supply because she was married and a mother. "I do not want to cause problems for her *ménage*," he told police.[18] In this way he also established his personal virtue by protecting a woman's reputation.

Women also made a case for their own respectability, which by extension was inconsistent with the commission of a political offense. Police described Angèle Cousin as Lefébure's "mistress," which she denied. They accused her of hiding her lover, a dangerous terrorist. By denying the relationship, she also denied the motive ascribed to her by police. In defense of her respectability on both moral and political grounds, Cousin admitted to having sheltered

Lefébure, but only because he could not return home due to marital problems.

Forty-nine year-old postal worker Léonard Marcellesi, who was married and the father of a child, claimed to have been lured to the site of the demonstration by the prospect of a rendezvous with a former mistress. He readily confessed to his "infidelities," whether real or invented.

It was two or three days before the thirty-first of May that I received a letter sent to my home that I intercepted at the post office of the Fifteenth Arrondissement where I work.[19] This letter was signed "Raymonde." Having had numerous mistresses, I was unable to place this "Raymonde," who, in her letter, set up a meeting for Sunday, May 31 at 9:30 in the morning at Odéon. She signed the letter "affectionately."

I went to the rendezvous . . . and at the Odéon metro station, I saw Marguerite Bronner. I thought that this Marguerite Bronner was Raymonde. This Marguerite Bronner had at one time been my mistress and I had it in my mind that her name was Raymonde. I met this woman at the time of the exodus [the mass movement of French people fleeing their homes after the German invasion] and at that time she told me that I looked familiar, that she recognized me from before the war.

Marguerite Bronner explained to me that there was a demonstration planned that consisted of getting cans of sardines from a store and distributing them and taking some of them for oneself; she asked me if I had a bag. . . .

During this conversation, we had been walking toward the shop in question, and we were approaching the Eco market when I invited Marguerite Bronner for a coffee. When we came out [of the café] I saw groups [of people] around the store. It seemed to me that these people were forming suspicious-looking groups. I then told Marguerite Bronner that I did not want to get mixed up in this business because I was a civil servant.[20]

Marcellesi does not deny his presence at the site, nor does he deny his association with Bronner, herself fully implicated in the demonstration. Having been drawn to the site by his former mistress, fearful for his job as a civil servant, he eschewed any involvement.

Perhaps Marcellesi chose to place the blame on Bronner for bringing him to the area because he knew she was already compromised. Or perhaps Bronner had in fact been his "mistress" and Marcellesi focused on this aspect of their relationship to deflect attention from his questionable presence on the rue de Buci. Whatever the case may be, what matters is the use of an illicit relationship to cover an illicit activity. Marcellesi played on presumed male complicity concerning a sexual exploit and the awkwardness of admitting to adulterous intent.

Marcellesi's strategy did not go well, to say the least. Marguerite Bronner was outraged at the accusation. In a confrontation with Marcellesi, Bronner adamantly denied that he had been her lover or that she had drawn him to the site of the incident. While Marcellesi tried to mask his political involvement behind the story of a secret romance, Bronner's strategy was predicated on her respectability as a women and her role as family caregiver. In her letters to authorities from behind bars the leitmotif of her argument for release was her role as a mother and daughter. She agonized about her sixteen-year-old son and her aging mother, both of whom depended on her for financial support and care. In this case, expectations of masculine vice and feminine virtue that the accused shared with police were deployed as self-defense, albeit at cross purposes.

What is gender-specific about telling a story about an illicit amorous relationship is that only men did it. While women protesters banked on their respectability and their roles as mothers and wives, two men resorted to telling tales about sexual exploits—and in the case of Marcellesi, impugning a fellow demonstrator's morality in order to construct an alibi.

For the investigators, the most valuable sources of information about the demonstration were the suspects themselves. The first twenty-four hours after arrest were the most critical. The basic playbook for clandestine agents advised resisters to make every effort to hold on for twenty-four hours, time enough for coworkers to disseminate news of the arrest, change hiding places, warn others, and fail to show at prearranged meetings. Police knew that any leads they might obtain from interrogations would run cold soon after a suspect was taken into custody. Investigators were prepared to extract useful information by any means possible: witnesses were interviewed, suspects were questioned, "evildoers" were interrogated.

Efforts to obtain information from people became increasingly vigorous, with pressure applied in the form of threats, pain, or torture. It was extremely difficult to withstand such treatment indefinitely without giving away the identities of one's coworkers, though somehow many resisters did. The ability to do so was not taken for granted. Some imprisoned resisters resorted to suicide rather than face repeated interrogations, seizing the opportunity—where one existed—to end their own lives.[21] It was impossible for anyone to know how much physical or psychological abuse a person could withstand, including oneself.

The participants I interviewed rarely mentioned torture at the hands of their captors, be they French or German, and I refrained from asking. In weighing my need to know against the human cost of asking someone to relive their nightmares, the choice was clear. On occasion, an interviewee made a subtle allusion or uttered a euphemism; rarely were the details volunteered. It was Maté Houet who told me that Marzin had been repeatedly beaten upon arrest. When the subject of interrogation came up in our meeting, Marzin said that she was always questioned with a revolver on the table between her and her interrogator. Her street clothes were stripped from her and she wore only her slip. The underground Communist press reported that she had been paraded naked through the police station "amid mocking sneers," but Marzin did not mention this.[22] "La matraque, la matraque, la matraque." That is how she described her interrogations: repeated blows of the billy club, over and over again.[23]

Marzin supplied additional details in a summary of the Buci affair that she wrote in 1951:

> I heard Yvonne Chauviré screaming in a distant room, where the men of the BS II [Brigades spéciales II] were hitting her.
>
> I personally was in a room by myself, handcuffed, where I was beaten with billy clubs and flogged with a whip the entire day of June 1. From time to time the men of the BS II took a break to throw water in my face. Then they started up again. . . .
>
> Rottée (*sic*) [head of the BS II] had me taken to his office; the cops dragged me there because I could no longer walk.
>
> "Ah, there she is, the little woman, the little revolutionary!" . . . He wanted to have me sit on a velvet-covered chair. He knew full well that I could not sit down. I was in pain with anger and I told him off.[24]

The authorities' written record of Marzin's interrogation betrays none of that. Words are recorded but voices are inaudible. There are no tremors or hesitations. The evasive stare, the nervous gesture, the reluctant nod: all are invisible. The pounding fist, the slashing whip are off the page, out of range. The only traces of a statement extracted under duress are the flat, smooth characters of the stenographer's typewriter. When the utterances of the accused are duly recorded in the file but the questions, threats, and physical violence of the interrogators are absent from the written record, the oral testimony of survivors is critical.

Marguerite Bronner's fate was sealed when she lost her pocketbook, complete with identity papers, during the scuffle inside the Eco supermarket. Soon to be divorced, Bronner worked at a print shop to support her mother and son. She lived in a rented room on the rue de la Convention in the Fifteenth Arrondissement. According to her police profile, she had a history of "sympathies for the far left-wing groups, and the Communist Party in particular." At the time of the demonstration, Bronner was involved in the women's committee of her arrondissement to protest food shortages and other injustices. No doubt she knew that she was taking a risk by participating in an illegal protest, but she could not have fathomed what lay in store.

Bronner had the misfortune of being arrested on the day of the demonstration. The names she gave police were those of people central to the demonstration, including that of Marzin herself. Many paths led to them and they might well have been rounded up anyway. However, it was the information Bronner gave police that enabled them to make some initial arrests and to extract yet more information from those arrestees. Nor was Bronner the only suspect who was forced to name names.

It was not surprising that some survivors had harsh words for the woman who was responsible for their arrests. Knowing this, I asked Madeleine Marzin how she felt about Bronner and her role in the first roundup of demonstrators. Maté Houet, Marzin's friend and co-worker, had previously told me, "Madeleine takes people as they are." It was an apt remark, for Marzin bore her accuser no ill will. Through the prison grapevine she had learned that Bronner's testimony had been extracted by interrogators under threat of harming her family.[25] It was a critical element that Marzin had learned in prison—*and it completely changes the story.*

The written record bears no indication of such a threat. It might have if a letter Bronner wrote to her family from prison had not been intercepted by the prison censor. In it she recounted the threats made in the course of her interrogation. But the letter never reached its destination.

The authorities were in full control of the written record. Yet, ironically, there is no police voice at all, no trace of the threats used to extract her testimony. Bronner's wrenching dilemma would never have surfaced without Marzin's oral testimony. It is a humbling re-minder of the limits of documentary records, and of the importance of the context in which such records are generated.

Bronner was ostracized by her fellow prisoners for having led police to individuals who were central to the demonstration. Louise Sézille de Mazancourt and her sister, Raymonde Van den Branden, were among those who knew of Bronner's role in the arrest of some of the demonstrators. They testified in 1988 that after receiving death threats, Bronner had been moved to a cell in another part of the prison away from the other political prisoners.[26]

Bronner's repeated pleas for clemency or release became ever more desperate. She denounced the Communist Party, claimed it had misled her, and informed her captors that she was severing her membership. She begged for her sentence to be commuted on the basis of her poor health. Most of all, she was tormented by the prospect of leaving her son without a mother. It was not until May 1943 that she learned that her requests had been denied. For all her "cooperation," Bronner was sentenced to life in prison and ended up in a concentration camp along with her peers.

In the transcript of a prisoner testimony, "S.I."—*sur interrogation,* upon questioning—is a fateful acronym. The record of an interrogation is a certain kind of testimony, a dialogue in which only one person speaks. It can read like a seamless narrative, or it may be punctuated by questions. The questions themselves are not always recorded; the reader gleans from the answer the nature of the question, but not how it was posed. What words, what voice, what looks, what gestures, what movement delivered it? A suspect is summoned for questioning a second, third, fourth, fifth time. Tensions mount and pressures build with each successive interrogation. The same questions may be asked or further elaboration called for.

Which brings us to the interrogation of Pierre Benoit. The interrogator questioned, the accused responded, and at the end there was the verification: "*persiste et signe.*"[27] The accused authenticated his statement by signing his name to the deposition. One rather suspects that Benoit was incapable even of that. His mark on the first interrogation is strong; the second is faltering; the third is sloppy and weak. By his fourth interrogation, Benoit's initials, while still legible, have staggered to a scrawl and bear little resemblance to earlier iterations. By the end of the last interrogation, the accused could barely hold a pen. The weak grip and the misshapen letters suggest the probable condition of the accused at the time of signing. Having suffered a terrible beating, perhaps barely conscious, Pierre Benoit affixed his broken hand to the damning chronicle of his "crimes." A mangled autograph is here the last trace of a seventeen-year-old body in agony.

The imprisonment, deportations, and killings of the protagonists are a critical part of the story of the demonstration on the rue de Buci. But the impact of the affair far exceeded its human cost, exorbitant though it was. The individual stories of two of the demonstrators, Madeleine Marzin and Pierre Benoit, provide further insight into the reach and significance of the Buci affair.

A tous Services Préfecture de Police, Police Nationale
Gendarmerie Nationale
-o-o-

Il y a lieu de rechercher très activement et d'arrêter :

M A R Z I N, Madeleine, Marie,
née le 21 juillet 1908 à Loudeac (C. du N.) de feu François et de
MORVAN, Marianne, ayant demeuré : 110, avenue Victor Hugo à Vanves.

Signalement :

taille : 1 m. 48, yeux légèrement truités, cheveux châtain-moyen,
maigre - peut être vêtue d'un costume tailleur en tissu gris uni et
d'une cape en tissu imperméable beige. Est généralement nu-tête.

Condamnée à mort pour menées terroristes, peine commuée, s'est
échappée à la Gare Montparnasse, au cours de son transfert à la Prison de Rennes.

En cas découverte, prendre toutes précautions. Peut être accompagnée d'un groupe de protection, composé de militants terroristes
chargés de veiller à sa sécurité.

Doit être munie de faux papiers à un nom qui n'est pas connu.

En cas d'arrestation, aviser Préfecture de Police - Direction
Générale des Renseignements Généraux, Turbigo 92 09, Odéon 43 80,
automatiques 301 et 304, de nuit : 317.

Le Directeur Général,

L. H. ROTTEE.

The wanted poster for Madeline Marzin, issued by the infamous Rottée, Director-General of the *Renseignements généraux* (police intelligence) alerted police and gendarmes to her escape. "If found," advises the circular, "take all precautions. May be accompanied by a security team comprised of terrorist activists assigned to protect her."

The description of the escapee notes that she may be wearing a beige raincape, the same clothing identified by witnesses on the day of the demonstration. Textiles were so scarce that many people had only one or two changes of clothing; their clothes were as much a part of their physical description as eye and hair color. That said, Marzin had probably long disposed of this incriminating garment, just as she removed it upon leaving the scene of the demonstration in order to change her appearance.

Archives de la Préfecture de Police de Paris, Le Pré-Saint-Gervais, France.

THE TEACHER AND THE TRUANT

Madeleine Marzin and Pierre Benoit were both condemned for their participation in the same affair, but they were strangers to each other. Each attained iconic status, Marzin as the heroine of the rue de Buci, Benoit as one of the students of the Lycée Buffon. Marzin was on the political side of the operation; Benoit was a member of the security team. Although both shared important features with other demonstrators, their backgrounds, roles, and destinies were as different from those of their peers as they were from each other's. Their personal stories were unique. Their itineraries converged on the rue de Buci and diverged in the aftermath.

Madeleine Marzin was an elementary schoolteacher and an old party hand with a lifetime of activism behind her. She came from a Catholic family that was also heavily involved in PCF politics. She had joined the PCF in 1932 in her native Brittany. When the party was forced underground in 1939, she maintained contact and ultimately resumed her work in the political branch of the underground Communist Party. Until May 31, 1942, she led a double life, teaching by day and organizing women, enlisting new recruits, and overseeing propaganda operations the rest of the time. The demonstration on the rue de Buci fulfilled two missions at once: it was both a public protest against hunger and a form of performative propaganda. Marzin was condemned to death by a French court, but in a bizarre and unprecedented series of events she resumed her activism, survived the war, and lived to her nineties.

Pierre Benoit was a newly politicized, inexperienced high school student who had joined the Front national des étudiants

(FNE, National Student Front), a broad-based movement of high school and university students organized by the Communist underground. From the FNE Benoit had moved into "direct action" operations under the auspices of the paramilitary wing of the party. In April 1942, in fear for his life, he went fully underground and never returned to school. Nor did he return to his parents' home on the rue Desnouettes in the Fifteenth Arrondissement. He was ultimately convicted of terrorism and executed by a German firing squad at the age of eighteen.

Of the four principals condemned to death by the Tribunal d'état for "assassination, attempted assassination, complicity in assassination, and association with evildoers," only Madeleine Marzin was fortunate enough to have her sentence commuted to life imprisonment. Her lawyer's request for a revision of her sentence traveled as far as the head of state himself, Maréchal Pétain, and his cabinet, the Conseil d'état.

Marzin had indeed recruited unarmed security teams to protect the demonstrators, and she had also organized the demonstration in concert with the paramilitary branch of the underground movement. However, she had not had a direct role in the deaths of the two policemen. Marzin testified in an interview that she had not known in advance there would be armed men on-site. It is not clear that she said this before the Tribunal d'état, or even that it would have mattered.

Marzin had fully admitted to her role in the demonstration from the very beginning. The only false or insufficient information she gave investigators concerned the identities of other demonstrators. Julia Cartier, who stood trial with the second batch of demonstrators, stated that Marzin had spared her a worse fate by her "extraordinary conduct," meaning that Marzin had protected her identity.[1] This accords with what coworkers and friends had said about Marzin all along. She was known for her integrity, probity, commitment, modesty, and selflessness.[2]

When the unnamed woman charged with singing "La Marseillaise" failed to deliver, Marzin took a huge risk by launching the action herself. As an organizer, her job was to discreetly observe the operation. No person in a command position would ever take on so public a role. That made organizers vulnerable, and the loss of an organizer had repercussions for the entire underground enterprise, not just the operation at hand.

Marzin rushed the Eco market and was seized by a shop employee, who later reported how furiously she had fought to free herself. He identified her to police as "the woman in the beige coat," as did other witnesses. But Marzin immediately removed her beige cape and left the scene undetected, wearing a gray suit. Later that afternoon she had the audacity to return to the scene, still dressed in the gray suit, to survey the area.[3]

She was a skilled and clever woman. Under questioning, Marzin was asked about a certain "Legros." As we know, Lucien Legros was a teenage member of the security team. But Marzin replied that "Le Gros" (the fat one) was the nickname or nom de guerre of a coworker whom they called fat because he was so skinny! Her spontaneous response was perfectly credible—and perfectly false.

When Marzin's case was set to go before the Tribunal d'état, she declined representation. She had assumed full responsibility for her actions. She made no pretense of innocence and had no need for a defense. The court, however, required that each defendant have legal representation; it was not optional. Marzin could have asked for a like-minded lawyer with Communist sympathies.[4] The party-as-family included people from every walk of life, even lawyers who could be called upon to defend underground activists. Instead she had a court-appointed lawyer assigned to her. "I did not want a *camarade* to be compromised in this affair," she told me.

Marzin did not have kind words for her court-appointed lawyer, Pierre Masson. "How did he plead?" I asked. What I expected to hear in reply was the basis for his legal argument, not a two-word description. *"Très moche"* (crappily) was her response.[5] When I pressed for a more substantive answer, Marzin replied that her lawyer had pleaded illness in her defense. Earlier bouts of tuberculosis had in fact left her quite frail. If ill health formed the basis of her lawyer's defense, then it was indeed a derisory argument considering the life-and-death stakes of the ruling.

Following the verdict of the Tribunal d'état, Masson appealed for a commutation of Marzin's death sentence. His letter is not in her file, but the Minister of Justice at the time, Joseph Barthélemy, remembered the gist of her defense. In his postwar memoirs he writes: "The young teacher who, if I recall, was named Marzin, defended herself by emphasizing that she had not herself taken part in the killing, had not acted with malice or out of self-interest, but in the service of an ideology: the ideology of communism. She was condemned to death just the same."[6]

That is not to say that Marzin was not genuinely motivated by the issues of food scarcity and hunger when she organized the demonstration. They were part and parcel of the "ideology" she was defending. She spoke movingly of one of her students, twelve-year-old Mireille, a tall, pale girl with sunken cheeks, who rummaged through garbage cans on her way to school each morning. As for the fall of communism after the 1989 dissolution of the Soviet Union, Marzin was circumspect. It had been a painful surprise. The ideas, the values, were just, she said; it was men who had ruined a beautiful project for the future.[7]

The state prosecutor, Colonel Farge, had opposed a commutation of the sentences of all of the accused. He made no exception for Marzin. Pétain's cabinet, however, was divided on the issue. Those who vehemently objected to clemency cited the "exemplarity" of the sentence, which was intended to dissuade would-be perpetrators of "terrorist crimes."

Barthélemy himself opposed capital punishment for all women, "even the most hideous of monsters." Most of all, he feared the effect Marzin's execution would have on public opinion. The minister of justice therefore pressed Pétain for a reprieve. According to Barthélemy, Petain was not inclined toward clemency but was open to argument. " 'For a long time now,' I said to [Pétain], 'women have not been decapitated; avoid going down in history as the one who brought [the practice] back.' "[8]

Whatever the stance of the members of the Conseil d'état, whether for or against clemency, the least of their concerns was the actual fate of the victim. Their arguments were based exclusively on how Marzin's execution would look to the public. That said, they had different publics in mind. The public that Marzin's detractors hoped to reach was "the terrorists"; the public Barthélemy had in mind was ordinary people.

Those government officials who opposed catering to public opinion might well have agreed with Minister of Education Abel Bonnard. He was famously dismissive of public opinion, perhaps because it was rarely on his side. In a striking turn of phrase, he invoked this highly gendered notion of the state and the people: "The government is male," he is reported to have said. "Opinion is female."[9]

In fact, the repeated executions of hostages and resisters by both the French and the Germans had deeply eroded public support for the regime. Partisan attacks remained undeterred. The savagery of state repression was a gift to party propagandists and recruiters. While the state-censored papers such as Le Temps began to relegate reports of executions to the back pages, the underground press placed them front and center. Such reports were powerful recruitment tools for bringing fighters, both women and men, into the ranks of the underground movement.

The authorities feared that reports of their own brutality would alienate public opinion, and they were right. The cheese merchant on the rue de Seine, otherwise well informed, had been unaware of the beheadings of Dalmas, Lefébure, and Meunier until I mentioned it in an interview. He was clearly unsettled by the news. A wave of shock and incredulity passed across his face, and he exclaimed, "Come on now, you don't guillotine just like that!"[10] And yet Félix

Barthélemy had been no more a fan of the Communist Party than of the demonstrators.

On July 17, 1942, Pétain signed the order to spare Marzin's life. Her sentence was reduced to "hard labor in perpetuity." He did not specify a reason, but his decision was in keeping with a practice inherited from the Third Republic. In granting a reprieve to Marzin, Pétain aligned himself with the republican heads of state who had preceded him.

As for Barthélemy, his last thoughts on the matter were for himself. "I am certain that if the Marzin woman had been executed, she would occupy a place of honor among martyrs of the Idea, and I am even more certain that responsibility for her death would have been ascribed to me."[11] When Barthélemy wrote these words in his prison cell in 1945, he did not know that Marzin would become famous anyway—just for staying alive.

Madeleine Marzin's "life sentence" lasted exactly one month from the day Pétain issued his reprieve. On August 17, she escaped from custody.

On that morning, a group of women prisoners that included Marzin was being transferred from the women's section of the prison at Fresnes to a more secure facility in Rennes, some 350 kilometers to the west. The women were loaded onto a police van and escorted to the Montparnasse train station in Paris. It was a small group of sixteen prisoners—nine women and their seven young children. The women were political prisoners who had been arrested for resistance activities. Some of them had been pregnant upon arrest and had given birth in detention. When the procession descended from the van and began its march to the platform, the women burst into "La Marseillaise."

Once again the national anthem figures in this story. The first time, "La Marseillaise" was intended to be the signal to demonstrators to enter the Eco market and "distribute" cans of sardines to the crowd. It would have signed the event as a patriotic act of people's justice, but the woman charged with launching the distribution never stepped up. As far as Marzin knew, she may not have shown up at the demonstration at all.[12]

This time the same strategy was used, but to successful effect. The prisoners parading through the Gare Montparnasse were seasoned Communist Party activists. They knew how to identify what we would call today a "teachable moment." They seized the opportunity to influence the public and make known their cause. By singing "La Marseillaise" as they were escorted through crowds by prison guards, they identified themselves to onlookers as fighters and patriots. The fact that many had children in their arms only served to drive the message home. Moreover, the women were not in prison garb. Due to the wartime scarcity of textiles, they wore their own clothes. This must have made the group appear all the more inoffensive and their detention all the more scandalous.

Lucienne Rolland was one of the women who participated in the small-scale "demonstration." She had been arrested on May 18, shortly before the demonstration on the rue de Buci, while distributing underground propaganda. Rolland was known to authorities and had already been condemned to death in absentia before her arrest. She was subsequently sentenced by the Section spéciale to "only" five years of hard labor; there was no hard proof of her other activities. Rolland gave birth to her first child in prison. They were separated when she was deported to Ravensbrück. She remembers alighting at the Gare Montparnasse en route to Rennes.

> It was a chance to create a spectacle and to shame the guards, all French just like ourselves. We didn't want people to think we were common criminals—prostitutes, thieves, murderers. We were French patriots, arrested by French police and confined to French prisons.[13]

According to Rolland, the other women prisoners were aware of the rescue plan. Making noise, creating a spectacle, had another purpose: to distract the guards.

The rescue of Marzin had been orchestrated in advance through an underground network that linked prisoners to the outside. Before leaving Fresnes, a fellow prisoner had given her a button with an embroidered cover, inside of which was some change; another had given her a metro ticket. This would be her feeble capital for survival in the post-escape phase.

The operation had been prepared with the help of complicitous railway workers. As the women boarded the train, Marzin slipped out a window on the side of the train opposite the platform. She landed on the tracks, where a railway worker was waiting. "He didn't know who I was," said Marzin, "and it was all for the better." He relayed her to another worker, who directed her to a small shed where the rail men kept supplies. A uniform, bucket, and broom were waiting for her. Marzin donned the uniform, exited the shed newly attired as a cleaning lady, and swept her way out of the Montparnasse train station to freedom.[14]

Meanwhile, the guards had been busy helping the women and children onto the train, along with their luggage. The women, encumbered with children, had no free hands for their bags. While they boarded the compartment reserved for them on the train, the guards handed bundles and bags from the platform below through the windows to the prisoner passengers. Minutes before the train was scheduled to depart, the guards performed a final head count. Madeleine Marzin was missing.

Security personnel—gendarmes, prison escorts, police, and railway security men—had to answer to their superiors for the disaster. They had no idea how Marzin managed to escape. One guard said that he was certain that Marzin had boarded the train. He speculated that she had taken advantage of the crowded corridor on the train to disappear into the bustle of regular passengers. The hypothesis that Marzin had exited through the window was ruled out. "It is difficult to believe," said the deputy chief of the train station, "that the Marzin woman was able to escape through the window of her compartment, two meters and thirty centimeters off the ground, by climbing over the windowsill, and this without attracting the attention of people on the facing platform."[15]

Security men searched the station and checked the exits, but to no avail. The guards deduced that Marzin was still somewhere on the train, which was scheduled to make several stops en route to Rennes. Station personnel at those stops were alerted ahead of time, but no one saw her get off the train. The chief inspector also alerted his colleagues in towns to the south of Paris nearest the Montparnasse train station—Chartres, Versailles, and Vanves, Marzin's last known address—but without success. Vichy's infamous woman prisoner was in the wind.

Marzin's escape made front page news. Maté Houet learned of Marzin's escape from the newspapers, and Marzin's mother learned from Maté. The legal, censored press carried the story. Needless to say, it was featured extensively in the underground party press.

Marzin's escape had far-reaching consequences. It sent shock waves throughout the prison system. It cost the jobs of the prison guards responsible for her safe conduct. It affected the prisoners already in custody and prisoners in the future. It precipitated policy changes at the highest levels. Most important of all, it alerted the authorities to the political potential of women.

An investigation was under way even before the prison escorts had returned to Paris from Rennes. According to the men in charge of the prisoners, the transport had taken place under challenging conditions. The prisoners had been unruly, singing and shouting "Free the patriots!" The fact that the prisoners were not identifiable by prison uniforms helped them to blend into the crowd, which had made it much more difficult to keep an eye on them. Finally, the throngs at the station had been such that members of the group got separated on the platform.

Although a total of twelve men had been mobilized to oversee a convoy of sixteen women and children, the chief investigator concluded that security precautions had been inadequate and security agents too few. Guards were also faulted for reserving a car in the middle of the train where it was harder to monitor the prisoners, for not restricting them to their compartments once they had boarded the train, for permitting them to hang outside the windows that faced the platform, and for timing the transfer at the end of a holiday weekend when traffic was at its most intense. Moreover, security personnel were criticized for having failed to conduct a thorough search of the train once Marzin had been discovered missing, even if it had meant delaying the departure of the train and calling for reinforcements.

Marzin's escape had been so spectacular, so inexplicable, there was even some speculation that the guards had helped her. The penal code called for sanctions against guards who "out of negligence or complicity, allowed the escape of prisoners suspected or accused of crimes punishable by death or life imprisonment." Marzin fit the bill on both counts. That same day, two prison guards were taken to the Santé prison. In October the two guards were given a suspended sentence of two weeks for dereliction of duty. Ever zealous, the prosecution argued for a stiffer sentence to set an example for others, but the judge ruled that the guards had performed their duties to the best of their abilities under extenuating circumstances.

According to one press account, the superintendent of the Fresnes prison was fired for failing to alert his men to the special "quality" of one of the detainees, who required extra surveillance.[16] The whole affair had been a huge fiasco. The authorities were mortified.

The escape prompted a new level of vigilance in the prisons. The authorities were on high alert and they were on edge. Shortly after the escape, the prefect of police denied the request of Denise Véron and Jean Atlan to be married because it was deemed too risky.

> The request presented by Atlan . . . to marry Véron at the town hall of the Fourteenth Arrondissement is denied. Indeed, the removal from prison of Atlan and Véron presents a double danger.

First: possible escape. (These prisoners were intimately connected to 'la Demoiselle Marzin' whose recent escape has made a considerable impact.)

Second: [the risk of] direct or indirect clandestine liaisons or communications with communist elements on the outside.[17]

Both Véron and Atlan had been arrested in the wake of the demonstration on the rue de Buci. Véron was the daughter of Eugénie Dietrich, whose home had been a nexus of illegal activities. At the time of Marzin's escape, Dietrich was being held at the Caserne des Tourelles, a prison in the Twentieth Arrondissement of Paris.

Dietrich stated in postwar testimony that she helped Madeleine Marzin to escape. Dietrich had long served as a link among activists, so it is not unlikely that she continued to do so, both within and outside the prison.[18] However, her role in the escape remains a mystery. There is no mention of her involvement in police or court records. The chain of complicities in Marzin's escape is as invisible to us now as it was to the authorities in the summer of 1942.

In his review of the missteps leading to Marzin's escape, Paul Cervoni, the director of the Fresnes prison, also faulted the guards for failing to handcuff the prisoners during transfer.[19] Although women were not routinely handcuffed, he said, "there is no rule that forbids the guards from doing so."[20] The oversight had been a failure of initiative on their part, wrote Cervoni. He did not mention how handcuffed women could be expected to carry their small children, some of whom were not yet walking on their own.

Marzin's escape occasioned a significant change in policy. A new directive ordered that henceforth, women prisoners were to be chained during transport. Thus was a gender-specific practice discarded in favor of one that was gender-neutral. The authorities had come to recognize women as dangerous political agents on a par with men.

It is probably safe to say that anyone else in Marzin's position—having suffered interrogations and beatings, then condemned to death—might be inclined to take a break from risky resistance activity. Not so Madeleine Marzin. After her spectacular escape from custody, she jumped back into the fray and joined the growing ranks of "illegals." She assumed a series of new identities, including that of "Jacqueline R.," a woman who had died in a hospital in the Fifteenth Arrondissement, and resumed her political work organizing women. From Paris, the epicenter of the occupied zone, she moved to its fringe in eastern France, where she was far less likely to be recognized as the infamous ringleader of the demonstration of the rue de Buci.

Flash forward to 1944. The scene is a train station in Saumur, France. Madeleine Marzin, aka "Marcelle," is waiting on the platform when she sees a group of women being escorted by a female prison guard. Marzin is appalled to see the women are in chains, one connected to the next.

"I hope they are not Communist resisters like us," she says to herself. Marzin inquires of the prison escort whether the women had been convicted of serious crimes. "Abortion," the guard replies. She is taking them to the women's prison in Rennes, the same prison Marzin was destined for when she made her escape. The women appear "placid, resigned, a bit sad"—hardly dangerous criminals likely to make a run for it.

"Why chain these women?" asks Marzin. "It must hurt their wrists and arms. Is it necessary?"

"They are liable to escape," replies the prison guard. "Have you never heard of a certain Madeleine Marzin?"[21]

All three interconnected cases—the Buci demonstration, the Lycée Buffon, and the partisan camp on the edge of the Fontainebleau forest—come together in the singular person of Pierre Benoit.

Benoit's clandestine work would be short-lived but intense. It began in 1941 when he joined the Front national des étudiants, a Communist Party–run organization to mobilize students against the regime and the occupiers. Their primary work was propaganda—writing and distributing flyers aimed at channeling student frustrations and anger into resistance. Benoit excelled at the work.

He showed initiative, daring, and zeal. Benoit must have been persuasive, as he was also a first-rate recruiter.

Before beginning his underground work, Pierre Benoit was already known for his role in the impeccably planned five-minute demonstration in the courtyard of the Lycée Buffon.[22] It was this emblematic action that secured the legend of the "students of the Lycée Buffon." On April 16, 1942, students from Buffon were joined by students from other Parisian high schools to protest the arrest of Raymond Burgard, a teacher at Buffon and one of the founders of the resistance group Valmy. Burgard had expressed his patriotic views in editorials for an underground paper of the same name, as well as in the classroom. He had been arrested by the Gestapo earlier that month.

During the morning recess, about fifty students from outside the lycée swarmed the courtyard, where the Buffon group was waiting. They sang "La Marseillaise," demanded the release of Burgard, and threw flyers into the air. Benoit and Arthus attempted to cut the phone lines, but a lycée staff member managed to report the disruption. Demonstrators scattered. The French police and the Gestapo arrived and searched the school. Legros and Arthus got away with the help of the school's *agent-chef,* or caretaker. Benoit, Baudry, and Grelot hid in the basement for two hours. All five organizers escaped detection, but they were now on the radar of the French and German authorities.

By May 31, 1942, the day of the demonstration on the rue de Buci, Pierre Benoit had already been on the run for six weeks. After the Lycée Buffon episode, fearing arrest, Benoit never returned to his family's comfortable apartment on the square Desnouettes in the Fifteenth Arrondissement. Benoit had gone fully underground and cut contacts with family and friends. After moving from place to place, he finally landed in the partisan camp in the forest of Fontainebleau.

Known by a series of aliases, he was "Maxime" for some, including the members of the group he commanded on the rue de

Buci, who also knew his real name. According to the false papers furnished him by the Resistance, he was thirty-five-year-old Lucien Dupré—an unconvincing identity for a boy who had not yet reached his eighteenth birthday. By late August, "Maxime's" real identity had been established by the Première brigade régionale, and he had been linked to a series of partisan actions: attacks on German soldiers, raids on town halls in neighboring districts, train derailments, and the planting of explosives.

On August 23, Pierre Benoit appeared under his own name on the wanted list that was circulated to police headquarters in and around Paris: "Looks 18–20 years old, approximately 1.80 m tall, dark brown hair, long face, pale complexion, slight build; distinguished appearance. Distinguishing feature: always wears glasses; nearsighted."[23] Benoit was in illustrious company. On the same wanted list appeared Pierre Georges, or "Fredo," who was to become Colonel Fabien, the military commander of the Communist underground—a legendary, even romantic figure killed while fighting in Alsace in 1944. French Communist Party headquarters in Paris is situated on the immense square in the Twentieth Arrondissement that bears his name.

In August the police located a partisan camp pitched on the edge of the Fontainebleau forest at Moret-sur-Loing, the command center responsible for a spate of "terrorist" activity. Albert Ouzoulias, the FTP commander of the Ile-de-France, called it the very first maquis, or group of rural partisan fighters, of the Paris region.[24] From his base at the partisan camp in the woods to the southeast of Paris, Benoit had launched many a partisan attack, both on his own and with others.

It was at Benoit's direction that Legros and Arthus made an unsuccessful May 19 attempt on the life of a German air force officer. This was the operation that placed them squarely on the occupiers' agenda. Benoit also threw a grenade onto a barge moored on the Seine where the Germans were having an event, while Legros stood lookout. The explosive device was presumably fashioned from materials that Benoit had directed Grelot to take from the lab at the lycée.

For Benoit, the fight for France's independence was all-consuming. While Legros, for example, had plans for a career in music and Arthus to be an electrical engineer, Benoit's sights were set on the present, not the future. His mother remembered him as a principled if misled young man who was intensely focused on his patriotic activities.[25] Others saw him as a fanatic.

Among Benoit's recruits were four other boys in his cohort, Arthus, Grelot, Legros, and Baudry. (As previously noted, Baudry had not been involved in the Buci affair, but his case was joined to that of the other four when they were prosecuted by a German military court.) Benoit "controlled" Arthus, Grelot, and Legros, meaning that he was the leader of their commando group. It was Benoit who issued the orders, set up their clandestine meetings, and stocked and distributed the weapons.

On the morning of May 31, 1942, Benoit, Grelot, Legros, and Arthus met by the fountain in the gardens of the Palais Royal. Benoit issued instructions and distributed revolvers to the others under his command. They were given their marching orders: to protect "our own" in the event of physical intervention from police or others. From the Palais Royal they made their way on foot to the rue de Buci. They crossed the river and approached the marketplace from a direction opposite that of the other demonstrators, who had convened at the Duroc and Odéon metro stations.

According to the boys' testimony, none of them fired a shot. Arthus and Grelot both told police that their revolvers never left their pockets. When they heard two shots ring out, they fled the scene through a narrow street. Nor did either of them see Benoit use his gun. When the three of them met up at the prearranged location after the demonstration, Benoit reported that he had managed to free one of the demonstrators by merely brandishing his weapon.[26]

Meanwhile, Legros reported having second thoughts as soon as he reached the scene where the demonstration was to take place. He gave his gun to a young woman he knew as "Suzanne," who tried to convince him to keep it, but without success. When it came time to return the revolver to Benoit, Legros insisted on keeping it because he was embarrassed to admit that he no longer had it.[27]

Benoit later testified that he had been unable to fulfill his mission on the rue de Buci. "When the fight broke out, the situation became confused and I was unable to follow the instructions conveyed to me by a man named Raoul. . . . He was certainly a boss."[28] Benoit knew very well that "Raoul" was a "boss": he was Georges Vallet, commander of the partisan actions on the rue de Buci and a wanted terrorist living, along with Benoit, in the camp at Moret-sur-Loing.

The fact that the boys had been on the rue de Buci and in possession of arms was enough to implicate them in the affair. Arthus, Grelot, and Legros were tried for their role in the Buci affair by the Tribunal d'état and condemned to hard labor for life (as previously mentioned, Benoit was condemned to death in absentia). Two days later they were handed over to the Germans, who wanted them in connection with a host of other partisan actions; with them went Jacques Baudry, who had been arrested on other charges on June 4. In addition to the attacks cited above, Legros and Arthus had made a botched attempt on the life of Hungarian student Tibor Berger, who was reputed to be a Gestapo agent. When Benoit was finally apprehended on August 28, he joined the other four at the Santé prison.

As soon as the boys were turned over to the Germans, the father of Lucien Legros knew his son's prospects had become all the more dire. Even before the Germans handed down the five death sentences, he had begun petitioning French authorities to intervene to save Lucien's life. Jacques Baudry's father also initiated an appeal through the same channels. Their letters landed on the desk of the chief French liaison with the German occupation authorities, Ambassador Fernand de Brinon.

Benoit and his cohorts were from "good families." Benoit's father was a police inspector. A sympathetic colleague in his local commissariat had warned him in advance of an impending police search of their home.[29] When a police investigator visited the Legros home, he noted that it was furnished "with taste." The salary of Legros *père* was also noted in his son's police file. The other young men's fathers were mid- or high-ranking civil servants, a doctor, and an engineer, all of whom earned comfortable livings. (By contrast, demonstrator Louise Berthelet, a laundress, earned one-tenth as much as the elder Legros.)

Moreover, although the story has it that all five boys were students at the Lycée Buffon, in fact both Benoit and Legros attended the prestigious École Alsacienne, a highly ranked private Protestant high school that was—and remains—favored by families of means.

The French authorities recognized that they were dealing with people of standing and culture, people like themselves. Benoit and his cohorts were all good students; Legros was a truly outstanding one. None of them fit the imaginary profile of a Communist grenade-wielding guerrilla fighter.

Maréchal Pétain, who had received a "particularly moving" letter from Baudry's father that described the younger Baudry as a studious boy who never went out and who was preparing for the entrance exam to a *grande école* in engineering, directed Brinon to press the Germans for a lighter sentence.[30]

As for Legros, in evidence were his stellar academic and musical accomplishments; his community service for the poor, the sick, and the infirm; and his abiding patriotism. Speaking on behalf of his wife and himself, Legros's father offered this explanation for his son's illegal activity:

> Terribly stricken to the core of our beings, we have searched with the greatest possible objectivity for what could have led an exemplary child to have taken part in a criminal demonstration. . . . Lucien was very affected by his brother's departure for the front and he despaired of being unable to follow him. The defeat was

profoundly upsetting to him. It was therefore easy to exploit his profound patriotic sentiment....

Moreover, this opinion was confirmed to me during our only visit at the Fresnes prison after the sentence was pronounced. He swore to us on his honor that only his love of country [*patrie*], his compassion for the unfortunate, and love for his dear parents guided his conscience and explained his behavior, and that he belonged neither to the Communist Party nor to a Gaullist group.[31]

In his October 20 communication with the German authorities, Brinon asked for clemency for all five boys, first and foremost on the basis of their ages. Benoit and Legros, he emphasized, had yet to reach their eighteenth birthdays at the time of their arrest. To drive home his point, he referred to them as "children." The oldest of the group was Baudry, who topped out at twenty years of age.

Brinon also argued that three of the five had already been sentenced by the French Tribunal d'état to a life of hard labor because they were threats to the public order. A heavier sentence (that is, a death sentence) for the same crime, he added, was disproportionate to the offense. Although the youths had contravened the law that forbade the carrying of guns, they had not made use of their arms.

Once again, as in Marzin's case, the issue of public opinion was foremost in his reasoning. The execution of five boys, two of whom were still minors, would "arouse ardent emotions" among the French public, he said.[32] But the Germans had no interest in public opinion. Nor did they make any pretense of "exemplarity." The question of public opinion would be handily preempted by killing the condemned in secret. The execution of the boys had but one purpose: to be rid of them once and for all.

What Brinon did not seem to understand even as late as October 1942 was that the Germans wanted the five students for crimes that dwarfed their roles as members of the security team in the Buci affair. All five students were wanted for numerous attacks on German installations and two assassination attempts (albeit botched)—one against a German officer and the other against a supposed Gestapo agent.

Newly infused with hope for a commutation of her son's death sentence, Legros's mother wrote her son's lawyer a letter of thanks:

> Like a good and beautiful fairy, you have eased [my husband's] pain by giving him the slim hope that he might see his dear child again, a hope he has helped me to share.... We have suffered so much ever since our dear angel left us.... Despite all appearances, my child is worthy of your efforts. He was all grace and goodness. The enemy of all violence, he was snatched from us and led astray![33]

"Angel," "child," "grace," "goodness": these were certainly not words that either the French authorities or the German occupiers would have used to describe a wanted "terrorist" and would-be assassin. Yet the appeal for clemency had reached as far as the head of state and his prime minister, Pierre Laval, whose private secretary also inquired about Legros's status. No doubt Laval was unaware that his own name and address had been found in Legros's pocket when he was arrested—Laval himself was in the partisans' crosshairs.

Alas, Madame Legros's hopes were in vain. Brinon's appeals were not just denied; they were never even acknowledged. The only correspondence the French liaison got in return was a February 22, 1943, confirmation from the Germans that the executions had already taken place. On October 15, 1942, Benoit, Arthus, Grelot, Legros, and Baudry were sentenced to death for terrorism by the military tribunal of the Luftwaffe, the German air force. They were executed by firing squad on February 8, 1943. The executions took place in the Fifteenth Arrondissement, not far from their own homes, at the firing range at Issy-les-Moulineaux.

The condemned were denied a final visit from family members. The deaths were not publicized, nor were they even announced. Indeed, their families were still frantically trying to save them when they learned that the sentences had already been carried out.

On the morning of their execution, the condemned were permitted to write last letters, but the letters were not conveyed to the addressees until the summer of 1944.[34] They had waited for nearly a year and a half for the fleeting solace of a final message, hastily scribbled in the hours or moments before their beloved sons, brothers, and friends faced a hail of German bullets.In his letter of adieu, Pierre Benoit reassured his family that after six months in prison, it was not that hard to die.[35]

Taken together, what do we make of the stories of Madeleine Marzin and Pierre Benoit—a prominent member of a Communist family and the son of a prosperous bourgeois family, a successful appeal and a failed one, a life sentence and a death sentence? Although Marzin and Benoit came from different social worlds, both were fully committed to the fight to free France. But Marzin had had far more responsibility for the demonstration on the rue de Buci than any of the boys on the security team. How is it that she lived to be ninety while the boys did not survive their teens?

It all goes back to the originary gender divide, where women and men were assigned different tasks from the outset. Throwing cans of sardines to the crowd was a threat to the public order; armed combat was an act of war. Although Marzin's reprieve was based on the fact that she was a woman, the fact that she was a woman was also the basis for her role as the organizer of a "women's" demonstration for food. This same distinction had ripple effects—in men's and women's defense strategies, in the price they paid for their activism, and, ultimately, in the ways in which the demonstration on the rue de Buci would be defined, distorted, remembered, and forgotten in the decades to come.

André Dalmas, Edgar Lefébure, and Henri Meunier were the first casualties of the Buci affair. Dalmas' identification card was among his personal effects. Lefébure's photograph probably comes from a similar personal document.

Photographs taken by police show Meunier on the day he was taken into custody. His disheveled appearance is likely a result of the chase and capture.

Archives de la Préfecture de Police de Paris, Le Pré-Saint-Gervais, France.

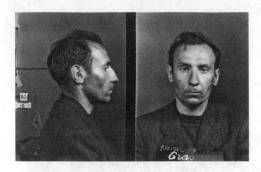

Elie Gras does not appear in any documentation of the Buci affair, although we know from Maté Houet's postwar oral testimony that it was Gras who prevented her from being trapped inside the Eco market on the day of the demonstration. Elie Gras was ultimately arrested on October 8, 1942. It proved to be his last day on earth. After a severe beating and mutilation by the sadistic Rottée of the *Brigades spéciales II*, Gras' broken body was returned to his cell, where he died that same night.

After the war, Rottée himself was condemned to death and executed. Among the worst crimes attributed to him at his trial was the beating death of Elie Gras.

Archives de la Préfecture de Police de Paris, Le Pré-Saint-Gervais, France.

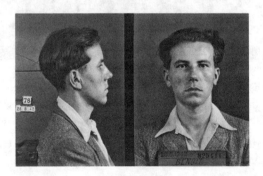

Pierre Benoit's police mug shot was taken on August 28, 1942, the day of his arrest by French police. By that time, his prospects were already quite bleak. Two months earlier he had been condemned to death in absentia by a French court. Upon his arrest, Benoit was handed over to the Germans at their request. Together with Arthus, Baudry, Grelot, and Legros, he was condemned to death a second time by the German Luftwaffe. All five were executed by firing squad on Feburary 8, 1943.

Archives de la Préfecture de Police de Paris, Le Pré-Saint-Gervais, France.

THE ECONOMY OF MEMORY

France had the distinction of being on the losers' side of the war and the victors' side of the peace. It was humiliated, invaded, and defeated in May 1940, but after four years of the collaborationist Vichy regime and German occupation, France emerged victorious alongside the Allies in May 1945. Vichy France, the France of Pétain, had been discredited; the upstart proto-regime of Charles de Gaulle moved into position as heir and victor both. These were the two Frances: one the guardian of order, the other champion of the universal principles of the rights of man. As the new republican France eclipsed the Vichy regime, a new set of values, viewpoints, and visions settled into place. Accordingly, erstwhile "terrorists" became heroes, "looters" became resisters, and the "riot by housewives" became a courageous act of defiance.

In reality there were and are many Frances, each with its own particular memory. There was Gaullist memory and Communist memory, the memory of the villages and that of the cities, the memory of the five zones, both occupied and "free." There was the memory of the victims and that of the perpetrators, hunters and hunted. There was the gray zone of memory, fraught with all the ambiguities of the in-between. And sometimes, in the interest of national reconciliation after a Franco-French conflict that had borne all the hallmarks of a civil war, there was only one France, one memory: that of the fighters and sometimes victims, a France absent of perpetrators past and present. The memory of the demonstration of the rue de Buci was shaped within this kaleidoscopic array of memories of the war, the Resistance, and the Occupation.

From the postwar period to the present, historical representations of the affair have cleaved along much the same lines as they did in 1942. There is still tension between the PCF's version of the event (a "women's" demonstration, a protest by housewives) and that of its critics (a pillage operation, a terrorist attack by armed men). At the heart of these contested memories lay the putative roles of women and men. In survivor memory, the event has been inseparable from the violence of the men—that of the security team and that of the executioners. In official Communist memory, the participation of partisan men has been elided or erased; the event has remained first and foremost a women's protest for food—when it is remembered at all.

What accounts for the disparities? How was the legend of the "women's demonstration of the rue de Buci" shaped, how did it take hold, and how has it traveled through time?

The Buci affair originally captured my imagination because it was everywhere yet terribly elusive at the same time. It was abundantly referenced in the underground Communist women's press and in postwar Communist testimony and literature. It was cited in both Communist and non-Communist histories of the Resistance, if only in passing.[1] In fact, the demonstration on the rue de Buci seemed to be a recurring metaphor for women's resistance in general.

More intriguing still, the women's demonstration of May 1942 figured in the oral testimony of the Communist women I was interviewing in the 1980s about women's role in the Resistance movement. "And of course, there was the demonstration of the rue de Buci," or "Don't forget the rue de Buci," I was told. When pressed to elaborate, though, no one was able to furnish information beyond the familiar and rudimentary details. In fact, some of the speakers who cited the Buci demonstration in oral testimony were already behind bars or barbed wire when the demonstration took place. They could have had no firsthand knowledge of the event.

When demonstrators Yvonne Chauviré, Marguerite Bronner, Norma Nicoletti Bléron, and the Berthelet sisters were sent to the women's prison in Rennes and then deported to Ravensbrück, they brought their story with them. They were joined by the women in Marzin's convoy, including Lucienne Rolland, who had witnessed her escape. Along the way these women transmitted the story of the Buci affair to fellow prisoners. Betty Jégouzo, like another Communist resister, Raymonde Reynal, learned of the demonstration through hearsay while in detention. They had played no role in the event themselves, yet they became unofficial spokeswomen by passing the story along. And so the legend made the rounds, traveling from Paris and Brittany to Germany and back again to France.

It was these women's memory of the event—that of a food demonstration by housewives and mothers—that would become fixed as the legend in subsequent accounts, both written and oral. From the very outset, however, there were fiercely competing versions of the story. Gaining and holding control of the narrative would be critical, both for the sponsors of the demonstration and for its critics. For organizers, at stake was the very legitimacy of the operation. For the opposition, what mattered was the legitimacy of the repression.

The day after the demonstration, the battleground shifted from the street to the papers. The state-sponsored, legal press lost no time responding to the event. Reports of the events emblazoned the front page of the major dailies throughout the northern and southern zones the very next day. Versions in the Vichy press differed very little. The official assessment was categorical: the incident was a case of "Bolshevik subversion."

Taking its cues from police reports drafted within hours of the event, the Vichy-approved press described it as "a despicable attack," "an incident [that was] clearly Communistic and terrorist in nature." The violence and tragic outcome of the operation were the leitmotif of such press accounts, from the morning after the event until the state funeral for the police victims—an event attended by dignitaries including the prime minister, Pierre Laval and the chief of police, Admiral François Bard. The main protagonists of these reports were the policemen who had lost their lives on the battleground.[2] Officers

Camille Morbois and Eugène Vaudrey were felled by "terrorists" who, it was claimed, "opened fire on the crowd."[3] They were "martyrs of the same persecution, heroes of the same cause." Warned one police officer on May 31, the very day of the demonstration: "[A] struggle to the death is being waged between the authorities and the agents of disorder, whose principal objective, now proven, is to eliminate those whom they consider to be a major obstacle to their nefarious enterprise."[4]

For the Vichy authorities, the event was the insidious work of foreigners. In a speech several days later, the Minister of Information, Paul Marion, linked the Buci affair to a grander scheme involving the Soviets and, even more absurd, the British. The recent bombing of the Paris region by the Royal Air Force and the "acts of professional terrorists commanded by Russian Soviets" showed that the Soviets and British were working hand in glove, he alleged; they were partners in "assassination, collective and individual." "Thus," concluded a radical right-wing paper, "English and Communists have joined forces once again to spill French blood."[5]

A month later, a similar claim was made about the demonstration on the rue Daguerre. Organizer Lise Ricol was reported to have climbed atop a display table outside the Prisunic grocery store and cried "Revolt! The Americans said so!"[6] This was not just the opinion of professional fabulists. In his memoir, lawyer Maurice Garçon reported speculation that the Communist Party recruited young shooters from Gaullist ranks to do their dirty work and take the blame.[7] Later some even speculated that Marzin's escape from prison had been orchestrated by resisters working for de Gaulle.

The state-censored papers such as *Le Temps* described the Buci operation as a "pillage attempt conducted at gunpoint" and "a crime against the public peace." The participants were denoted as "Communist provocateurs" and Madeleine Marzin as a "Communist rioter." Attorney Jacques Isorni, who represented the logger Raymond Estrade before the Tribunal d'état (and later defended Maréchal Pétain), claimed in his memoir that the affair had been a deliberate attempt by Communists to provoke German reprisals against the population.[8] At its most benign, the operation was merely disparaged as a "clumsy skirmish." However, most of the time it was defined, by authorities and by the press, as a "criminal attack" (*attentat*).[9]

Defining the affair was not merely a matter of semantics. Whether deemed a "criminal attack," on the one hand, or a demonstration of hungry and righteous French women, on the other, representations of the incident had profound consequences. At stake were the fate of the activists and, ultimately, the legitimacy of the entire underground enterprise.

The war of words continued throughout the summer of 1942. News reports compared the demonstration of the rue Daguerre, which took place on August 1, to its predecessor on the rue de Buci. In an interview, Lise Ricol, the organizer and main protagonist of the demonstration on the rue Daguerre, proudly recalled the headlines in the paper the next day: "The second front goes from the rue de Buci to the rue Daguerre." That women's food protests even made the papers, much less the headlines, was a source of deep satisfaction for her.[10] That such actions were deemed analogous to a *military* offensive was more noteworthy still.

Such was Ricol's memory of the headline in a 1988 interview. When I located the original newspaper, I found something quite different: "The only second front they have found so far is the one that runs from the rue de Buci to the rue Daguerre."[11] Critics of the regime had been eagerly anticipating the inevitable Allied landing, the second front that was expected to turn the tide of the war. But for the far-right journalists of Marcel Déat's *L'Oeuvre*, comparing the women's demonstrations to the elusive "second front" was a way to belittle the hopes and aspirations of the opposition: the "second front" was the long-awaited rescue that would never come. It would be no more significant than a couple of derisory "food riots by housewives."

The creation of the Buci legend was partly the result of a self-conscious political strategy and partly an attempt to salvage a disaster. To a large extent, it was also a consequence of the manner in which the demonstration was planned and organized, with women aboveground, visible, and at center stage, and men underground or hidden in the wings.

Oxymoronic as it may appear, the first "memory" of the women's demonstration of the rue de Buci actually predates the event itself. This was the version composed in advance of the event by party organizers in the form of the leaflet that was distributed on-site as the event unfolded. It contained an idealized representation of what was supposed to happen—without the gunfire and without the arrests. And it is precisely this version of events that party organizers and propagandists sought to impose as the authoritative one. Indeed, subsequent accounts in the party press and in participants' testimony conformed in large measure to this originary representation of the event. The purpose was to identify the demonstration as an act of people's justice by innocent mothers on behalf of their hungry families.[12] Women were making reasonable demands, the better to fulfill their nurturing roles.

Initial accounts in the underground press portrayed the demonstration on the rue de Buci as the very embodiment of women's resistance—a version of the story that survives today. Staging the event on Mother's Day only served to reinforce this representation. A Communist Party flyer distributed for Mother's Day of 1942 proclaimed that "mothers' love is a struggle" and exhorted mothers to take action to combat state-imposed hunger: "For our holiday this year a special task is incumbent upon us. We will show our power. . . . Together, in cortèges from town halls to the warehouses [stocked with food], the mothers of France will made their powerful voices heard."[13]

The underground women's press pilloried the official speeches, luncheons, and festivities honoring French mothers, instead using the occasion to denounce the hypocrisy of state policies and turning Vichy's discourse on "terrorism" against itself. In this account, the overnourished head of state, Maréchal Pétain, is depicted as the enemy of the French family.

This sinister old man, well fed and satisfied . . . dares to make a tearful call to courageous French mothers on their traditional day. WE SCREAM TO HIS FACE: THIEF! ASSASSIN! BANDIT! To save [our children] from death we are ready to dare everything, to risk all. We need BREAD![14]

In answer to Pétain's feeble and "tearful call," women were exhorted to scream and threaten. The head of state was depicted as a criminal, not the doting, protective "father" who shields the nation with his own body.[15] It was up to France's mothers to meet Pétain's passivity with forceful speech and actions. In order to fulfill their mission—feeding the family—women had to take decisive action. Taking action did not mean stepping outside traditional roles; rather, it was the logical and necessary extension of those roles. In short, mothers must intervene where the "father" has failed to fulfill his duty, that of provider.

This militant expression of patriotic motherhood flew in the face of Vichy's prescriptions for women's behavior, according to which women were to be docile and subservient.[16] Women demonstrators and propagandists pushed their responsibilities as mothers far beyond acceptable bounds by taking to the streets and making demands. Thus did the female protagonists of the demonstration both exploit and transcend the roles ascribed to them.

Not incidentally, the Buci demonstration was also a countercelebration of the official, state-sponsored version of Mother's Day, where propaganda was joined to action. The party press highlighted the collective, grassroots nature of the activity. A special June 1942 edition of *L'Humanité* reported:

On May 31, rue de Buci in Paris, an important demonstration took place, the significance of which was recognized by the Vichy clique. The example it set will be useful to all housewives and mothers who are not resigned to letting their children die of starvation. . . . It was Mother's Day, and these women were thinking of the meager meal that awaited their children, when some courageous patriots among them took the initiative of distributing canned goods, which otherwise would have gone to the *boches*.[17]

In reacting to Vichy's version, the Communist press reappropriated and reinterpreted the event in its own terms. Central to this representation was the historic role of revolutionary women.

> As in 1789 when the shop women of the central market in Paris [Les Halles] went to Versailles looking for the king to deliver bread, as in 1791–92 when housewives forced the Public Authorities to feed the Population of Paris . . . by forcibly entering shops and raiding boats and carriages on supply routes. So too in 1942, on May 31, rue de Buci, in the 6th arrondissement of Paris, holding their own this time against the invaders of our country for whom canned goods were intended, housewives stormed, INVADED AND PILLAGED one of the biggest retailers . . . working with the *boches* to ruin the health of Parisians by starving them, the better to dominate them and reduce them to nothingness.[18]

The term "pillage," typically used by the right-wing press to describe the theft of stocks from inside the store, was here a form of people's justice where women take what is rightfully theirs.

Thus the Vichy press and the Communist propagandists posited starkly antithetical versions of the same event. The operation was an "underhanded machination and not "a good way to celebrate Mother's Day," an "armed commando raid" rather than a "women's demonstration." The protagonists were "rioters," not "honest housewives" and "brave French mothers," "terrorists" as opposed to "patriots" who act in "self-defense." Word for descriptive word, the struggle to define the event was intense and unremitting.

In only one version of the event featured in the clandestine party press is there any allusion to the violence that erupted during the demonstration. Here both the French regime and the German occupiers were targeted as the enemy.

> These women were right to take what was intended for the *boches*; but the police, in service to the Gestapo was there not to protect the French but to defend the *boches* who pillage and kill, and the cops came to the rue de Buci to attack the housewives who were committing a just and restorative act. The patriots defended themselves and they were absolutely right to do so.[19]

Roles and responsibilities were thus reversed. Not only did the Communists redistribute the wealth, they also redistributed the roles of the actors in the drama. It was not housewives who stole goods, but the occupiers who were stealing food from the French people. The aggressors were not the patriots but rather the Gestapo and the Germans, aided and abetted by the French police in slavish service to their German masters. In yet another account, the Eco grocery store was denounced as a shady establishment known to truck with collaborators and Germans.[20]

The party's account was not merely a skillful reordering of good and evil where one person's terrorist is another person's freedom fighter. It was above all an effort to mold opinion, mobilize support, and shape the contours of a story that would become a legend in the months and years to come.

Yet the most significant aspect of the Communist representation is not so much what was included as what was missing. Although the eruption of violence was mentioned in passing in the earliest accounts, it was omitted from subsequent versions of the story. Only in reacting to official accounts published in the Vichy papers did the underground press refer to the violence that ensued. The shootings and deaths disappeared from Communist Party accounts entirely.

The omission of the violence made it possible to portray the event as a demonstration, and in particular, a demonstration by women. "In future demonstrations like the one on the rue de Buci," continues the article quoted above, "when women serve themselves in warehouses and stores that feed the *boches*, they will energetically fight back any show of force directed against them." Thus the women will defend themselves. There is no mention of a male security group that will be posted to protect them.

Downplaying the tragic outcome made sense in light of the intended purpose of the demonstration, which was to bring women into the struggle. The risks of the operation had to be discounted if others were to join the movement. Marzin and other women's organizers have indicated how difficult it was to organize protests of the sort and to galvanize housewives to action.[21] Neighborhood women were often afraid of taking risks by resorting to illegal public action, and with good reason. In instances such as this, we are reminded that the purpose of the clandestine press was not only to inform but also to incite.

While the government and pro-German press were keen on highlighting the killings of the policemen, they were far more discreet when it came to publicizing their own killings.[22] Articles on the executions of Dalmas, Lefébure, and Meunier were relegated to the back pages of the Vichy papers. Nowhere at the time or in subsequent months did the Germans' executions of the five high school students appear in the legal newspapers. Even French authorities at the highest level of government were not informed of the executions by their German partners, but only later, and incidentally, by the families of the young men. In any event, the Vichy government would have been loath to publicize its own loss of control over dissidents.

The French government used the press in much the same way as their opponents. The oft-made argument in favor of so-called exemplarity—the deterrent capacity of capital sentences to warn the public and stave off further attacks—was superseded by the desire to keep their own violence out of public view.

By executing the men, the Vichy and German authorities also destroyed the human evidence of the so-called terrorist raid, thereby leaving the Communist legend—a demonstration of women—to stand. As a result, some key male activists have suffered a double erasure. Their physical elimination meant that surviving participant memory of the Buci affair would be first and foremost a women's memory. It is an ironic reversal of the status quo, where men have historically overshadowed women.

For the Communist underground, the perceived legitimacy of the operation was predicated on its being a demonstration and not a commando raid. The presence of partisan men not only contradicted the preeminent characterization of the event as a women's demonstration, it introduced the notion of risk. It meant that protesting women needed protection because they were risking arrest—and worse. If such actions were to be repeated in the future, then the prospect of violence had best be minimized or obscured altogether. Thus the clandestine party press defined the incident on the rue de Buci as a women's protest for food. That said, there was another reason for representing the event in such a way.

Some of the men who were erased from the Buci affair were not forgotten at all, but were detailed to populate another narrative. Arthus, Grelot, and Legros were arrested and tried in a French court for their involvement in the Buci affair. They were later joined in prison by Benoit and Baudry. All five of them were tried a second time, this time by the Germans, and executed for their commission of "terrorist" acts. Although actively sought by the police, none of them was arrested for their involvement in the student demonstration of the Lycée Buffon, which in fact was the least of the offenses attributed to them. Moreover, two of the five, Arthus and Legros, did not even attend the Lycée Buffon at the time. And yet they all became immortalized as the "five students of the Lycée Buffon." Indeed, they are far better known by the general French public than any of the demonstrators of the rue de Buci, including its ringleader, Madeleine Marzin.

The students of the Lycée Buffon became emblematic figures in French Communist memory, both together and separately. During the war they were celebrated in clandestine flyers and newspapers.

In 1944 they inspired a tribute by Communist poet Paul Éluard, who wrote a poem dedicated to Lucien Legros.[23] Since that time, their memory has been preserved in brochures, secondary literature, memorials, and even a postage stamp. In fact, the story of the five students has transcended Communist memory to become part of Resistance memory more generally. In most public tributes—plaques and monuments in Paris—their connection to the PCF is not even specified. The emphasis is on their sacrifice or "martyrdom," their youth, and their active commitment to an ideal.

Why are the women participants remembered for the rue de Buci, while the young men, originally prosecuted for the Buci affair, are remembered for something else? It was a wise and frugal deployment of meaning in keeping with the logic of front politics. A broad-based movement under Communist direction that aimed to group all patriots, Communist and non-Communist alike, the Front national reached out to different constituencies based on profession, workplace, residence, age, and sex. The story of the students and the story of the demonstrators would be framed as separate chapters in the same epic narrative of resistance, a great pluralist movement encompassing every element of the French population.

Thus were the five young men written out of the story of the demonstration in order to constitute a story of their own. Separating the action of the male high school students from that of the female demonstrators served a double purpose: it created a signature women's event and a signature event for high school students. Different constituencies, same struggle. Like a wartime recipe that uses every last crumb of a desiccated stump of stale bread, one story could become two. It was an economy of meaning where each element is mined for maximum value. And so was the representation of the Buci affair further secured as a women's demonstration, absent the critical, life-changing actions of the male security team.

What became of the protagonists of the Buci affair after their trials? By the time the gates of the prisons and internment camps swung open and political detainees were freed, some prisoners had already served their time and more. Others had embarked on remarkable itineraries that deviated from the sentences handed down by the courts. The postwar dossiers of the Ministère des anciens combattants (Veterans Ministry) reveal how sentencing by Vichy courts actually translated into time served and where.

The people associated with the demonstration received judgments ranging from outright acquittal to death. However, the only penalties that were carried out to the letter, exactly as stated in the rulings, were the death sentences: three beheadings by the French and at least six executions by German firing squad.[24] As for the other penalties, sentences were often carried out in ways not intended by the courts. Vichy courts handed down a Third Republic type of penalty, hard labor, for a given time period. Those time periods implied that the regime and its system of justice had a future. In the Vichy era, however, hard labor often translated as deportation.

Ten people, five women and five men, were deported to concentration camps, where they spent the rest of the war. Political prisoners who were deemed particularly dangerous were sometimes extracted from prisons by the French and turned over to the Germans, who in turn deported them to concentration camps in the East. All but one of the people prosecuted for their involvement in the Buci affair, Émile Blanchon, survived the camps. They were not liberated until the spring of 1945. Their actual sentences varied wildly, from five years of hard labor to hard labor for life. Yet despite the differences in the levels of responsibility imputed to them, they suffered similar fates, all of which were far worse than their actual sentences.

The Berthelet sisters, Louise and Raymonde, were condemned to terms of ten and five years of hard labor, respectively. They left the Rennes prison for Ravensbrück, the only concentration camp for women, located northwest of Berlin, in May 1944. Their itinerary was typical of many women resisters: from La Petite Roquette, the women's prison in Paris, to the prisons in Fresnes and Rennes, and ultimately to the camp of Romainville, from which they left for Germany. The sisters were separated in June 1944, when Louise was sent to Neuengamme, then detailed to a work commando outside Hanover. She was repatriated on the day the armistice was signed, May 8, 1945. Raymonde spent the last month of her deportation in Mauthausen. She left the camp on April 9, 1945, and was ultimately repatriated via Switzerland.[25]

Marguerite Bronner, who was sentenced to a life of hard labor, was deported to Ravensbrück and later transferred to Sachsenhausen.

Yvonne Chauviré, sentenced to five years of hard labor, was deported to Ravensbrück.

Norma Nicoletti Bléron was deported to Ravensbrück, transferred to Flossenberg, and ultimately assigned to a work commando in Holleischen. Her husband, Roger Bléron, who had been condemned to twenty years of hard labor, remained in a French camp at Melun, from which he was liberated in August 1944 after the liberation of Paris and some parts of France.

The men who were deported to concentration camps included Marcel Leclerc. His itinerary began at the Santé and Tourelles prisons, both in Paris. From there he went to the holding camp at Compiègne, from which he was deported to Sachsenhausen in May 1943. He was subsequently transferred to Buchenwald. Also in Buchenwald were Robert Desvignes (by way of Sachsenhausen) and André Martin. Albert Barrachi was sent to Mauthausen and Raymond Pluvinet to Sachsenhausen.

Some men who had even stiffer sentences were not deported at all but remained interned in French prisons and camps. Émile Sézille de Mazancourt's life sentence translated into detention in Fresnes and the Centrale de Melun, from which he was liberated on August 25, 1944, the day of the liberation of Paris. Yet his wife, Louise, who was condemned to "only" ten years of hard labor, ended up in Ravensbrück.

Demonstrators whose cases were dismissed for lack of evidence, or who were judged but acquitted, expected to regain their freedom. Alas, many of them remained in custody. Charges against Swiss chocolate maker Julien Baudois and his wife, Georgette Duperray, who was Swiss by marriage, were completely dropped. However, they remained in French prisons until August 1943, whereupon they were extradited to Switzerland thanks to the intervention of the Swiss consulate. They returned to France after the war.

Other people arrested by the police and later exonerated by the courts were less fortunate than the Baudois couple. Those deemed to represent a potential threat to the public order could be placed in "administrative detention" by local authorities, usually the departmental prefect.[26] Moreover, prison directors were required to report imminent releases to the German authorities, who had the final say over the disposition of a prisoner. This is very likely why some men and women who were actually acquitted of wrongdoing were not freed but instead sent to one of the internment camps intended for Jews, foreigners, and other "enemies of the state" that were scattered throughout France. A few were fortunate enough to be liberated before the end of the war. Others served their sentences in French prisons (Fresnes, Tourelles) or were transferred to French internment camps (Melun, Pithiviers, La Lande).

The disparities between the sentencing of the courts and the actual trajectories of the prisoners suggest the complexities of French and German systems of justice and incarceration, operating in tandem or independently, that were without precedent. How and why some people remained in prison while others were consigned to internment camps in France or deported to concentration camps in the East is a complex story in which a number of variables—the pressures of time and space, political decisions, the personal dispositions of officials, their perceptions of a given prisoner—came into play in each individual case.

On February 26, 1945, an extraordinary thing happened: the Buci affair was judged anew. It was the second time that the first batch of demonstrators would be judged for the same "crimes," and the third such judgment for four of the five high school students.

The June 25, 1942 verdict of the Tribunal d'état that had sent three men to the guillotine, meted out life sentences to five people, and sentenced twelve to varying years of hard labor was annulled. The condemned were fully exonerated.[27]

Dalmas, Lefébure, and Meunier had already perished at the guillotine. Of the five people condemned to a life of hard labor, four had been executed by the Germans. Ten of the remaining thirteen accused were still in concentration camps. For all of them, the least that could be said is that it was too little too late.

What in the world was the purpose of overturning the original verdict? What were the circumstances that led to such an astonishing measure?

France had yet to be liberated and the Germans were still on the scene when, in 1943, the Comité français de Libération nationale (CFLN) had begun meeting in Algiers to guide the nation's transition from authoritarian state to postwar democratic republic. It revoked the most iniquitous of the Vichy decree-laws, including the decrees of August and September 1941 that established the "exceptional" jurisdictions, the Section spéciale and the Tribunal d'état. An ordinance of July 6, 1943 stated that "all acts committed after June 10, 1940 that were infractions of the law then in effect, and committed in service to the cause of the liberation of France, are declared legal."[28]

The ordinance was worded that way because the original intention of simply nullifying the decisions of the courts in one fell swoop was deemed too broad. The Tribunal d'état had prosecuted not only political "crimes" but other offenses that were still illegal: attacks on the food supply (burning harvests, trafficking in ration tickets, stealing food packages meant for prisoners of war, black marketeering), and performing an abortion or having one. There could be no blanket erasure because some of the convicted were in fact ordinary felons, murderers, and thieves.

Resisters therefore had to be distinguished from common criminals. Politically motivated decisions rendered by the Tribunal d'état and the Section spéciale had to be reexamined. The task of reviewing their judgments fell to a newly established section of the

Paris appeals court, the *chambre des révisions.* The case of the rue de Buci was reopened. The condemned had perpetrated their "crimes" for the purposes of resistance, ruled the court. They were thereby exonerated (*réhabilités*) and the judgment against them nullified.

It was the first time that the state would recognize the demonstration on the rue de Buci as an act of resistance. Such was the view of the court in 1945, but as we will see, later historians, jurists, and other commentators would judge it differently.

The status of the Buci affair, however, was far from evident from the beginning. Revision of the original judgment was a tortuous process that reveals the instability of definitions of "resistance" at a liminal moment in the transition from authoritarian state to republican democracy.

Public protest, stealing sardines, looting a shop, and distributing illegal propaganda were all common criminal offenses in May 1942. The provisional government thus redefined these and other "crimes" committed by resisters in the course of their political activities as patriotic acts. Even killing a policeman, an unfortunate but sometimes unavoidable byproduct of the struggle to free France, no longer justified incarceration or, worse, death. Resisters with criminal records now could have their records cleared.

The government originally considered a more sweeping measure: declaring the Tribunal d'état and the Sections spéciales illegitimate to begin with. The decisions of illegitimate institutions would have no standing; it would be as if their rulings never existed. This was a critical distinction. Victims of the courts would be neither pardoned (*graciés*) nor exonerated (*réhabilités*) because they had committed no crime in the first place. The only crime in question had been committed by the courts themselves.

It was thus determined that each ruling be examined separately in order to ascertain whether it met the requirements of the new statute. A special appeals process was established through the *chambre de révision,* the jurisdiction created for the express purpose of reviewing the decisions rendered by Vichy courts. A resister or the family of a resister could petition the court to overturn such rulings, which in turn would enable imprisoned patriots to be freed. Reviewing decisions one by one was a painstaking process. It required time and personnel, and there was little of either. The onus was put on the convicted, not on the court, to pursue revision. Moreover, the first version of the law required that appeals be submitted within a three-month period. This article was later revised and the period extended.

It was the French Communist Party deputy Mathilde Péri who brought the Buci affair to the floor of the newly constituted National Assembly. Péri advocated the repeal of the original court ruling that had resulted in five death sentences and fifteen prison terms. The condemned had been sentenced as common criminals but they were in fact political activists working to free France, she argued. They should no longer bear the stigma of their sentences, even— especially—posthumously. The victims were patriots and martyrs. Moreover, survivors of the affair would be unable to vote because they had criminal records.

The protagonists of the Buci affair had another advocate in the person of Étienne Legros, the father of Lucien. Together with Mathilde Péri he had cofounded the Association des veuves et familles de fusillés et massacrés, a lobby representing the widows and families of murdered resisters. Legros *père* acted on the new legislation by petitioning the *chambre des révisions* to invalidate the Tribunal d'état ruling of June 25, 1942. While his son's killers were German, it was the Tribunal d'état that had originally condemned Lucien Legros to a life of hard labor, and it was the French who had handed his son over to the Germans. Now it was the French who would be called upon to restore his reputation and honor his legacy.

Legros's request was denied. The investigating judge ruled that the Buci affair had been prosecuted as a criminal offense that had nothing to do with the liberation of France. The original ruling did not meet the criteria set forth by law and was therefore left to stand. The failure of the appeals court to overturn the Tribunal d'état's ruling on the Buci affair made it abundantly clear that there was no reliable consensus on what distinguished a politically motivated judgment from one that was based on law.

On February 20, 1945, Communist deputies Auguste Gillot and Mathilde Péri once again brought the Buci affair to the attention of the National Assembly. The news of the court's refusal to invalidate the Tribunal d'état's ruling on the Buci affair met with outrage. In the following transcription of Péri's remarks and the spirited debate that followed, audience reaction on the floor of the assembly is duly recorded. The stenographer's parenthetical remarks convey a sense of the temperature in the chamber.

> <u>Madame Péri</u>: M. Gillot has just shown that the purge and republican reorganization of the judiciary have not gone far enough and have not offered the French any guarantee of justice.
>
> Permit me to cite a fact, which, in all its brutality, illustrates the continuity of the Vichy court system. It concerns the affair of the rue de Buci of May 31, 1942.
>
> The people of Paris remember Madeleine Marzin, who courageously distributed to housewives food that was stocked in a shop on the rue de Buci. The young students Lucien Legros, Pierre Benoit, Jean Arthuss [*sic*], and Pierre Grelot protected the housewives to keep them from falling into the hands of the Gestapo and Vichy's *milice* [*sic*].[29]
>
> On June 25, 1942 the tribunal [*sic*] d'état, presided over by the all too well-known Devise, handed down a judgment concerning the participants, including the four students whose names I have just cited. It was a judgment that condemned three of them to a life of hard labor, and the last student, Pierre Benoit, was condemned to death in absentia. These young people were then handed over to the German authorities and shot after several months of torture.
>
> What crime had they committed? *Fighting against Hitler's plan to exterminate the French race by starvation.*[30]
>
> . . . [T]he families asked for a revision of the sentence.

One of the families has just been notified that there are no grounds for revision. (*Exclamations from the audience.*)

M. Jacques Debû-Bridel: It is a scandal.

Madame Péri: You must observe, *M. le Garde des Sceaux,* . . . that the judges of 1945 did not even bother to examine the file, as the assistant prosecutor, M. Ruellan, admitted to a representative of the association of the families of the shot and massacred, M. Legros, whose son was among those shot by firing squad.

The only excuse M. Ruellan could come up with was that "the short timetable of three months was not long enough to study the files." The judges of 1945 approved the decision of the judges of 1942, rendered by Devise, who was serving the enemy, against the young patriots whose only crime was fighting for the liberation of France.

That notwithstanding, General de Gaulle glorified the acts of the victims of the Buci affair. The radio, the French press, and the press of our allies paid homage to these young martyrs imbued with patriotic spirit.[31] But just the same, the odious ruling issued by Pétain's judges of 1942 was confirmed by the judges of 1945.

Are the same judges still in place? If that is the case, then they must be replaced and placed under investigation for acting in service to the enemy. (*Applause.*)

Have the judges been replaced? If this is the case, then you have replaced one group of Vichy servants [*vichyssistes*] with another, and they must be tried immediately for treason.

This observation, *Monsieur le minister,* . . . I bring to you on behalf of the association of the families of the shot and massacred. The association would like to be assured that the thinking of the men of Vichy has been banished, and thoroughly, from our entire judicial system; it would be pure justice. (*Lively applause.*)[32]

Members of the Assembly challenged the Minister of Justice and Keeper of the Seals, François de Menthon, to answer for the decision of the Appeals Court. On February 22, 1945, Menthon addressed the Assembly in person. His remarks gave rise to a boisterous discussion on the floor.

> M. le Garde des Sceaux, Ministre de la Justice: I cannot comment on all the cases mentioned here because I cannot violate the confidentiality of the office of investigations or the work of the prosecutor. (*Interruptions.*) However, I will address in broad terms the most serious cases that have been cited here and which have roused legitimate passions.
>
> Regarding the affair of the rue de Buci, the purpose was to review actions that were technically matters of criminal conduct because they were committed for the purpose of the liberation. It is true that on January 4, 1945, the Chamber of Revisions of the Paris Court of Appeals rejected the request presented by M. Jean Grelot on behalf of his son Pierre, who was shot by the Germans after having been previously condemned by the Tribunal [*sic*] d'État. (*Interruptions.*)
>
> The public prosecutor, who alone receives instructions from the Minister of Justice, presented the case for revision. As early as February 7, the case was taken up by the office of the prosecutor. M. Etienne Legros, who had also filed a request for revision on behalf of his son Lucien, also shot by the Germans following the same affair, was asked by the prosecutor to prepare a file that was essential to the review of the case.
>
> For the past several days, the case has been back on the docket for a [new] hearing on March 1. The prosecutor will also request a revision for all of the people sentenced in the same affair, including those whose families have not submitted a request for review.
>
> M. Pierre Villon: What if the court rules once again to deny the revision?
>
> M. le Garde des Sceaux: How can the prosecutor be held accountable for a negative decision of the court? The prosecutor acted according to the general instructions issued by the ministry.

The court ruled against repealing the original decision. The judges were poorly informed ... (*Interruptions.*)

M. Pierre Villon: You mean they were poorly chosen!

From various quarters: The former judges [of the Vichy regime] have been kept on!

M. le Garde des Sceaux: ... The public prosecutor is refiling a request for review. The ruling of January 6 [*sic*] that everyone deplores was a scandal.

Believe me, there is your explanation!

All of us know about the Buci affair, if only because we heard about it on the radio. But these judges were basing their decision on the file presented to them, and since they were men of the court who were out of touch with what was being said in the public domain ... (*Lively and prolonged interruptions.*)

M.Vincent Auriol: They listened to the Vichy radio, not the BBC!

M. le Garde des Sceaux: ... [T]hey issued a ruling based solely on the evidence supplied to them by the families, who were justified in thinking it unnecessary to elaborate the facts of a case that was so well known.

This is the psychological explanation for the lamentable error in judgment, which obviously is not the fault of the office of the prosecutor. (*Interruptions.*)[33]

The minister's explanation struck some members of the audience as disingenuous. One representative, Édouard Depreux, expressed his incredulity.

You spoke of the affair of the rue de Buci. Do you realize that what you said clearly is this: the judges who were mistaken in their ruling should be excused because they are men of the bar and therefore unaware of what was being said in the public domain?

What?! Public discussion, the eloquent and moving remarks of our friend [Maurice] Schumann [spokesman for the Free French] on the radio from London, in praise of those who were fighting for the sacred cause of the Resistance against the Germans? Public discussion stating that twenty-year-old Frenchmen like young Legros, whose father I know and whom I like very much, were assassinated by the Germans after having first been condemned by a French court? How is it possible not to know that this is Resistance when both the father and brother were also arrested by the German authorities as hostages?[34]

The minister's responses had fallen far short of satisfying the National Assembly. Members faulted him for the slow pace of justice, and for the failure to replace the judges of the Vichy regime with nonpartisan, republican judges worthy of the universalist French tradition of the Declaration of the Rights of Man. They decried the fact that the judges reviewing decisions issued by the courts under the Vichy regime were the very same ones who had issued those rulings to begin with. The new Minister of Justice charged with purging the justice system, they agreed, was not performing his job, or at least not doing it fast enough. Some members suggested that his salary be reduced by 100 francs. The proposal garnered support but was never put to a vote. It was a symbolic rebuke, but a rebuke just the same.[35]

On February 26, 1945, several days after Menthon's upbraiding by the Assembly, the Buci affair was put before the same court once again. This time the judge ruled in favor of the plaintiffs: the June 25, 1942, ruling of the Tribunal d'état was rendered null and void.

In the first round of revision, the state had been divided. The legislature and judiciary had different notions of what constituted "resistance." External pressures had brought the judges around, but only on a second appeal. The official position had become unitary and incontrovertible: the demonstration on the rue de Buci had been an act of Resistance committed for the liberation of France. Thus did the legislature and the executive branches of the postwar state redefine and reconfirm the demonstration on the rue de Buci affair in a way wholly consistent with the first representations of the event in the underground Communist press.

During the debates on the floor of the National Assembly, only the Lycée Buffon protagonists and Madeleine Marzin were mentioned by name. There was total silence surrounding André Dalmas, Edgar Lefébure, and Henri Meunier, who had arguably suffered the worst fate of all: the French guillotine. Dalmas, Lefébure, and Meunier were just as dead and just as patriotic as the four young men, but no one spoke for them. Their death sentences had been declared and meted out by the French alone.

Although they were not explicitly named on the floor of the chamber, however, the state prosecutor's original request for the revision included the three men, together with Raymond Estrade and Arthur Lathulière. What about the other participants? Aside from Marzin, the "honorary man" who was condemned to death along with the three men, where were the women?[36] Why did the women enter the conversation only belatedly, as an afterthought? It was not until later that the appeal was amended to include *all* of the protagonists of the rue de Buci, protesting women as well as partisan men.

It cannot be said that the focus of the Assembly and the court was only on those participants who had been accused of violence. Nor can it be said that the focus was on those with the stiffest penalties: Yvonne Chauviré and Louise Sézille de Mazancourt were condemned to five and ten years of hard labor, respectively. Arthur Lathulière and Roger Bléron got twenty years. Something more pernicious was at play here: the abiding invisibility of women.

Throughout the debates, the event is consistently referenced as the "Buci affair," not "the women's demonstration on the rue de Buci," as it would later become known. Moreover, the four young patriots had yet to fully assume their identities as "the students of the Lycée Buffon."[37] The constituent elements of the story were in place, the emblematic status of the affair had been consolidated and reinscribed, but the legend had yet to take hold.

With the revision of the court decision, the first official recognition of the Buci affair focused on the event itself. In subsequent years, beginning in the 1950s, state recognition focused on individual protagonists. Protesters and partisans alike were acknowledged for their contributions to the Resistance, which included and often transcended their involvement in the demonstration.

Although very few resisters were engaged in combat missions per se—known to the Germans as "terrorism"—their roles and responsibilities in the underground movement were later assessed and translated into military terms. Unprecedented and innovative ways of challenging the regime, such as demonstrating for food, had no language or institutions of their own. The new French state thus recast unusual forms of "fighting" into traditional military categories, accorded military rank to resisters, and honored remarkable service with military-style decorations.

For the French Communist Party, demonstrating for food was defined as women's political work. Ironically, the most quintessentially feminine form of resistance was reconfigured in memory in what were then the most masculine of terms. The postwar state translated levels of responsibility into ex post facto military rank, and rank translated into pensions and privileges. Female demonstrators, once considered enemies of the state, now found themselves accorded official military rank. Louise Berthelet Sézille de Mazancourt and Norma Nicoletti Bléron, for example, acquired the respective ranks of sergeant and soldier.[38] Partisan men also acquired ex post facto rank, but urban guerrilla operations had more in common with traditional warfare. As a rule, postwar government officials ranked underground activity under Communist Party auspices lower than comparable activity associated with Gaullist groups and networks, and they also accorded lower status to noncombat activity, where women predominated.

The deep rifts and mutual distrust that had characterized relations between the French Communist Party and the non-Communist resistance were not overcome, but subsequent republican regimes acknowledged, if begrudgingly, the contribution of the party to the Resistance effort. So, too, did the French voting public. From the immediate postwar period and into the mid-1950s, the French Communist Party garnered between 26 and 29 percent of the popular vote, in large part because of its role in the struggle to liberate France from collaborators and occupiers both.[39] However, memory of the demonstration on the rue de Buci remained largely confined to Communist Party members and fellow travelers.

The schoolteacher and the seamstress, the garage renter and the cheese merchant, the housewife and the logger: all had their own personal recollections of the event. There was no personal memory that belonged to the post office worker, or the high school truant, or the retiree. They did not survive the war. Their memory was not of them but for them. It would be forged by others in the name of France, the French Communist Party, or both.

There was also the memory of second-generation victims. As a ten-year-old child, Denise Leclerc had talked her way into the Santé prison to show her father, Marcel, her outstanding report card. Fifty years later, Denise was still struggling to understand her father's role in the demonstration, searching for answers that had defied her for a lifetime. The event that had deprived her of a father for nearly three years hovered over her like a cloud, heavy and opaque. Denise Leclerc Boyer devoted her retirement to researching the Buci affair until she hit a dead end: the archives were closed to her. She died before the hollow bits could be filled in. We are left to wonder what Marcel Leclerc may have told his daughter, if anything, after his return from Buchenwald.[40]

We first heard Leclerc's voice and those of his fellow demonstrators in the summer of 1942 when they attempted to deny, explain, or justify their presence on the rue de Buci to police investigators. Their statements were shaped toward a desired result: an acquittal, a more lenient sentence, liberation. In that moment, the discursive strategies they adopted were exculpatory. What later became of the testimony of the same person in describing the same activities when the desired result was radically different? What if the speaker's goal was to recast her once illegal activity before a different audience, in a positive light?

This was precisely the case after the tide had turned in favor of the Resistance, including the Communist resistance. By the 1950s, the same people who had struggled to diminish their underground roles before the police and the courts were then in a position to establish their Resistance bona fides. Participation in the Resistance, detention, and deportation became valued forms of social capital. They accorded prestige, honor, and pride.

Before others would recognize the contributions of women to the resistance movement, women had to recognize themselves. Women were far less likely to file for these benefits, at least in the short term, just as they were less likely than men to write memoirs of their resistance experiences until the 1980s. Recognition for wartime service in the form of military honors and decorations also came to women much later than for their male coworkers, and for Communist women later than for their non-Communist counterparts.[41]

The application process for postwar recognition of resistance activities began with the assembly of a dossier. The candidate detailed her activities, dates of service, group or affiliation, and, where appropriate, a chronology of her time in detention. Her declarations were seconded by surviving supervisors and coworkers who could vouch for her. Her dossier was assessed by state officials at the Ministère des anciens combattants (Veterans Ministry), who rendered a decision.

Information extracted by the police about a resister's activities and information volunteered by the same person many years later both derived from the same source: the resister herself. In each circumstance, however, the purpose, the audience, and the desired result were radically different. Here again we are confronted with first-person testimony preserved in written form. Wartime police files and the postwar files of the ministry are two very different sets of documents, yet both are derived from the same witness about the same activity. How does self-representation change from one circumstance to the next?

This is not to suggest that one kind of testimony is reliable while the other is suspect, or that some claims are necessarily understated while others are exaggerated. Rather, the jarring disparities display the primacy of context and intent in the shaping of a document. Indeed, in the case of the Buci affair, wartime and postwar testimony often complement each other in enlightening ways. Context is all the more important when personal survival is at stake, in the one instance, and when private memory and public recognition are being reconciled, in the other.

The postwar statements of some people arrested by police reveal that they very likely played more consequential roles in the demonstration, or in underground Communist activities more generally, than offical records would have us believe. Some "second-stringers"—people arrested in the wake of the demonstration and prosecuted in the second batch by the Tribunal de première instance—appear to have been quite successful in dissimulating the extent of their illegal activities in their statements to the police.

One such woman was Angèle Cousin, a factory worker in the Paris suburb of Courbevoie, who was arrested for having given refuge to Edgar Lefébure. Cousin was part of the Communist "family," both literally and figuratively: her husband had been arrested in January 1942 for Communist activities and was in the custody of the Germans at the time of her own arrest. The police investigation and her declarations to police make that much clear. Cousin was convicted of having sheltered a "terrorist," but no other illegal activity had been attributed to her. A 1955 document in her file at the Ministère des anciens combattants, however, reveals that she was engaged in far more dangerous activity: the transport of arms for the FTPF of Ile-de-France, the greater Paris region.[42]

So, too, Julia Cartier, a retired teacher in her sixties, who was acquitted of Communist activity altogether in January 1943 and released from prison after seven months of detention. Yet despite her acquittal, and according to postwar documents, she had in fact been thoroughly engaged in a wide range of clandestine support tasks. As a member of a Communist Party–run group in her home arrondissement, the Fifteenth, Cartier distributed the underground press and collected money to help the families of political prisoners. She was also responsible, among other things, for finding hiding places for hunted illegal activists.

The author of a letter on her behalf mentions that even before the demonstration on the rue de Buci, Cartier had participated in several other street protests "with tricolor flags flying." This detail was furnished as a way of insisting that the protests in question were fully patriotic in nature, despite the fact that they had been organized by the underground party in 1940 and 1941, before Hitler's invasion of the Soviet Union. That careful letter writer with a fine eye for nuance was none other than Cartier's supervisor, Madeleine Marzin herself.[43]

Another case is that of Raymond Estrade, a member of the security team who was prosecuted by the Tribunal d'état with the first batch of suspects. That he was on-site to defend the women is well established in both sets of documents. But a critical element furnished in the postwar period is absent from his testimony to the police: Estrade was armed. Had the authorities been aware of that, it would have made the difference between the life sentence he got and the death sentence meted out to the other armed men.

A second disparity between the testimony activists gave to the police and their testimony in the postwar period concerns the timing and duration of their involvement in French Communist Party–sponsored activity. In their interrogations by police, the overwhelming majority of demonstrators claimed that they had had no contact with the party before June 1941. The party, it should be remembered, had been outlawed in September 1939 following the signature of the Hitler-Stalin nonaggression pact. Any activity in association with the PCF was thus automatically deemed criminal. Hitler's invasion of the Soviet Union on June 22, 1941, did not change the legality of the party, but it did restore the party's legitimacy. Thereafter, the PCF could be seen to be fighting both the Germans and the Vichy government.

In the postwar period, these same activists dated the onset of their activism much earlier. In fact, for many, there had been no "onset" per se; their wartime political work was an extension of the work they had been doing in the 1930s. When the men who rented the garage on the rue de la Clef were arrested in June 1942, they told police that they had lost or severed ties with the party and with former party comrades. Marcel Leclerc admitted having been approached by a party comrade who had asked him to distribute propaganda, but he claimed to have refused. Yet according to information they gave the Ministère des anciens combattants, and despite interruptions, their participation in PCF activity had been all of a piece with their earlier political work. As we now know, most protagonists of the Buci affair were not newcomers to political activism when they staged the demonstration. Many of them had been involved in illegal activity, however sporadic or sustained, before June 1941.

May 31, 1992, was not only a Sunday but also Mother's Day, exactly as it had been a half century before, to the very day. I had invited two surviving participants, Madeleine Marzin and Berthe Houet, to meet me on the rue de Buci to commemorate the fiftieth anniversary of the demonstration. It was a beautiful spring morning. The Buci-Seine marketplace was bustling with shoppers buying provisions for the midday Sunday meal, and café terraces were spilling over with people enjoying drinks and conversation. All in all, it was a typical weekend market scene.

We met on the sidewalk in front of a shop that occupied the corner of the rue de Buci and the rue de Seine, exactly where the *magasin* Eco, at that time a chain store with branches throughout the capital, had once stood. It was a moving reunion with Maté Houet, whom I had not seen for several years, and a stirring first encounter, at long last, with the noted ringleader of the operation, Madeleine Marzin herself.

I arrived in advance of the women to observe the market in full Sunday animation. On the very spot where the demonstration had occurred fifty years earlier, a local party activist was selling *L'Humanité de dimanche*. Hawking the party newspaper at the Sunday morning market had for decades been the iconic task of the party rank and file. Seeing him there comforted my longing for a sign, some indication of historical continuity.

I bought the paper, but there was no reference to the Buci affair in the Communist daily. The French Communist Party, responsible for staging the demonstration, shaping its narrative, and crafting the legend, did nothing to mark its fiftieth anniversary. When I asked the newspaper vendor if he was aware of the significance of the day and the site where we were standing, I drew a blank stare. The demonstration on the rue de Buci did not resonate with him, either. The concerns of France in May 1992 were very different. The major news story of the day was the upcoming vote on the Maastricht treaty in favor of European integration and the adoption of the euro, which the French would approve by a slim 51 percent. It was a very different market and marketplace from the one Jacques Prévert had elegized in 1942.

Marking the moment with Houet and Marzin was exhilarating for me, but their mood was one of overwhelming sadness. That infamous sidewalk had been a battleground that sent comrades to their deaths; it had also been a perilously close call for both women. On the modern awning that framed the main shop entrance in May 1992 was the inscription *boucherie*—literally "butcher shop," figuratively "slaughter." It was a terrible irony that had escaped my notice until the two women stood posed beneath it. For these two surviving participants, the anniversary was no occasion to honor a past victory, but a sobering reminder of lives lost.

May 31, 1992, passed unnoticed by the French Communist Party, the creator and bearer of its own historic legend. Even Houet and Marzin, the survivors of the operation, had been unaware of the fiftieth anniversary of the event until I phoned inviting them

On May 31, 1992, at the carrefour Buci (the intersection of the rue de Buci and the rue de Seine), shoppers are enjoying the first fruits of the spring season. *Photo by author.*

to meet me at the site. Despite the recent surge of World War II commemorations, both official and officious, no one acknowledged the glorious symbol of women's resistance on its fiftieth anniversary, not even the women themselves. But not commemorating is not the same as not remembering. On the contrary, the lively conversation we shared at a neighboring café that same day confirmed that participant memory of the event was very much intact.

It was obvious that Marzin and Houet had remained close friends since that fateful day in May had set them on separate paths. The two women shared a certain complicity, but they could not have been more different in personality and demeanor. Each made a remarkable impression in her own way. Maté stood out; Madeleine blended in. One was voluble and outgoing; the other was reserved and self-effacing. It was hard to imagine that the women before me,

Madeleine Marzin (left) and Maté Houet (right) returned to the scene of the incident on the afternoon of May 31, 1992. The iron grate of the Eco supermarket is drawn and the Sunday market has closed for the rest of the day. It was not a joyous occasion for the two women. Their pose and facial expressions betray their discomfort. Each is holding a single rose to commemorate the fiftieth anniversary. *Photo by author.*

Madeleine Marzin (left) and Maté Houet (right) seated at a café on the corner of the rue de Seine and the boulevard St.-Germain, where we repaired to discuss the event that had transpired fifty years earlier. *Photo by author.*

ages seventy-eight and eighty-four, respectively, had once been dangerous, subversive agents in an underground war.

Many decades had passed since either woman had revisited the site of the demonstration. Both lived in working-class neighborhoods located in Communist-run districts far from the Sixth Arrondissement. Although the rue de Buci was by then quite removed from them in space and in character, their lives had in many ways been defined by it. This was particularly true of Madeleine Marzin, who was tapped to become a standard-bearer of the party when France was liberated.

Even before the close of the war, the French Communist Party was holding up Marzin as the living exemplar of women's resistance and promoting the demonstration on the rue de Buci as an emblematic event. The fact that she had both eluded a death sentence and escaped capture further secured her reputation.

The deportees had yet to return home. Paris had been liberated, but other parts of the country remained under German control. Slowly but surely, the Resistance was moving into place to recover the reins of power, preparing to govern, and reconstituting republican institutions. A provisional government was established and with it, new personnel culled from the ranks of the Resistance.

Madeleine Marzin was one such person. Marzin had several valuable assets. First, her personal qualities: she was known for her probity and integrity. Second, she had first-rate credentials as a Communist resister, one whose activism had begun well before the German invasion of the Soviet Union in June 1941 legitimized Communist activity as "patriotic." Third and not least, she was a woman.

Just as the PCF was the only resistance entity that had aimed to mobilize women as a group and to create women's committees, so too was it the first political party to nominate women to stand for office in the postwar period. This was before French women got the vote and before they became eligible to serve in elected office, a scandalous omission in a democratic state that did not grant women these rights until 1944.[44]

In 1944 Marzin returned to Paris and was appointed to the Comité parisien de la Libération (CPL). A provisional governing body that would become the city council once peace was restored and the Germans evicted, the CPL was formed from the clandestine popular committees organized by the PCF during the war.

Marzin also helped lay the groundwork for the Union des femmes françaises (UFF), a nationwide, PCF-run women's organization that drew its legitimacy and its leadership from women who had played important roles in the Resistance movement. The building blocks of the UFF were the popular women's committees like the ones Marzin had organized throughout France: in the Fifteenth Arrondissement, in other neighborhoods in Paris and the Paris region, and in the eastern and central regions of the occupied zone, where she continued her underground work after her escape.

Following the immediate postwar period and her stint on the CPL, Marzin held two elective offices. From 1945 to 1951 and again from 1965 to 1971, she represented her home arrondissement, the Twentieth, on the Paris city council. She was designated by the PCF to serve on the party list and was elected to the National Assembly, where she represented the Department of the Seine from 1951 to 1958. One of Marzin's main priorities in the early postwar years was food supply and rationing. She remained faithful to the values that had motivated her in 1932 when she first joined the PCF in her native Brittany: her pet projects as a legislator included public education and low-cost housing for her predominantly working-class constituents.

The French Communist Party thus promoted the chief protagonist of what critics had derided as a "terrorist raid." But Marzin was ultimately recognized not so much for her role in the demonstration as for her lifetime of public service. In 2006, eight years after her death, a street in the Twentieth, the arrondissement where she had lived most of her life, was baptized in her name. The plaque identifies her as "teacher, resister, city councilor, and representative of the Seine." Her role in the demonstration is of course subsumed under the qualifier of "resister," but the demonstration itself is not specified. Nor is there any reason it should rise to that level. It was but one of many of Marzin's contributions to the underground movement.

Scattered throughout the Parisian cityscape are many such reminders of the Resistance and the Second World War. They take many forms: street names, monuments, memorials, and plaques. Some markers are extremely subtle, noticeable only to well-trained eyes; others are more striking. On national holidays such as Bastille Day (July 14), Armistice Day (November 11), Victory in Europe Day (May 8), and the National Day of the Resistance (May 27), family members or municipal workers decorate these sites with wreaths, bouquets, ribbons, or even a single flower.[45] There are tablets in town halls, post offices, police stations, and railway stations listing the names of workers who surrendered their lives to the fight to free France. There are plaques in metro stations, like the one at Pasteur opposite the Lycée Buffon in honor of Serge Boldrini, who was felled on that spot during the battle for the liberation of Paris. So, too, on the corner of the rue de Buci and the boulevard St.-Germain, a stone's throw from the Buci-Seine marketplace, a plaque marks the place where Fred Palacio was killed in street fighting to liberate Paris. Many of the resisters whose names appear on these plaques are ordinary people unknown to the general public.

A stone tablet on a latticed path near the town hall commemorates the citizens of the Sixth Arrondissement "who fell before firing squads, on the barricades, and on the battlefield during the struggle against Nazi Germany."[46] There is no mention of the guillotine that took the lives of André Dalmas, Edgar Lefébure, and Henri Meunier. Perhaps the omission results from the relative obscurity, at least in some quarters, of the first victims of the Buci affair. The only place the three are mentioned together is on a plaque erected on the stone wall outside the Santé prison, where they were guillotined. Their names are listed along with those of the other fifteen men who were executed in the prison courtyard for political activities during the war.[47]

Of all the participants in the Buci affair, it is the so-called students of the the Lycée Buffon who have been the most widely commemorated, in numerous forms and in various venues. They are honored first and foremost, and most of the time exclusively, for their defense of Professor Burgard. Their role in the Buci affair, their affiliation with the Communist Party, and their long résumés of "terrorist" activity are largely unknown and only very rarely recognized.

Arthus, Baudry, Benoit, Grelot, and Legros enjoy iconic status at their former high school, in their neighborhoods and *arrondissements*, and in the literature and historiography of the Resistance. A commemorative stamp devoted to the "Five Martyrs" was issued in April 1959.[48] At the Lycée Buffon there are no fewer than eight memorials to the group.[49] In the main entranceway that leads to a central courtyard, there is a monument to the "student martyrs" of 1942. Their names appear again on a monument honoring former students who died during the Second World War. Five classrooms are individually named, each for a different student. Their portraits hang in the main assembly hall. Alumni of the school have published brochures and testimonies about them.[50]

The five students have a prominent place in the public spaces of the capital as well. Jacques Baudry is the only student among the five who has a street in Paris dedicated to him alone. It was named for Baudry in 1954 and runs through the Fifteenth Arrondissement. In the quarter of the Montparnasse train station, a square and a bridge were named for the five students in 1992: the Place des Cinq Martyrs du Lycée Buffon and the Pont des Cinq Martyrs du Lycée Buffon. The inscription on a neighboring plaque focuses on their grisly fate and, in particular their ages at the time of execution. (The spare design of the memorial calls attention to their youth, so it is all the more curious that the ages inscribed on it are off by two years.)[51] In Bagnolet, a once Communist-run municipality on the eastern edge of Paris, a large and rather striking marble plaque is dedicated to the five students. Etched in gold are a few lines of text that specify the respective roles of the Vichy government and the Nazis.[52] In keeping with their signature "student" status, the ashes of four of the five were transferred to an urn in the crypt of the Sorbonne.[53]

Georges Vallet, the commander who revised partisan strategy after observing the unfolding of the demonstration on the rue de Buci, is also commemorated on two plaques in his native Nineteenth Arrondissement. He is listed along with three other prominent Communist resisters who were shot by the Germans. The earlier plaque belongs to a period when the derogatory term "boches" could be inscribed on a public monument. A later plaque, perhaps intended to replace the first one, is exactly the same in format and text, but revises that designation to read "nazis."[54]

The posting of plaques and the erection of monuments lay in temporal strata that reflect the evolution of different memories on

The "five martyrs of the Lycée Buffon, young students shot by the occupier in 1943" are commemorated on this post near the Montparnasse train station, a few blocks from the Lycée Buffon in the Fifteenth Arrondissement. It marks the tiny square to the right of the post off the boulevard Pasteur. *Photo by author.*

the part of different constituencies over time. Their unequal distribution in space also reflects the social geography of the capital. Streets named for resisters, particularly communist resisters, are disproportionately dense in working-class neighborhoods such as the Nineteenth and Twentieth Arrondissements. Foreigners, women, and some Communists—resisters who were acknowledged relatively late compared to some of their iconic peers—populate the most recent layers. The rue Madeleine Marzin belongs to this group. Named in 2006 and officially inaugurated in 2009, its creation corresponds to the decade when the placement of such markers seems to have proliferated. It is small wonder that this memorial activity has come precisely at the time when the Resistance generation has all but passed out of existence.

As far as I have been able to determine, there are no other monuments to Madeleine Marzin, although it would be appropriate that a school be named in her honor. The only physical trace in the Paris region of any of the other women who participated in the demonstration is a street plaque honoring Maté Houet in Vitry, the Communist-run suburb of Paris where she lived for most of her life. Survivor memory of the demonstration, ephemeral and now altogether gone, may well have been female, but the lasting physical traces in the public arena belong overwhelmingly to the men who lost their lives.

Of some 1,600 commemorative plaques in the city of Paris, 1,250 are associated with the Second World War.[55] That number has doubled since 1993.[56] Many if not most of them pay tribute to a notable person, place, or activity in Resistance history. Yet the site of the legendary women's demonstration for food at the heart of a bustling market, frequented by Parisians and now tourists, remains unmarked and unremarked. Its time is yet—or soon?—to come.

FROM SARDINES TO
SMOKED SALMON

A few generations have passed and the Resistance, more than ever, belongs to history. "Forty-five years ago was yesterday," said the police commissioner in charge of the archives. It was 1995 and he was making his case for restricting my access to the police files of the affair. Those words have come back to me many times. Decades later, I have a new appreciation for the point he was making and the telescoping of time. Madeleine Marzin led other women in the storming of the Eco grocery store in what now may seem like a distant universe. Yet in many ways, public memory of the demonstration, where it exists at all, has changed very little.[1]

At the same time, contemporary scholarship has brought the Buci affair back into view with some of its unique features intact, in particular the dynamics of gender roles and expectations that cast housewives as protesters and male partisans as protectors.[2] It was the opening of the archives that marked a real turning point. The first revised accounts of the demonstration restored its lost dimensions, thanks to the unearthing of the court records and their consequent, though limited, accessibility.[3] This cleared the way for moving beyond the legend.[4] Most important, it opened a narrow window of time when it was possible to put the written record and the oral testimony of surviving activists into dialogue with each other. That window has now closed for good.

Archival access is critical, but access alone does not guarantee the production of new historical knowledge. For one, the questions being asked have everything to do with discovering the files in the first place, as we saw in the preface. Those sets of questions, or *problématiques*, shaped and were shaped by the meta-trends of a given moment: "history from below," microhistory, women's history, oral history, and, later, gender studies. A generation of historians influenced by feminism and other social movements of the 1960s and 1970s pursued new lines of inquiry and forged new methodologies.

The polarized politics that dominated postwar historiography until the late 1970s ultimately gave way to more nuanced approaches to the study of the Second World War. Since then, scholarship on the Resistance and the war in general has been far more sensitive to the gray zones and moral ambiguities of the period.[5] Most important, perhaps, daily life is no longer treated as a mere backdrop against which events played out, but as a rich and deeply textured story unto itself. Food, hunger, and food supply are now acknowledged as deeply imbricated in the evolution of public opinion, political motivations, public policy, and even the very conduct of the Second World War across several continents.[6] Yet while much has changed, the role of the French Communist Party in the Resistance movement continues to pique and to polarize. The demonstration on the rue de Buci lays at the tangled nexus of these trends and threads.

In remembering the events of May 31, 1942, there has been much at stake: for history; for the legacy of the party; for participants, their families, and their descendants. In the immediate term, defining the event had life-and-death consequences; clearly the demonstration of the rue de Buci was "resistance" from the perspective of those to whom it posed a threat. In the postwar period, definitions of the event affected the recognition, reputations, and attribution of state benefits for surviving participants. Subsequent interpretations, by scholars and others, have gone to the very heart of what qualifies as "resistance"—with or without a capital *r*—and, by extension, a certain idea of how the French see themselves.

In short, the memory of the demonstration of the rue de Buci has been a matter of some consequence, as we saw from the 1945 overturning of the original court decision that condemned some demonstrators to death and others to prison. But no single type of memory exists in a vacuum. Official memory, group memory, family memory, personal memory—these and other types of memory exist in tension with one another and fluctuate over time. Like that of any other event, the memory of the Buci demonstration has been expressed in various ways, at different times, by different constituencies. Equally significant is the absence of memory, those moments when the demonstration seems to have been forgotten.

In the initial version of the story you are reading, there was another erasure of men, albeit an unwitting one. When chronicling the human toll of the operation, it had never occurred to me to consider the men whose deaths were at the heart of competing versions of the story. Officers Morbois and Vaudrey lay in the blind spot of my own revision of the Buci affair. It was an unintended omission and thus all the more insidious. I had cast the police as investigators, interrogators, and torturers. There was no role for the local beat cops who lay dead in the street in the aftermath of the affair.

Their invisibility had something to do with Manichean notions of the Resistance that affected my own deeply ingrained perspective on a history I had set out to complicate, not reproduce. But there was something else at play: I never expected to be able to say anything much about them until, to my surprise, I was granted access to their personnel files. I had caught myself in an inadvertent act of self-censorship. I had not asked for the files initially because I assumed they would be off-limits. Thanks to the archivist at the Préfecture de police, the officers who lost their lives could be restored to the story.

The manuscript registry in the guardian's hut at the Montparnasse cemetery confirms that Vaudrey and Morbois are buried in the *caveau du devoir*, the crypt dedicated to policemen who fell in the line of duty. Their names are artfully inscribed on the crinkly pages of a bound inventory, where every burial has been recorded for nearly two centuries. On the day following their deaths, the men were promoted to the respective ranks of *brigadier chef* and *brigadier*, a gesture entitling their bereaved families to a larger compensation from the state. Both men were forty-three years old when they died, were married, and were fathers. Morbois left behind an eleven-year-old son and Vaudrey a fourteen-year-old.

Camille Auguste Morbois and Eugène Louis Vaudrey belonged to the generation that experienced two world wars. In fact, Morbois also lived in the shadow of an earlier conflict, the Franco-Prussian War. He was born and raised in the department of Meurthe-et-Moselle when it was part of Germany from 1871 to 1918, before it reverted to France. A "civilian prisoner" during the Great War, Morbois "performed work of all sorts and was subjected to harsh treatments," according to his own statement.[7] His engineering studies were interrupted by wartime captivity and then military service. He entered the police in 1931, and from then on was assigned to the Sixth Arrondissement. Morbois said he was naturally inclined toward police work because protecting the public gave him "a moral satisfaction that no other profession could offer."[8] In 1941 his alleged mistress tried to pressure him into marriage by threatening to denounce him to German authorities. She claimed that he and others in the Sixth Arrondissement were hiding revolvers, hunting rifles, and pistols, a charge he successfully denied. At the time of the demonstration on the rue de Buci, Morbois was a *gardien-cycliste*, meaning that he made his rounds by bicycle.

Like his fallen colleague, Vaudrey left school after obtaining his *certificat d'études primaires*. He went right to work at the age of twelve, helping his parents run their small farm in the Haute-Saône, a department in Burgundy. At eighteen, Vaudrey was called up to serve at the front. He was injured in a gas attack but returned to the front a few days later, where he served until the armistice. In 1922 Vaudry entered the police force but left soon thereafter, again to help his then-aged parents with farm work.[9] He later returned to law enforcement, where superiors praised his discipline, devotion to duty, and professional knowledge. Vaudrey was commended for "knowing his place" and singled out for his future command potential.

The two policemen who died during the exchange of fire were given full honors: an official mass at Notre-Dame, the Médaille d'or des belles actions (gold medal for good deeds), and the Médaille d'or du dévouement (gold medal for devotion). In late 1942, Maréchal Pétain named them both Chevalier de la Légion d'honneur, by far the most prestigious of their awards.[10]

In October 1945 an internal committee reviewed the policemen's records for a possible revision of their honorific status. If the transition from French state to French Republic was to be credible, then civil servants who had served the enemy had to be deposed and punished. The "purge," as it was called, was never complete and sometimes merely symbolic. Emphasis was on big fish and low-hanging fruit. For France to function and to rebuild, the nation needed its elites and its civil servants.

The committee's report on Morbois states: "Among his neighbors and those in his immediate entourage . . . we hear only positive remarks. He was known as a good patriot. The concierge of his building declared that her renter showed evidence of anti-German sentiments." The report concludes, "Friends and colleagues in the Sixth Arrondissement are unanimous . . . [Morbois] did not engage in politics [*ne faisait pas de politique*]."[11] As for Vaudrey, those same coworkers were again "unanimous in saying that [he] was a good brigadier and a good comrade who never talked politics, but rather showed evidence of anti-German sentiments."[12]

The results of the investigation confirmed that both men had been devoted civil servants killed in the line of duty, "*victimes du devoir*."[13] Because neither had exhibited "political" motivations, it was determined that they had given their lives in an attempt to restore public order, not in a street fight against resisters. No revision in their honorific status would be necessary, as both men were good patriots who were not involved in "politics," here implicitly defined as a certain kind of politics.

"Not engaging in politics" suggests a stance of neutrality, a requirement for a public servant in close proximity to the local population in a time of social and political strife. In October 1945, having expressed opposition to the Germans before June 1942 is considered respectable conduct. Anti-German sentiment is located *outside* the realm of politics. There is no mention of attitudes toward the Vichy government. "Politics" in this context meant performing the very same tasks, but in the service of pro-Vichy, collaborationist, or pro-German sentiment.

In the end, the official investigators found that the fallen policemen had performed their duty by protecting the public from thievery and violence. Yet the very same thievery and violence were recast as "resistance" by the court that revisited the Buci affair that same year. In both instances, it was the state who made the rulings.

Was the state at odds against itself?

How can the very same activity be defined, by the same definer, as both illegal and meritorious at the same time?

This makes sense only if we acknowledge that the state is not a unitary bloc and that something bigger was at stake. The ministries, the executive, and the legislature; local, departmental, and national administrations; remnants of the old régime and the new: each had its own interests at heart, but they also had something in common. France had to move on. France needed its elites and its institutions to rebuild. If it was to heal, France needed to sanction the criminals and make peace with the past, even if the criminals were never fully punished and the peace was never perfect. A consensus had to be built, however fragile. That consensus rested on a shared sense of national purpose and identity.

Official narratives help make that possible.

Negotiating the uncertainties and ambiguities of a troubled past involves the skillful management of perceptions. There was more than one way to interpret the incident on the rue de Buci, as shopkeeper Félix Barthélemy wisely pointed out. For him, the incident on May 31, 1942, qualified as a disturbance of little import. It was not an act of resistance.

During the occupation, [an incident like the one on the rue de Buci] could easily pass for an operation against the occupiers, you understand. Uncertainty [*équivoque*] was always hovering in the air. People could say they didn't do it to pillage the shop, they didn't do it to steal, they did it to annoy the occupiers, you see? So obviously [such activities] were ambiguous or open to interpretation.[14]

Defining what exactly constitutes "resistance" remains a matter of debate, then as now. Factors that come into play include type of activity, chronology or timing of activism, patterns of activity, motivations, even results. The focus is usually on the doer, not on the position of the one defining the activity, although situating the definer may be as important as the definition itself. The question of what counts as "resistance" is particularly thorny when applied to people who spent the war in service to the Vichy regime: jurists, judges, appointed officials, prefects, administrators, police.

Walking down the boulevard Saint-Germain one day, I stopped to read a plaque on the corner of the intersection with the boulevard Saint-Michel, a plaque I had seen hundreds of times but never really noticed. The inscription reads:

On August 19, 1944, Robert BOTTINE, *brigadier des gardiens de la paix* of the 6th arrondissement, was mortally wounded on this site for the liberation of Paris.[15]

I was struck by a shock of recognition—*that* Bottine?

On May 31, 1942, Robert Bottine had been one of several local officers who rushed to the scene of the disturbance at the intersection of the rue de Seine and the rue de Buci. He shopped at the Buci market and policed those same streets. From the viewpoint of the neighborhood beat cop, Bottine intervened on May 31, 1942 to quell a public disturbance that began with looting and ended with the killing of his two colleagues. Along with other witnesses, Bottine

The plaque on the corner of the boulevard Saint-Germain and the boulevard Saint-Michel marks the spot where Robert Bottine died fighting for Liberation on August 19, 1945. The ring under the plaque is affixed to the wall for the purpose of holding a bouquet of flowers. *Photo by author.*

had given testimony in the police investigation of the events that had led to the deaths of officers Vaudrey and Morbois.

Two years later, a few steps away from the rue de Buci, Bottine gave his life fighting for the liberation of Paris.[16] Between May 31, 1942 and August 19, 1944, he had gone from battling street fighters to becoming one himself.

Does Bottine's activity in 1944 imply an evolution in his thinking, or was it consonant with the opinions he held all along? If the former, then Bottine was not unlike the majority of the French population who initially supported the Vichy regime and later repudiated it. In any case, support for Pétain, together with or apart from support for the Vichy régime, was not necessarily inconsistent with the desire to rid France of German occupation.

Did Bottine go over to the Resistance? Or had he been involved in some form of resistance all along? Complicities between police and their prisoners were not out of the question. Indeed some police attempted to mitigate the effects of state repression by warning Jews of impending roundups. Others were conduits of information from imprisoned resisters to contacts on the outside.[17] One of the guards who escorted the women demonstrators from the prison to the courthouse for their trial confided to Marzin that he had been directed to elicit additional information from the women.[18] The *équivoque* or ambiguity cited by Félix Barthélemy with regard to resisters applies here just as well to the opposition.

When the perpetrators were called to account for their actions, there was no agreed-upon definition of what constituted "resistance." For some, looting, thievery, and killing—especially when committed by Communists—were indisputably *criminal* activity and would remain ever so. The afterlife of the Buci affair reveals the extent to which such notions prevailed among members of the judiciary who had been involved in the prosecution of demonstrators. A postwar initiative undertaken by Yvonne Chauviré and Madeleine Marzin is a telling example.

After the Liberation, the women were outraged to learn that the *juge d'instruction* in the Buci affair, Pierre Ménégaux, had been named to a high post in the Ministry of Justice.[19] Together they asked to see the new Minister of Justice to protest Ménégaux's appointment. Ménégaux should be sanctioned for his role in the fierce repression of resisters, they argued, and in any event, certainly not promoted. Marzin, it should be remembered, had been condemned to death; Yvonne Chauviré had been acquitted but remanded for one year, which in her case meant deportation to a concentration camp. She had just returned from Ravensbrück.

The minister, François de Menthon, did not deign to receive them. Instead the women were met by his chief of staff. Their

A plaque commemorating the policemen of the Sixth Arrondissement who died during the Liberation of Paris and in deportation is located at the entrance of the Commissariat de police of the Sixth Arrondissement (rue Bonaparte). Robert Bottine figures in the first category. There is no plaque commemorating Officers Morbois and Vaudrey. Is this because Morbois and Vaudrey were killed in the line of duty in the course of a criminal act, rather than one having to do with the Resistance? Is it because they were indeed killed by resisters, which would situate them on the "wrong" side? Or is it because no one remembers them in the twenty-first century? *Photo by author.*

complaint against Ménégaux had no basis, they were told. He had prosecuted a matter of common law, not resistance.[20] It is not clear whether their visit occurred before or after Menthon's aforementioned appearance before a boisterous and hostile assembly.

Several years later, in 1949, Colonel Paul Farge, the state prosecutor who tried the Buci affair before the Tribunal d'état, displayed the same unrepentant attitude. This time, Farge was the one on trial. The charge against him was *intelligence avec l'ennemi*, or high treason, and it was punishable by death. It was Farge who had called for the death sentences that were eventually meted out to Dalmas, Lefébure, and Meunier. He had vigorously opposed their lawyers' request for clemency and insisted that Marzin be executed along with her "co-conspirators."

At his own trial Farge refused to disavow his condemnation of the perpetrators of the events of May 31, 1942. His decision had been made in accordance with his conscience, he said, and was in no way politically motivated.

> The Meunier affair was a *case of pillage of a store on the rue de Buci and the voluntary homicide of agents of the state*. The gravity of the offenses justified the death penalty that I asked for, which is why in my report of 26 June 1942 to the Minister of Justice I opposed the requests for clemency entered by the lawyers of the condemned. . . .
> I only asked for the death penalty, even for rulings against those accused in absentia, in cases where my conscience dictated it. . . .
> I protest the accusation of high treason. I never had any relationship with the Germans, neither in my capacity before the Tribunal d'état nor elsewhere. I always served my country as a loyal officer to the best of my ability. I have been in the army since the age of 18 and *have never engaged in politics*.[21]

Once again we see the Buci affair defined as a purely criminal case having nothing to do with political opposition to the Vichy regime or the German occupation. This court, this time, implicitly ruled against such a characterization of the Buci affair by condemning Farge to a life of hard labor. He narrowly escaped a death sentence because medical experts diagnosed him as senile. According to the doctors, Farge was already mentally incompetent in 1942 when he prosecuted the Buci case.[22]

Judge Paul Devise, who was infamous for his zealotry, presided over the prosecution of some of the protagonists of the Buci affair before the Section spéciale. He, too, was deemed by medical experts to be too mentally incompetent to withstand trial. He was neverless condemned to death and executed. The six other members of his court successfully escaped prosecution by invoking the inviolability of confidentiality. The judges could not be forced to reveal how they had voted in the Buci case, they successfully argued, because judicial deliberations are protected.[23]

The "insignificant" Buci affair was notable enough for key players in the Justice Ministry to comment upon it in their testimony and memoirs, if only to vilify it. Twenty years after the events on the rue de Buci, lawyer Yves-Frédéric Jaffré, who had defended Pierre Laval in 1945 when the former prime minister was on trial for his life, had this to say about the demonstration[24]:

> In any case, these acts had nothing to do with the fight against the occupiers, nor even with resistance against the Vichy government. The pillage of a food store cannot be considered an act of war, nor can the fostering of disorder be considered an acceptable form of action. Moreover, by placing killers charged with slaughtering police whose intervention was inevitable, the Communist Party showed abominable premeditation. This planned operation was a *purely criminal act.*[25]

And twenty years after that, in 1985, Félix Barthélemy, the owner of the cheese shop on the rue de Seine, offered a similar assessment of the operation.

You know, it is a subtle thing to grasp. During the German occupation there was a joint effort because the Communist Party was trying to take control of the Resistance. They succeeded in part because de Gaulle gave them a certain recognition. . . . *There were authentic, pure acts of resistance, and then there were machinations for political reasons.* It is difficult to tell them apart because both of them were against the German occupation, but they did not share the same motives. . . . *It was an organized commando raid, not a spontaneous crowd action.*[26]

The marketplace disturbance of May 31, 1942 was still drawing fire from its critics in the post-Liberation period and into the 1980s. Since that time, it has continued to defy easy categorization. No ready consensus has emerged on what exactly it was. Some have called it a riot in the tradition (if not the mold) of the bread riots of prerevolutionary France. But a riot is disorganized, spontaneous, unbridled, not meticulously prepared. For others the role of the PCF in planning the operation wholly disqualifies it either as a "demonstration" or as "resistance." Their reading of the event is based on the political orientation of the actors, not on the action itself.

Whether deemed "spontaneous" or "organized," "authentic" or "criminal," the "women's work" of the underground movement—particularly such work as the organization of women's protest in markets and market streets—never emerged as a consequential or well-known form of resistance. For a long time, and often even now, the activism of women resisters had generally been eclipsed by that of men. This is why the fact that the demonstration survived in *women's* memory is so ironic.

Armed combat, precisely the area in which women were a small minority, has been prized as the quintessential form of resistance. Women connected to Communist-run groups like the popular women's committees were doubly invisible, both as Communists and as women. But public protest was as integral to the underground movement as gunrunning, illegal publishing, or intelligence collection.

No less important, organized displays of opposition such as the demonstration on the rue de Buci carried symbolic weight. When free speech and freedom of assembly are outlawed, symbols are all the more important as vectors of public opinion. Demonstrating for sardines was never about sardines; it was a public condemnation of a politics of food supply that left little more than sardines on French grocery shelves. Demonstrating for bread was not just about bread in a culture where bread is a powerful metaphor for food and life. Demonstrating for food was not just about diminished bodies and struggling families. It was about a nation forcibly starved of its independence, a nation both cannibalized and cannibal. It is this symbolic dimension of the demonstration that has been so often missed or discounted by its critics.

Admittedly, symbols do not stand a chance against tanks and firing squads. The resisters' ranks were thin, their armory poorly stocked. And so they fought with their wits, their voices, and their bodies. In this respect the Buci demonstration, a fiasco by some measures, shares much with the myriad other forms of resistance in this period: it was meaningful even if it did not turn the tide of war. "The price [was] very high for a propaganda operation without much effect," said one scholar.[27] Such was evidently the assessment of the party leadership. After a similar scenario on the rue Daguerre, aboveground displays of this nature and magnitude were discontinued altogether. The demonstration was expertly mined for its abundant propagandistic potential and more. The abiding importance of a demonstration for food at a time of dire restrictions and fierce repression, then as now, derives in no small part from its rich symbolic value.

In both public and private venues, commemoration and celebration have figured the Resistance past, as have their counterparts, forgetting and erasure. Public memory of the Buci affair has taken a variety of forms: street signs and the absence of signs, monuments and the absence of monuments. Official memory of the affair has been expressed by postwar recognition in the form of awards and pensions. The surviving protagonists themselves carried their personal memory of the affair. The victims' families carried and carry the burden of knowing and not knowing. In writing, both scholarly and memorial, the demonstration has traveled forward in time, whether ignored or contested, acknowledged or condemned.

What remains to be examined is another form of public or historical memory: imitation, emulation, reenactment. Events also traverse time by attaching themselves to exemplars of the past. We have already seen how Communist resisters situated their struggle along a historical through line running from the French Revolution to the Paris Commune.

As the Communist women of 1942 styled their protest after the market women of Paris who marched for bread in 1789, so the Gauche prolétarienne (Proletarian Left), a left-wing party that emerged from the student movement of May 1968, looked for models to the partisan actions of the Resistance generation.

In another month of May some twenty-eight years after the demonstration on the rue de Buci, student activists protested class inequalities and hierarchies of power. Their political coming of age had been the events of May 1968. Like the protagonists of the rue de Buci, male and female protesters played separate roles in their raid on Fauchon, a chic right-bank purveyor of specialty foods. From there they went to the downtrodden outskirts of Paris to distribute their spoils to poor immigrants. It was an eloquent testimony to the transmission of memory and the symbolic power of public protest. What could be a more fitting display of the striking shift from wartime scarcity to postwar consumerism? While the resisters of 1942 seized cans of sardines packed in oil, their daughters and sons raided packages of smoked salmon and tins of foie gras.

In 2012, sixty years after that momentous and momentous day on the rue de Buci, I found myself once again at the archives of the Paris police. Like many years before, I had a case to make before the archivist. The files I wished to review had nothing to do with the demonstration of the rue de Buci or even the Second World War, at least not on the surface. What intrigued me now was a different demonstration from a different era, one that appeared to share some striking features with its predecessor on the rue de Buci. In March 1970, members of a small Maoist party, the Gauche prolétarienne, stormed a luxury food emporium at the place de la Madeleine. They were the sons and daughters of the Resistance generation, and they had some points to make about social inequities in the new consumer society. Several arrests had been made and one demonstrator, a woman, had been sentenced to prison. Now I wished to see the police files of the demonstrators.

This time I sat before Madame la Commissaire—twenty years earlier, there were few women in the police, fewer still in positions of authority. So much had changed, I thought. In presenting my case, I took care not to breach the invisible force field surrounding her desk, although this time it would scarcely have mattered. Things were different now, or so I thought.

Her answer was no.

I was taken aback. There had been no war, no occupier, no collaboration government in March 1970. No shameful deportations or summary executions or malevolent denunciations to be handled with discretion. True, the upheavals of 1968 and its aftermath had rent civil society, but this was no civil war.

I called her attention to a striking parallel. When I had finally been granted access to the police files of the demonstration of the rue de Buci, some forty years had elapsed since the event. When I requested access to the police files of the demonstration at the place de la Madeleine, some forty years had elapsed since the event. What was so different now? I wondered. Why were far less sensitive materials still off-limits?

The sixty-year rule protecting personal information could not be contravened, I was told. Not only were the individuals in question still living, but some had become public figures. The Ministry of Justice would not approve my request at present, but if I wanted to return in 2030 ...

I tried to take solace in the gift I had unwittingly been handed: a fitting bookend to my introduction, the perfect epilogue. This flattered my sense of irony, but I would have much preferred to focus on a different sort of parallel. The parallel I sought to explore was one of content, not of access to records. I wanted to show that memory functions in bodily *acts* as well as in collective and individual minds. Two emblematic street protests some fifty years apart, yet similar in nature, raised a series of questions: Was the demonstration on the place de la Madeleine inspired by the one on the rue de Buci? Were the parallels intentional or merely coincidental? If intentional, then a case could be made for the enduring significance of the Buci affair. If coincidental, then what deeper social meanings attach to public protest, gendered politics, and the politics of food? What explains the overlap?

On March 8, 1970, a group of young people, mostly students, stormed Fauchon, the legendary purveyor of specialty gourmet foodstuffs on the place de la Madeleine in central Paris. The women were "armed" with shopping bags, into which they stuffed cans of foie gras, caviar, cakes, and smoked salmon. The men were armed with crude implements—a sawed-off shovel handle, an iron bar. Their job was to protect the women. Once inside the store, they broke windows and displays, smashing bottles of aged wine, cognac, and other fine alcohols.

They did not try to blend into the crowd; on the contrary, the raiders reportedly wore identifying badges, small buttons featuring the image of Chairman Mao, and red scarves. The women wore turtleneck sweaters with the collars turned up for camouflage. They did not throw cans of foie gras into the waiting hands of other shoppers; their redistribution would take place later and elsewhere. Their objective was not only to scoop up as much merchandise as possible in the moment, but also to make some noise. The state prosecutor later called it a propaganda operation; he recognized that the purpose of the raid was both pedagogic and symbolic.

The next day, the raiders took their booty to an immigrant *bidonville* (shantytown) in Ivry, a home for elderly workers in Nanterre, and a housing project for French workers in Bagnolet. All of them were working-class communities in the "Red Belt," a string of Communist-run municipalities that ringed the capital city. The workers' typical midday meal was supplemented by luxury items that sold for the value of a full month's pay: foie gras with truffles, paté, candied chestnuts, fine cakes, fruits in syrup, chocolate, smoked salmon. As the Muslim immigrants consumed neither pork products nor alcohol, the fine wines and paté were reserved for their French counterparts. According to one press report, raiders chanted slogans as they redistributed their spoils: "Fauchon feeds the shantytowns," "It is right to steal from thieves." But the immigrant workers did not know what Fauchon was, nor were they acquainted with these foods.

Things had not gone according to plan. One of the women was seized inside the store by the resident pastry chef. She was handed over to police, who had been summoned to the scene by store employees. Meanwhile, one of the men, Bernard Marcade, a twenty-two-year-old art history student, had been neutralized by customers and shop personnel. He was badly beaten but escaped to the nearby metro station, where he was found by police. Marcade was arrested and taken to the hospital, where he remained for weeks. Three wounded shop employees were also taken to the hospital and released shortly thereafter.

The Gauche prolétarienne had no way of knowing that the doorman for Fauchon, stationed outside the store in his car, was a six-foot-tall judo champion. Thanks to him, intervention had been swift and furious. It was he who was featured in news articles the day after the raid, not the detainees or the activists. "The vigor and skill of the raiders proved inferior to their revolutionary zeal," reads a tongue-in-cheek commentary in the press.[28]

Several weeks later, a judge sentenced Frédérique Delange, a twenty-year-old sociology student, to thirteen months in prison and a fine of 3,000 francs. The decision was met with stunned silence in the courtroom. (Damages had also been estimated at some 3,000 francs.) For reasons unknown, the only other demonstrator who had been caught, Bertrand Marcade, was never charged. The defense considered the penalty excessive; the proprietor of Fauchon, who declined to press charges, testified in court that he was "inclined toward leniency."

In speaking for herself, Delange admitted her role in the operation, saying that her motives justified her actions. "I admit having participated in this political action. The point was to return luxury goods to hardworking people toiling in factories. Since legal means had not sufficed, it had become necessary to find another way. I thought that the cause was just."[29] But unlike the protesters on the rue de Buci who were judged on the basis of the motives ascribed to them—Bolshevik subversion—Frédérique Delange would be judged solely on the basis of her actions. In the 1970 case, motives were beside the point.

Her father also spoke for the defense. Because Delange was a minor, her parents were considered liable for their daughter's crimes. Ultimately they were found not to be responsible because she was no longer living under their roof. M. Delange, an economist and jurist by training, made no effort to conceal his disapproval of his daughter's act. Yet he extolled her intent: "When I learned that what had been stolen at Fauchon had been redistributed in a shantytown, everything became clear to me. I could not imagine Frédérique caught up in a violent affair. But I recognized her, fighting as she could, against injustice. On a political level, I judged her as mistaken, and I still do. On a human level, I thought, 'Good for you!' [*Bravo ma petite!*] for having the courage that few people with the same convictions would have had."[30]

The defense attorney also focused on the motives of Delange's act rather than on the act itself. "Three-quarters of the world is dying of hunger while the other quarter is inventing weight-loss programs. Such absurdity is hard for a twenty-year-old to swallow. How can you, sons of the Revolution, condemn a just act in the name of an unjust order?"[31] The prosecutor rebutted: "The price of revolution is martyrdom. *It is not a question of a few canned goods, but of disorder, anarchy, and violence.* They must be condemned. It is childish to think that one can change the world with such derisory measures. There is even a certain disingenuousness in blaming some for the evils of consumer society, while having others [the people of the shantytowns] savor its fruits."[32]

That the commando raid had been carried out by the sons and daughters of the very people who shopped at Fauchon was not lost on the right-wing press.[33] Indeed, the raiders, students from middle-class and upper-middle-class families, had little in common with the schoolteachers, seamstresses, postal workers, and mechanics who staged the demonstration on the rue de Buci twenty-eight years before. A newspaper article that was well disposed toward the raid also lodged an attack against Fauchon's privileged clients. It pilloried the store for provisioning the residents of the Elysée Palace (home of the French president) and even the Kremlin.[34] By accusing the Soviet leadership of gastronomic indulgence alongside their French counterparts, sympathizers of the raiders condemned by extension the French Communist Party. The battle lines had shifted since 1942.

The parallels between the raid of the Eco supermarket and that of Fauchon are abundantly clear: both were street performances intended to galvanize the public and both waged a battle in the name of social justice around the issue of food. We see the same division of political labor on the basis of gender, with women in charge of "shopping" and men assigned their protection. In both cases, store employees intervened to foil the operation, and some demonstrators were arrested by police. In 1970 as in 1942, demonstrators sought to explain their action to the public after the fact: the *travail d'explication* in the Buci demonstration, the "victory communiqué" in the Gauche proletarienne's newspaper. Small shopkeepers were expressly avoided in each case; large food chains and the specialty stores who competed with them were singled out as sites for the action.[35] In form and in function, objective and result, the "commando raid" on Fauchon and the demonstration on the rue de Buci share important—even defining—features.

But they are not perfect mirror images of each other. It was a different world in 1970. The penury of the war and postwar years had given way to unprecedented prosperity. It had been built in good measure by an influx of new immigrants from North Africa, who had been recruited by French employers in dire need of workers to meet the demands of a booming economy. A consumer society had arisen from the economic and demographic surge of the 1950s and 1960s. This was a period known for the expansion of the middle classes, the growth of the service sector, the democratization of higher education, and the birth of babies who would grow up to question all forms of authority: in civil society, in the workplace, in the schools, in the family. The raiders of Fauchon were those children, and they were angry. They repudiated the politics of the right and the politics of the left, including that of the Communist Party. Some say they were a generation in search of an identity. The preceding generation had had their defining moment, the Resistance. Now it was their turn; the torch would be passed.

The raid on Fauchon was shaped by a logic of political protest at a particular historical moment. Twenty-eight years later, it still made sense for women to pose as shoppers and for men to protect them. It made sense to target food, especially luxury items, as emblematic of social inequality. It made sense to enact a public spectacle as a means of raising awareness. But did the raiders of Fauchon model their operation on a relatively obscure food protest that had taken place a generation before?

It was Yves Cohen who first told me about the Fauchon incident. I met him after interviewing his mother, Marie-Elisa Nordmann, a Communist activist and young chemist who had survived deportation to Auschwitz and Ravensbrück. She and Yves's father,

Francis Cohen, had been prominent members of the Front national universitaire, the wing of the underground party that grouped
students and intellectuals for the Resistance effort. Yves was a
seventeen-year-old activist in the Gauche prolétarienne at the time
of the Fauchon raid, which he remembered as a contemporary version of food demonstrations like the one on the rue de Buci. He had
grown up in a household steeped in the memory and spirit of the
Resistance. For him, Fauchon recalled the Resistance protests of his
parents' generation. It was an inalienable part of his heritage, both
familial and political.[36]

That the Resistance served as inspiration and template is explicit
in some testimony, implicit in other. Georges Delange, the father
of Frédérique, gave this interpretation of his daughter's actions to
the court:

> My daughter met friends in our home who had committed illegal
> acts during the occupation. It was different then, of course, but she
> did not understand that. . . .
>
> My daughter did not understand that illegal actions are only
> permissible under certain circumstances. . . . Young people her age
> were raised in a unique context. My daughter saw that friends who
> committed illegal acts in the Resistance, and others who had been
> imprisoned during the Algerian war, were considered heroes.[37]

M. Delange was not alone in drawing such parallels. Former
members of the Gauche prolétarienne who participated in the
commando raid also cite the Resistance as a reference. Michel
Field, a sixteen-year-old Gauche prolétarienne member at the time,
remembers that such illegal demonstrations evoked the "mythic and
cinematographic qualities of the Resistance."[38] He was referring,
among other things, to the clandestine practices of compartmentalization where only one activist in a group of three knew the contact
person in the next group, mapping escape routes, and intercepting
police communications and adjusting logistics accordingly.

Just as resisters looked to the uprising of the Paris Commune in 1871, the student activists of May 1970 looked to the Resistance for their inspiration and their models. The gaze of both converged on the originary event at the very heart of French politics, culture, and identity: the Revolution of 1789. It is a lineage that stretches from bread to sardines, from sardines to smoked salmon.

A public protest for food that ended tragically became a rallying point for French women and men starved for bread and hungry for the reestablishment of republican ideals and institutions. The demonstration on the rue de Buci confirmed the worst fears of French government officials that food scarcity was undermining morale and popular support for the regime. For the police, it was the long-dreaded explosion of citizen anger that had been festering in markets, shops, and food lines since the beginning of the war. Alas, the violence of the demonstrators was no match for the violence of the French state and the German occupiers. The executions, deportations, and prison sentences suffered by the protesters and their families are without question the saddest part of its legacy. That legacy is still being shaped in the France of today, in its schools, streets, monuments, literature, and media.

The Buci affair will remain a moving target. Like other versions of the story, this one will be unstable. The discovery of a new document, another testimony, a fresh interpretive lens, will shape the next one. In the end, memory is a perishable commodity like any other, and so too this book, stacked on a vendor's table like canned sardines packed in oil, on display inside a shop.

NOTES

Introduction

1. *Buci* is pronounced "bu-SI."

2. Natalie Zemon Davis, *The Return of Martin Guerre* (Harvard University Press, 1983); Carlo Ginzburg, *The Cheese and the Worms: The Cosmos of a Sixteenth-Century Miller,* trans. John and Anne Tedeschi (Johns Hopkins University Press, 1980, 1992); Robert Darnton, *The Great Cat Massacre and Other Episodes in French Cultural History* (Vintage Books, 1985, 1984). Examples of microhistorical studies of French twentieth-century subjects include Bonnie G. Smith, *Confessions of a Concierge: Madame Lucie's History of Twentieth-Century France* (Yale University Press, 1985) and Edward Berenson, *The Trial of Madame Caillaux* (University of California Press, 1992).

Chapter 1

The reconstruction of the events is based on court records and police files in the Archives nationales (AN) and the Archives of the Préfecture de police in Paris (APPP), and on the oral testimony of surviving participants that was collected in the 1980s and 1990s. Reference to these sources may be found in the Select Bibliography. Only direct quotations will be cited; all other information comes from these same archival series unless otherwise noted. All translations are my own.

1. The neighboring cheese merchant on the rue de Seine maintained that the Eco supermarket only appeared to be part of a chain because of its larger-than-usual size, but in fact was owned by an independent shopkeeper. Interview with Félix Barthélemy, Paris, October 17, 1985.

2. Interview with Madeleine Marzin and Maté Houet, Paris, May 31, 1992. Marzin gave earlier testimony on this exchange in Centre d'Histoire sociale du XXè siècle, Fonds André Marty, 2-AM-5A (1941–1951), boîte 13, "Témoignage de Madeleine Marzin sur la manifestation de la rue de Buci le 1 juin 1942 [*sic*]."

3. Centre d'Histoire sociale du XXè siècle, Fonds André Marty, 2-AM-5A (1941–1951), boîte 13, "Témoignage de Madeleine Marzin sur la manifestation de la rue de Buci le 1 juin 1942 [*sic*]."

4. Centre d'Histoire sociale du XXè siècle, Fonds André Marty, 2-AM-5A (1941–1951), boîte 13, "Témoignage de Madeleine Marzin sur la manifestation de la rue de Buci le 1 juin 1942 [*sic*]."

5. Maurice Garçon, *Journal (1939–1945)* (Les Belles Lettres, 2015), entry of June 1, 1942. He reports: "The affair is said to have occurred spontaneously, without preparation." Garçon had access to rumors on the ground as well as to the hypotheses of his colleagues at the Palais de Justice. In his entry of June 22, Garçon gives a fuller description of the event and surmises that Communist provocateurs and Gaullists were in league.

6. The Front national was the French Communist resistance movement. It was founded in 1941 as a broad, over-arching program designed to bring all elements of the population, regardless of political leanings, social class, sex, religion or profession, under a unifying umbrella.

7. Italics mine.

8. Serge Klarsfeld, *Le Mémorial de la déportation des Juifs de France* (Serge and Beate Klarsfeld, 1978).

Chapter 2

1. Jacques Hillairet, *Dictionnaire historique des rues de Paris* (Editions de Minuit, 1997), 1:249, 2:510–512. Another source states that the rue de Seine got its name around 1510. Félix Lazare and Louis Lazare, *Dictionnaire administratif et historique des rues de Paris et de ses monuments*, (F. Lazare, 1844), 612.

2. As of the last census (2012), the population of the Sixth Arrondissement was 44,000. INSEE, *Base de données, recensement populations*, http://www. insee.fr/fr/ppp/bases-de-donnees/recensement/populations legales/ commune.asp?depcom=75106&annee=2012. Figures for 2019 put the population at 41,000. https://ville-data.com/nombre-d-habitants/Paris-6e-Arrondissement-75-75106 (consulted on November 20, 2019).

3. Demographia, "La Ville de Paris" (online site), December 21, 2010.

4. Interview with Félix Barthélemy, Paris, October 17, 1985. He continued: "With the housing crisis that followed the war, many of these same people still had children living under their roofs, there could be multiple households living together. Later the children were able to move out on their own when new housing was erected on the periphery of Paris. So the big apartments in the area emptied out, and there were fewer residents in the neighborhood."

5. Jacques Prévert, "La rue de Buci maintenant . . . ," in *Paroles* (Gallimard, 1997 [1949]), 213–217. The excerpt referred to here is:

... *et la misère debout fait la queue aux portes du malheur*

aux portes de l'ennui

et la rue est vide et triste

abandonnée comme une vieille boîte au lait

et elle se tait.

Pauvre rue qui ne veut plus qui ne peut plus rien dire

pauvre rue dépareillée et sous-alimentée . . .

... And destitution waits in line at the doors of misfortune

the doors of boredom

and the street is empty and sad

discarded like an old milk pail

and it falls silent.

Poor street now devoid of meaning or words

Poor street mismatched and malnourished . . .

6. For fuller discussion of food scarcity in Paris and the occupied zone, see Kenneth Mouré and Paula Schwartz, "*On vit mal*: Food Shortages and Popular Culture in Occupied France, 1940–44," *Food, Culture and Society* 10, no. 2 (Summer 2007): 262–295.

7. Meunier letter to Marcel Leclerc, June 26, 1942. I am grateful to Pierre Boyer for sharing the original of the letter Meunier wrote to his grandfather.

8. Interview with Cécile Borras, Paris, April 17, 1986.

9. Interview with Marie-Louise Claudé, Paris, December 1, 1985. I am indebted to Sarah Fishman for putting us in contact.

10. Jacques Le Roy Ladurie, *Mémoires, 1902–1945* (Flammarion/Plon, 1997), 325. Le Roy Ladurie was appointed to his position on April 18, 1942. On April 23, the day he installed his new office in Paris, he enjoyed "a superb lunch served by an impeccable headwaiter that bore hardly a trace of the restrictions then in effect" (319–320).

11. APPP B A/1808, Ministère du Ravitaillement, report of December 22, 1940, files d'attente.

12. Telegram of February 21, 1941, in APPP B A/1806, Ministère du Ravitaillement, correspondance, June 1940–December 1941.

13. Report of June 7, 1941, in APPP B A/1807, Ministère du Ravitaillement, état d'esprit de la population, rapports divers, 1940–1941.

14. Report of June 17, 1944, in APPP B A/1806, Ministère du Ravitaillement, rapports divers, 1942–1944.

15. Maurice Garçon, *Journal (1939–1945)* (Les Belles Lettres, 2015), entry of June 1, 1942. My thanks to Michel Gabrielli for this reference.

16. The number of German troops and administrative personnel in France, which fluctuated between 1940 and 1944, is subject to some debate. According to Lieb and Paxton, the number of soldiers in France never exceeded 100,000 at any one time. However, this figure does not include administrative personnel. Peter Lieb and Robert O. Paxton, "Maintenir l'ordre en France occupée. Combien de divisions?," *Vingtième Siècle: Revue d'histoire* no. 112 (2011): 125.

17. Lizzie Collingham, *The Taste of War: World War II and the Battle for Food* (Penguin Books, 2011).

18. Dominique Veillon, *Vivre et survivre en France, 1939–1947* (Payot, 1995), 113–114.

19. Rhoda Métraux and Margaret Mead, *Themes in French Culture: A Preface to a Study of French Community* (Berghahn Books, 2001 [1954]), 57.

20. Gertrude Stein, *Wars I Have Seen* (Random House, 1945), 228.

21. Édouard de Pomiane, *Cuisine et restrictions* (Éditions Corrêa & Co., 1940), 101.

22. de Pomiane, *Cuisine et restrictions*, 156.

23. Stein, *Wars I Have Seen*, 45–46.

24. Interview with Félix Barthélemy, Paris, October 17, 1985.

25. Adélaïde Blasquez and Gaston Lucas, *Gaston Lucas, Serrurier* (Plon, 1976), 218. Thanks to Rosalie Fisher for calling my attention to this reference.

26. APPP B A/1808, Ministère du Ravitaillement, report of December 22, 1940, files d'attente. (Emphasis mine.)

27. Ernst Jünger, *Journaux de guerre, II. 1939–1948* (Gallimard, 2008), 316, entry of July 4, 1942. (Emphasis mine.)

28. Ernst Jünger, *Second journal parisien, Journal III, 1943–1945* (Christian Bourgois, 1995), 170, entry of September 29, 1943. Sometimes fear—or dignity?—trumped hunger: "I bought some grapes and offered them to some children sitting on the street. . . . Almost all refused to take some or were frightened, suspicious." What Jünger concludes from the experience is even more striking. "People," he remarks, "are not accustomed to gifts"!

29. Léonie Villard, untitled manuscript, 1940–1944, Mount Holyoke College Archives and Special Collections, 16. I am indebted to Karen Remmler for bringing this document to my attention.

30. Stein, *Wars I Have Seen*, 139. On the front leaf is this note: "'V': This is a Random House Wartime Book. It is manufactured under emergency conditions and complies with the government's request to conserve essential materials in every possible way."

31. For more on this topic, see Paula Schwartz, "The Politics of Food and Gender in Occupied Paris," *Modern and Contemporary France* 7, no. 1 (February 1999): 35–45.

32. Ruffin or Anonymous.

33. Jean Galtier-Boissière, *Journal, 1940–1950* (Paris: Quai Voltaire, 1992), entry of July 8, 1941, p. 46.

34. Although her official duties were in the women's sector, Georgette Wallé also worked with her husband, Louis, in the FTP, transporting arms, running messages, performing surveillance, and procuring food and lodgings for partisans. The Wallé constituted another husband-and-wife team that worked together in the Communist underground despite the fact that party leadership formally forbid it. But sometimes the needs of the organization trumped security. More important, perhaps, was the fact that it was simply not realistic to expect all couples to separate, work, and live apart. Finally, as Wallé herself put it, she had an independent nature and was not always inclined to follow orders. Interview with Georgette Wallé, November 22, 1985.

35. Fonds Lise Ricol-London, Collection Musée de la Résistance nationale, Champigny-sur-Marne, France, note, "Manifestation 27 juin (1942)".

36. Fonds Lise Ricol-London, Collection Musée de la Résistance nationale, Champigny-sur-Marne, France, note, "Manifestation 27 juin (1942)".

37. Interview with Georgette Wallé, November 22, 1985. However, in what appears to be an excerpt from another report by Wallé, she expresses regret that the women responsible for bringing the effigy arrived too late. "Too bad that the women who were supposed to bring the effigy and other materials arrived late, or our success would have been complete." Lise Ricol, "Dès 1940–1941, avec les femmes de la région sud de Paris, de Seine et Seine-et-Oise," in UFF, *Les Femmes dans la Résistance* (Éditions du Rocher, 1977), 187. Ricol indicates that an effigy of Laval was also in evidence at another women's demonstration for food on the rue Lafayette, but she does not provide a date.

38. Georgette and Louis Wallé were arrested in September 1942 by the Brigades spéciales II, the same specialized police unit that rounded up some of the demonstrators after the rue de Buci incident. There is no mention of Georgette in court records because she was never tried. From the prison of Fresnes, she transited through several prisons in Germany before ending up in Ravensbrück and ultimately Mauthausen. Interview with Georgette Wallé, Paris, November 22, 1985.

On October 6, 1943, Louis Wallé was executed by German firing squad at Mt.-Valérien. Interview with Georgette Wallé, November 22, 1985; Claude Pennetier, Jean-Pierre Besse, Thomas Pouty, and Delphine Leneveu, eds., *Les fusillés (1940–1944): Dictionnaire biographique des fusillés et exécutés par condamnation et comme otages ou guillotinés en France pendant l'Occupation* (Les Éditions de l'Atelier/Éditions Ouvrières, 2015), 1830.

Chapter 3

1. This figure is approximate because some people arrested for other "crimes" were subsequently found to have been present on the rue de Buci the day of the demonstration. Others were arrested in connection with the demonstration but their participation could not be established. Some were detained anyway, or detained and tried on other charges.

2. According to Lise London Ricol, Claudine Chomat was the party *responsable* in charge of women's affairs at the time. Lise London, *La Mégère de la rue Daguerre: Souvenirs de Résistance* (Éditions du Seuil, 1995). Chomat stepped in after the arrest of Danielle Casanova, who was deported to Auschwitz on January 24, 1943, in a transport known as the "31,000" for the series that was tattooed on their forearms upon arrival at the camp. It included many eminent Communist women resisters such as Marie-Claude Vaillant-Couturier and Germaine Pican, to name but two.

3. AN, 4W6, André Dalmas, [3è interrogatoire], June 5, 1942.

4. Claude Pennetier, Jean-Pierre Besse, Thomas Pouty, and Delphine Leneveu, eds., *Les fusillés (1940–1944): Dictionnaire biographique des fusillés et exécutés par condamnation et comme otages ou guillotinés en France pendant l'Occupation* (Les Éditions de l'Atelier/Éditions Ouvrières, 2015), 484.

5. The CGTU was the name of the PCF-led labor union from 1922 until 1936, when it merged with Socialists and became part of the CGT.

6. Jacques Baudry was the fifth member of the group. He was not involved in the demonstration on the rue de Buci.

7. Letter from Baudoin to the Military Tribunal of the German Air Force, October 16, 1942.

8. For the notion of a French Communist counter-culture, see an early overview in *La Culture de camarades*, dir. Antoine Spire, *Autrement 78*: March 1986, and the work of Marie-Claire Lavabre, including *Le fil rouge: Sociologie de la mémoire communiste* (Presses de la Fondation nationale des sciences politiques, 1994).

9. Serge Klarsfeld, *Le Mémorial de la déportation des Juifs de France* (Klarsfeld, 1978), 98.

10. Isabelle Von Bueltzingsloewen, ed., *Mort d'inanition: Famine et exclusions en France sous l'Occupation* (Presses Universitaires de Rennes, 2005). See the section on psychiatric facilities. For mention of Sainte-Anne, see Dominique Veillon, "Aux origines de la sous-alimentation: pénuries et rationnement alimentaire," 31–43 in the same volume.

11. Archives du Ministère des Anciens combattants, file of Jean Atlan.

12. Archives nationales, Z 4 73, "Lettres et divers," Jean Atlan to Grenier, Directeur de la Police judiciaire, September 30, 1942.

13. The age breakdown is as follows: 17–31: 11 people; 32–41: 15 people; 42–64: 11 people.

14. AN, 4 W 6, pièce 271, interrogation of E. Dietrich, June 1, 1942.

15. According to her 1951 testimony, Marzin recruited demonstrators "according to their age, their family situations, and the need to avoid deploying *camarades* more or less under surveillance by police." Centre d'Histoire sociale du XXè siècle, Fonds André Marty, 2-AM-5A (1941–1951), boîte 13, "Témoignage de Madeleine Marzin sur la manifestation de la rue de Buci le 1 juin 1942 [*sic*]."

Houet said that she was loath to attend the demonstration for fear of exposure. Interview with Maté Houet, Paris, May 31, 1992. Apparently Marzin thought the risk to Houet was minimal.

16. Interview with Roger Arnould, Paris, June 10, 1986.

17. Pennetier et al., eds., *Les fusillés*.

18. Charlotte Delbo, *Le Convoi du 24 janvier* (Les Éditions de Minuit, 1965), 225.

19. Delbo, *Le Convoi*, 225–226. Known as the "31,000"—so called because of the numerical series tattooed on their arms upon arrival—the group of 230 women included some of the most eminent women of the underground French Communist movement, including Danielle Casanova and Marie-Claude Vaillant-Couturier.

20. I am indebted to Pierre Labate for providing clarifications regarding Lucette Pécheux. The association Mémoire Vive maintains a website with updates and corrections to the biographical profiles published by Charlotte Delbo in 1965: http://www.memoirevive.org/lucie-dite-lucette-pecheux-nee-lable-31633. Many thanks also to Ghislaine Dunant, biographer of Charlotte Delbo, who shared copies of the original source material pertaining to Pécheux that Delbo used in the preparation of her book. Bibliothèque nationale de France (BNF), Département des Arts du spectacle, 4-COL-208 (105–106), Fiches de renseignement établies pour les 230 déportées du convoi.

21. Centre d'Histoire sociale du XXè siècle, Fonds André Marty, 2-AM-5A (1941–1951), boîte 13, "Témoignage de Madeleine Marzin sur la manifestation de la rue de Buci le 1 juin 1942 [*sic*]."

22. Centre d'Histoire sociale du XXè siècle, Fonds André Marty, 2-AM-5A (1941–1951), boîte 13, file "La Résistance dans le XIIIè arrondissement."

23. Richard Ledoux, Jean Chaumeil, and another man known sometimes as "Parmentier," sometimes "Patate," were *responsables aux cadres* with knowledge of the demonstration. Marzin named them as sources. However, it is not clear from her account whether they were present the day of the demonstration. Centre d'Histoire sociale du XXè siècle, Fonds André Marty, 2-AM-5A (1941–1951), boîte 13, "Témoignage de Madeleine Marzin sur la manifestation de la rue de Buci le 1 juin 1942 [*sic*]."

24. Conversations with André Tollet, Ivry, 1978, and Paris, 1998.

25. For a biographical profile of Vallet, see Claude Pennetier, Jean-Pierre Besse, Thomas Pouty, and Delphine Leneveu, eds., *Les fusillés (1940–1944): Dictionnaire biographique des fusillés et exécutés par condamnation et*

comme otages ou guillotinés en France pendant l'Occupation (Les Éditions de l'Atelier/Éditions Ouvrières, 2015).

26. Roger Bourderon, "Le colonel Rol-Tanguy," *Revue historique des armées* 248 (2007); Roger Bourderon, *Le PCF à l'épreuve de 1940 à 1943: De la guerre impérialilste à la lutte armée*, (Éditions Syllepse, 2012); Roger Linet, *1933– 1943, La traversée de la tourmente* (Messidor, 1990).

27. Interviews with Lise London-Ricol, Paris, August 11, 1988, September 12, 1988. See also her autobiographies: Lise London, *La Mégère de la rue Daguerre: Souvenirs de Résistance* (Éditions du Seuil, 1995) and its sequel, *Le Printemps des camarades* (Éditions du Seuil, 1996).

Chapter 4

1. The French terminology is *association de malfaiteurs; pillage en bande et à force ouverte en temps de guerre; assassinat et tentative d'assassinat; acte de guerre*.

2. This meant that Pierre Marzin had continued his activity in the French Communist Party after it had been declared illegal in September 1939.

3. AN, 4 W 6, dossier 6, "Forme et Frais," Letter, June 10, 1942.

4. AN, 4 W 6, unnumbered.

5. Quoted by Charles Tillon, *Les FTP: Témoignage pour server à l'histoire de la Résistance* (Julliard, 1971 [1962]), 137. Tillon quotes this excerpt from a written document dated June 25 [1942], but he does not identify the source.

6. Letter from the Commissaire du gouvernement près le Tribunal d'État to the Garde des Sceaux, Minister and Secretary of State for Justice, pièce no. 696, 4W6, dossier 6.

7. "La cour ... considérant que la publicité des débats dans la présente affaire peut être dangereuse pour l'ordre public ... ordonne que les débats auront lieu à huis clos." Extrait des minutes du greffe de la Cour d'Appel de Paris, AN, Z 4 73, no. 512.

8. As we will see in chapter 6, Legros' father appears to have had personal or profession connections that gave him access to high-ranking people in the Vichy government.

9. "Les douze petits yeux noirs du destin allemand," in Albert Camus, *Lettres à un ami allemand* (Éditions Gallimard, 1972 [1948]), 22.

10. AN, 4 W 6, interrogation of Henri Meunier, June 6, 1942, pièce 511.

11. AN, 4 W 6, interrogation of Arthur Lathulière, June 6, 1942, pièce 509.

12. AN, 4 W 6, interrogation of Raymonde Berthelet van den Branden, June 5, 1942, pièce 507.

13. AN, 4 W 6, interrogation of Estrade, June 5, 1942, pièce 513.

14. AN, 4 W 6, interrogation of Grelot, June 8, 1942, pièce 521.

15. The name "René" is in quotation marks in the text because it refers to another person by his nom de guerre.

16. AN, 4 W 6, interrogation of Louise Berthelet Sézille de Mazancourt, June 5, 1942, pièce 509.

17. AN, 4 W 6, interrogation of Norma Nicoletti Bléron, June 7, 1942, pièce 497.

18. AN, Z 4 73, interrogation of Lucien Menut, September 16, 1942.

19. It is interesting that Marcellesi refers to a mail intercept in his self-exculpatory testimony. When police questioned his entourage, a coworker accused Marcellesi himself of intercepting mail. If true, he may well have been intercepting letters of denunciation or other compromising material. So-called threshold resisters straddled the line, using their legitimate aboveground jobs in service of the underground movement. Marcellesi would have been strategically placed to play such a role.

20. AN, 4 W 6, interrogation of Leonard Marcellesi, June 7, 1942, pièce 493.

21. Two famous cases come to mind. Pierre Brossolette, de Gaulle's envoy to Occupied France, jumped to his death from the fifth-floor window of the Gestapo headquarters on the Avenue Foch (Paris) on March 22, 1944. Jean Moulin, prefect of Chartres and later head of the Conseil National de la Résistance, faced this dilemma in the summer of 1940 after his arrest by German authorities for refusing to sign a false statement. He attempted to end his own life by cutting his throat, but survived. In an iconic photograph, Moulin wears a scarf around his neck, a sartorial flair he had adopted to cover the scar. In June 1943, he was tortured to death by Klaus Barbie.

22. "L'institutrice, Madeleine Marzin fut promenée nue sous d'horribles sarcasmes dans les locaux de la police." Tract, "Des Policiers français aux ordres de la Gestapo torturent les patriotes parisiens," Le Comité Parisien de la Libération, n.d. Fonds Tollet, III, Appels CPL. Musée de la Résistance Nationale, Champigny, France. Marzin's ordeal is here dramatized with the invention of a gender-specific component—the exposure and humiliation of a woman prisoner by men and before an audience of men.

23. Interview with Maté Houet and Madeleine Marzin, Paris, May 31, 1992.

24. Centre d'Histoire sociale du XXè siècle, Fonds André Marty, 2-AM-5A (1941–1951), boîte 13, Témoignage de Madeleine Marzin sur la manifestation de la rue de Buci le 1 juin 1942 [*sic*], Marzin, "Ce que je sais de la manifestation du 31.5.42, rue de Bucci [*sic*]."

25. In another version the threat was against her daughter, who would be sent to a brothel on the Eastern Front if the mother did not cede to their demands. The grapevine is not always trustworthy; Bronner did not have a daughter. Such threats were actually made in other instances, but by Germans.

26. Interview with Louise Berthelet Sézille de Mazancourt and Raymonde Berthelet Van den Branden, Fleury-Mérogis, August 7, 1988.

27. Jacques Kahn, *Persiste et signe* (Editions sociales, 1973), 28. In his memoir, Communist activist Jacques Kahn recalls forcing himself to read the record of his interrogation with utmost care before affixing his signature. Kahn describes his own interrogation in December 1942 after arrest by the Brigades spéciales in Montpellier. "Racked with pain to the point of being nearly desensitized, in an altered, dreamlike state, one had to summon enough presence of mind to be vigilant before signing. To force oneself to decode each line, word by word. To be careful to sign right under the last typewritten line without leaving any space so that no lie could be added after the fact."

Chapter 5

1. Attestation de Julia Cartier, Service liquidateur du Front National, February 15, 1962, Archives du Ministère des Anciens Combattants.

2. Interview with Maté Houet, Paris, July 8, 1988; numerous conversations with André Tollet, late 1970s and 1980s.

3. Interview with Madeleine Marzin, Paris, May 31, 1992.

4. Marzin's brother, Pierre, was represented by Odette Moreau, a lawyer involved in Resistance activities who was later arrested and sent to Ravensbrück.

5. Interview with Madeleine Marzin, Paris, May 31, 1992.

6. "La jeune institutrice qui, s'il m'en souvient bien, s'appelait la femme Marzin, se défendit en faisant valoir qu'elle n'avait pas tué elle-même, qu'elle n'avait obéi à aucun motif bas, à aucune passion de cupidité, mais qu'elle entendait servir une idéologie: l'idéologie communiste. Elle n'en fut pas moins condamnée à mort." Joseph Barthélemy, *Ministre de la Justice, Vichy 1941–1943. Mémoires* (Éditions Pygmalion–Gérard Watelet, 1989), 456.

Joseph Barthélemy was Minister of Justice from February 1942 to March 1943. According to a report of the Commission du ravitaillement of the Comité parisien de la Libération, he was the cousin of Félix Barthélemy, the owner of the cheese shop on the rue de Seine. "There is a butter and cheese seller in the GIL (Groupement interprofessionnel du lait) [a dairy association], M. Barthélemy, cousin of the former Keeper of the Seals. He was charged with unlawful price hikes and sold eggs with falsified invoices but his cousin covered it up." Archives du Musée de la Résistance, Champigny, France. Fonds Tollet, boîte III, "Rapport d'André Tollet sur la situation du ravitaillement dans l'Île-de-France. Possibilités sabotées," (1945), 20–21.

7. Interview with Madeleine Marzin, Paris, May 31, 1992.

8. "Il a y longtemps, lui disais-je, qu'on ne décapite plus les femmes; évitez d'être devant l'opinion celui qui a recommencé." Barthélemy, *Ministre de la Justice*, 456.

9. "Le gouvernement est mâle, l'opinion est femelle." Reported by Barthélemy, *Ministre de la Justice*, 273 (italics added).

10. Interview with Félix Barthélemy, Paris, October 17, 1985.

11. "Ce dont je reste toujours bien sûr, c'est que, si la femme Marzin avait été exécutée, elle occuperait une place d'honneur parmi les martyrs de l'Idée, et encore plus sûr que sa mort me serait reprochée." Barthélemy, *Ministre de la Justice*, 457.

12. Interview with Madeleine Marzin, Paris, May 31, 1992.

13. Interview with Lucienne Rolland, Enghein-les-Bains, France, June 7, 1988; conversation with Lucienne Roland, Paris, 1989.

14. Interview with Madeleine Marzin, Paris, May 31, 1992.

15. AN, BB18 3454 dossier 1229/42. Arrêt du 29 December 1942, Cour d'Appel de Paris.

16. "La singulière évasion de l'émeutière communiste," *L'Oeuvre*, August 28, 1942, 3. "M. Cervoni [director of the Fresnes prison] n'aurait pas attiré spécialement l'attention . . . sur la personnalité des condamnées qui conduisait à la prison de Rennes." *L'Oeuvre* was the newspaper of Marcel Déat, the notorious collaborationist.

17. AN, Z 4 73. Letter from the Préfet de Police to M. le Procureur de l'État français près le Tribunal de 1ère Instance de la Seine, 2e section, September 22, 1942.

18. Dietrich also stated that aiding the escape was one of the charges against her when her case was referred to the Section spéciale. File of Eugénie Dietrich divorcée Véron, Ministère des Anciens Combattants.

19. BB 18 3454, dr 1229/ 42. Letter from the Directeur des prisons de Fresnes to the Garde des Sceaux, August 17, 1942.

20. BB 18 3454, dr 1229/42. Letter from the Directeur des prisons de Fresnes to the Garde des Sceaux, August 17, 1942. A brief *New York Times* article announces Cervoni's dismissal a mere four days after Marzin's escape. The timing suggests that Cervoni paid for her escape with his job. *New York Times,* "Vichy Ousts Prison Director," August 22, 1942.

21. Interview with Madeleine Marzin, Paris, May 31, 1992.

22. Of the many secondary accounts of the demonstration, the best is a booklet produced by the school for the twentieth anniversary of Liberation: Maurice Conquéré, *Les Cinq lycéens de Buffon fusillés par les Allemands,* n.d. [1964]. It was prepared with the help of surviving members of the boys' families and accords most closely with official records. Thanks to Cécile Hochard from bringing it to my attention.

23. AN, 4 W 6, 686, Pierre Benoit, summary of interrogations of August 29 and 30, 1942.

24. Interview of Albert Ouzoulias, Paris, June 15, 1988; Albert Ouzoulias, *Les fils de la nuit* (Grasset, 1975), 255–259.

25. Maurice Conquéré, *Les Cinq lycéens de Buffon fusillés par les Allemands,* n.d. [1964], n.p.

26. AN, 4 W 6, 686, Pierre Benoit, summary of interrogations of August 29 and 30, 1942.

27. AN, Interrogation of Legros.

28. AN, 4 W 6, 686, Pierre Benoit, summary of interrogations of August 29 and 30, 1942.

29. *Les fusillés (1940–1944): Dictionnaire biographique des fusillés et exécutés par condamnation et comme otages ou guillotinés en France pendant l'Occupation,* ed. Claude Pennetier, Jean-Pierre Besse, Thomas Pouty, and Delphine Leneveu (Les Éditions de l'Atelier/Éditions Ouvrières, 2015), 160.

30. AN, F 60 15775, pièce 48, "Note sur le jeune Legros," n.d.

31. AN, F 60 15775, pièce 48, "Note sur le jeune Legros," n.d.

32. AN, F 60 15775, pièce 14, "Note verbale," October 20, 1942.

33. AN, F 60 15775, dossier 584, pièce 27, Letter from Raymonde Legros, n.d.

34. "Here are their last letters, finally obtained from the occupant in 1944 after the Allied landing. Until that time, repeated appeals from the families were met with refusals, sometimes threatening, one of which was even accompanied by physical brutality." Conquéré, *Les Cinq lycéens,* n.p.

35. "Life will be beautiful. We leave singing. Have courage. It is not so terrible [to die] after six months in prison." The last letters of all five students are reproduced in the aforementioned brochure. For Pierre Benoit, see also *Ils aimaient la vie. Lettres de fusillés,* ed. Etienne Fajon (Messidor, 1985 [1958]), 67.

Chapter 6

1. Early histories of the Resistance that reference the demonstration on the rue de Buci include the encyclopedic *Histoire de la Résistance en France, de 1940 à 1945,* vol. 2, *L'armée de l'ombre, juillet 1941–octobre 1942* (Robert Laffont, 1969) by prominent non-Communist historian Henri Noguères (with M. Degliame-Fouché, and J.-L. Vigier). Henri Amouroux devotes several pages to women's demonstrations with a special focus on the rue de Buci in *La Grande histoire des Français sous l'Occupation: Les Beaux jours des collabos, le peuple réveillé, juin 1940–june 1942* (Robert Laffont, 1998), 653–656. See also Simone Bertrand, *Mille Visages, un seul combat* (Les Éditeurs Français Réunis, 1965), 501; Union des Femmes Françaises, *Les Femmes dans la Résistance* (Éditions du Rocher, 1977), 175, 187–189; "Madeleine Marzin," in Nicole Chatel, *Des Femmes dans la Résistance* (Julliard, 1972), 21–73.

2. *Le Temps,* June 1, 1942, June 2, 1942.

3. This accusation—false, according to police and witness reports—recurs after the August 1 demonstration on the rue Daguerre as well.

4. APPP, dossier 253, circular of May 31, 1942.

5. *L'Oeuvre,* June 7, 1942.

6. "Un nouvel attentat à Paris," *Le Temps,* August 4, 1942. Prisunic was part of a chain of grocery stores, comparable to the Eco supermarket.

7. Maurice Garçon, *Journal, 1939–1945* (Les Belles Lettres/Fayard, 2015), entry of June 22, 1942. This theory was likely a reference to the high school students who came from upper-middle-class families and therefore did not fit the speaker's notion of a "Bolshevik" or "terrorist."

8. Jacques Isorni, *Mémoires, 1911–1945* (Éditions Robert Laffont, 1984), 227. "How did [the demonstration] promote French interests? Or those of the French? It was about provoking reprisals. Nothing more. Public opinion was deeply shaken. The public did not support the provocateurs." If such was the opinion of Estrade's own advocate, one might well question the sincerity of his defense.

9. For examples of this language in the right-wing "legal" press, see *Paris Soir*, June 1 and June 4, 1942; *Le Temps*, June 5, June 13–14, and August 4, 1942; *L'Avenir*, June 1 and June 4, 1942. For the first police reports, see APPP, Rapport, Commissaire principal du 6e à M. le Directeur de la Police Municipale, May 31, 1942; Circulaire "Attentat sur Gardiens de la Paix," May 31, 1942.

10. Interview with Lise Ricol, Paris, August 11, 1988.

11. *L'Oeuvre*, August 5, 1942. "Comme deuxième front, ils n'ont encore trouvé que celui qui va de la rue de Buci à la rue Daguerre."

12. The flyer is presented in toto and analyzed in Chapter 1.

13. Musée de la Résistance, Champigny, France, Tracts 2 (femmes) 50 b.

14. Musée de la Résistance, Champigny, France, Tracts 2 (femmes) 50 b.

15. In June 1940, Pétain uttered the now famous phrase: "I offer to France the gift of my person." He later maintained that the Vichy government acted as a shield against the depredations of the German invaders.

16. For the definitive treatment of Vichy's policy on women, see Miranda Pollard, *Reign of Virtue: Mobilizing Gender in Vichy France* (University of Chicago Press, 1998).

17. "Femmes à l'action!," *L'Humanité*, special edition, June 1942, 4. "Boches" is a derogatory term for "Germans."

18. Musée de la Résistance, Champigny, Tracts (femmes) 23; "Femmes de Paris," n.d. [late June or July 1942], emphasis in original.

19. *L'Humanité*, June 5, 1942. A careful reader of the French might detect the presence of men: "*patriotes attaqués*" denotes a male or mixed group of patriots.

20. *La Voix des femmes*, n.d. [1942].

21. Interview with Josette Dumeix, August 27, 1988; interview with Madeleine Marzin, May 31, 1992.

22. According to law, notice of an execution was to be posted at the site of the victim's residence and his place of work. I have not seen any indication in the official records that the rule was followed in the case of these men.

23. Paul Éluard, "Avis": "La nuit qui précéda sa mort / Fut la plus courte de sa vie / L'idée qu'il existant encore / Lui brûlait le sang aux poignets / Le poids de son corps l'écœurait / Sa force le faisait gémir / C'est tout au fond de cette horreur / Qu'il a commencé à sourire / Il n'avait pas UN camarade / Mais des millions et des millions / Pour le venger il le savait / Et le jour se leva pour lui." Paul Éluard, *Au rendez-vous allemand* (Les Éditions de Minuit, 1945).

24. The six men who died by German firing squad include the five students and Georges Vallet. Other armed men under Vallet's command were present at the demonstration. They too were executed but it is not clear which of them was present at the demonstration.

25. Interview with Louise Berthelet Sézille de Mazancourt and Raymonde Berthelet Van den Branden, Fleury-Mérogis, August 4, 1988.

26. Prison directors informed the local prefect before releasing a prisoner who had served his or her sentence. If a soon-to-be-released prisoner was deemed a potential threat to the public order, the prefect could have the "liberated" prisoner placed in preventive or administration detention and remanded to another facility.

In the event of an acquittal, discharge, or dismissal, it was the responsibility of the public prosecutor's office to notify prison and local authorities before the prisoner could be released. Again, such prisoners were often detained regardless of the outcome of their case. Alain Bancaud, *Une Exception ordinaire: La magistrature en France, 1930–1950* (Gallimard, 2002), 44. As of October 1941, French authorities were also required to alert the Germans prior to a prisoner's release. The Germans had the final say in the disposition of prisoners, even those who had already served their sentences. Bancaud, *Une Exception ordinaire*, 80–81.

27. "L'affaire de la rue de Buci en révision," *Sud-Ouest* 161 (March 2, 1945), 1.

28. Archives Nationales, Ministère du Justice, 19950395/24 dossier S.L. 1012-3.

29. The militia (*milice*) was not formed until late 1943.

30. Italics mine. Péri's use of language here ("French *race*") is redolent of far-right discourse of the period. Her claim that Hitler aimed to "exterminate" the French by starvation was a popular notion, as discussed in Chapter 2.

31. Efforts to find evidence of de Gaulle's "glorification" of the protagonists of the Buci affair, or mention of the demonstration by other speakers on the BBC airwaves, have proven unsuccessful. A similar claim is made by Lise London-Ricol: "Radio London and Radio Moscow . . . paid homage to the courage of

the population of Paris and to that of women in particular." Lise Ricol, "Dès 1940–1941, avec les femmes de la région sud de Paris, de Seine et Seine-et-Oise," in *Les Femmes dans la Résistance*, ed. Union des Femmes Françaises (Éditions du Rocher, 1977), 188. A glowing reference to the "operation" at the market on the rue Daguerre appears in a BBC broadcast of August 7, 1942: Jacques Brunius, "La France a faim," in *Les Voix de la Liberté: Ici Londres, 1940–1944*, ed. Jean-Louis Crémieux-Brilhac (La Documentation française, 1975), 184.

The demonstration on the rue de Buci, however, did make the front page of "the press of [the] Allies": "One Killed, 9 Hurt in Rioting in Paris," *New York Times*, August 3, 1942, 1, 4. The news article is based on official reports on the demonstration of the rue Daguerre (including misinformation that the instigator cried, "Riot! The Americans are calling for it"). The article includes a reference to the earlier "riot" on the rue de Buci. A *New York Times* article of June 3, 1942, reports that the Conseil des ministres referred the "authors and instigators of the recent riot in a Paris food store" to the Tribunal d'état.

32. *Débats de L'Assemblée Consultative Provisoire*, vol. 2, *Du 6 Février au 31 Mars 1945* (Imprimerie des Journaux Officiels, 1945), session of TK, TK–TK.

33. *Débats de l'Assemblée Consultative Provisoire*, vol. II, *Du 6 Février au 31 Mars 1945* (Imprimerie des Journaux Officiels, 1945), session of February 22, 1945, 165–166.

34. *Débats de l'Assemblée Consultative Provisoire*, vol. II, *Du 6 Février au 31 Mars 1945* (Imprimerie des Journaux Officiels, 1945), session of February 22, 1945, 167.

It should be noted that the arrest of the father and brother are not noted in the archival record. The speaker clearly had access to this information from the father of Legros himself. If he is correct, then the actions of the authorities have once again been omitted from the written record of the affair.

35. *Débats de l'Assemblée Consultative Provisoire*, vol. II, *Du 6 Février au 31 Mars 1945* (Imprimerie des Journaux Officiels, 1945), session of February 22, 1945, 167.

36. For the notion of "honorary man" as it applies to exceptional women resisters in traditionally male roles, see Paula Schwartz, "*Partisanes* and Gender Politics in Vichy France," *French Historical Studies* 16, no. 1 (Spring 1989).

37. Jacques Baudry, who was shot along with his co-conspirators, is missing from the appeals story. His presence at the Buci market on the day of the melee has never been established.

38. Ministère de la Défense, Secrétariat des Anciens Combattants, Délégation à la Mémoire et à l'Information Historique, Département des Archives, dossiers of twenty-seven individuals arrested in connection with the Buci affair. My deepest thanks to Madame Christine Diatta, who assembled these files for my use in August 1999.

39. Serge Berstein and Pierre Milza, *Histoire de la France au XXè siècle,* vol. II, *1930–1958* (Perrin, 2009), 388–391, 402, 437, 633.

40. I wish to thank Annie Chenieux for sharing memories of Denise Leclerc, and for putting me in touch with Leclerc's son, Frédéric Boyer.

41. For a fuller discussion, see Paula Schwartz, "Redefining Resistance: The Activism of Women in Wartime France," in *Behind the Lines: Gender and the Two World Wars,* ed. Margaret Randolph Higonnet et al. (Yale University Press, 1987), 141–153, and Paula Schwartz, "Resistance et différence des sexes: Bilan et perspectives," in *Les Femmes dans la Résistance en France,* ed. Mechtild Gilzmer et al. (Tallandier, 2002), 71–86. This chapter is a revised version of "Différence des sexes et Résistance: Bilan et perspectives," *Clio: Histoires, Femmes et Sociétés* 1, no. 1 (Autumn 1995): 67–88.

42. Ministère de la Défense, Secrétariat des Anciens Combattants, Délégation à la Mémoire et à l'Information Historique, Département des Archives, dossier of Angèle Cousin, letter of attestation from Albert Ouzoulias (FTPF), April 29, 1955.

43. Ministère de la Défense, Secrétariat des Anciens Combattants, Délégation à la Mémoire et à l'Information Historique, Département des Archives, dossier of Julia Cartier, letter of attestation from Madeleine Marzin, February 2, 1962.

44. French women were granted the right to vote in April 1944 and exercised their suffrage for the first time in the April 1945 municipal elections.

45. July 14 celebrates French independence and marks the anniversary of the taking of the Bastille in 1789. Unlike the United States, France has a separate national holiday for each world war: November 11 commemorates the 1918 armistice of World War I; May 8 marks the 1945 armistice of World War II. The Journée nationale de la Résistance, celebrated on May 27, was created in 2014 to honor resisters. It is a national day of remembrance but not a national holiday. The Conseil National de la Résistance (CNR) held its first meeting under the direction of Jean Moulin.

46. "Aux citoyens du VIe arrondissement tombés devant les pelotons d'exécution, sur les barricades et sur les champs de bataille durant la lutte contre l'Allemagne nazie, au cours des années 1939–40–41–42–43–44–45.

Que le Souvenir de leur sacrifice soit uni dans nos mémoires à celui des Glorieux Aînés de la Guerre 1914–1918." Located on wall bordering the Allée du Séminaire, Sixth Arrondissement.

47. Dalmas and Meunier are also remembered separately. Their names figure on commemorative plaques honoring members of their respective professions.

48. An accompanying text summarizing their activity mentions "patriotic demonstrations," but also commando raids and sabotage, aspects of their activity that are rarely mentioned.

49. I was unable to confirm the existence of a memorial to Benoit and Legros at the École Alsacienne. Efforts to obtain information or permission to visit the premises from the school's director were unsuccessful.

50. My deepest thanks to Isabelle Benistant, history professor at the Lycée Buffon, who toured the premises with me, introduced me to the sites, and provided a wealth of in-house literature on the students.

The youth of the boys is exaggerated here; it is falsely stated that none of them had reached their eighteenth birthday by the time of their execution. Ministère des Postes, Télégraphes, et Téléphone (PTT), no. 6, 1959, https://www.wikitimbres.fr/public/stamps/pdf/POSTE-1959-12.pdf.

On official memory of the Resistance in the form of commemorative postage stamps, see Laurent Douzou and Jean Novosseloff, *La Résistance oblitérée, sa mémoire gravée par les timbres* (Éditions du Félin, 2017). For the Lycée Buffon students, see page 88.

51. The memorial plaque straddles the Fourteenth and Fifteenth arrondissements. "A la mémoire des lycéens résistants fusillés le 8 février 1943. Jean Arthus, 15 ans; Jacques Baudry, 18 ans; Pierre Benoit, 15 ans; Pierre Grelot, 17 ans; Lucien Legros 16 ans." The correct ages are: Arthus, 17; Baudry, 20; Benoit, 17; Grelot, 19; Legros, 18.

52. "Arrested on the order of the government of the French State, shot by the Nazi occupiers."

53. Baudry is buried in a family plot, as per his wishes and those of his family.

54. "Dans ce hameau habitaient Lucien Sampaix, 1889–1941, Georges Vallet, 1912–1943, André Biver, 1921–1942, fusillés par les boches" on the rue Émile-Desvaux, and in the second, more recent version, on the rue des Bois, "fusillés par les nazis." "Boches" is a derogatory term for Germans that had currency during both wars. In the second iteration of the plaque, the insult is erased and in lieu of "Germans," "Nazis" is used to distinguish between the perpetrators

of the crimes and the German people as a whole. The language makes clear the fact that one plaque preceded the other.

Unfortunately, city authorities find no record of their respective dates: "In fact, after the Liberation of Paris numerous markers were placed spontaneously by private individuals.... On April 12, 1946, a decree from the Ministry of Interior established rules for the placing of commemorative plaques. However, from 1944 to 1954, most plaques, especially those honoring resisters, were hung without permission from the Prefect. Very often it was the family or friends of the victims who wanted to have such plaques engraved in the absence of grave markers or tombstones." Note of July 31, 2018, Céline Duval-Aveline, Département de l'Histoire, de la Mémoire et des Musées Associatifs, Direction des Affaires Culturelles, Mairie de Paris. Thanks also to Thérèse Teyssedre, Chargée de Mission, Cabinet du Maire du 19th Arrondissement.

55. See the website of the Mairie de Paris: https://www.paris.fr/services-et-infos-pratiques/culture-et-patrimoine/histoire-et-patrimoine/histoire-et-memoire-2419#. Consulted on June 1, 2017.

56. Mariana Sauber, "Traces fragiles. Les plaques commémoratives dans les rues de Paris," *Annales. Économies, Sociétés, Civilisations* 48, no. 3 (1993): 715. In 1984, there were 432 such plaques (Michel Henocq, cited by Sauber, 715 n. 1).

Chapter 7

1. Contemporary versions of the story contain errors of fact, some of which are rather fanciful.

2. The demonstration briefly figures in two recent general histories of the Resistance: Julian Jackson, *France: The Dark Years, 1940–1944* (Oxford University Press, 2001), 443, and Olivier Wieviorka, *Histoire de la Résistance, 1940–1945* (Perrin, 2013), 184 (the latter albeit with factual errors). Éric Alary et al. devote substantial attention to women's food protests throughout France but do not associate any of them with PCF organization or issues that transcend hunger: "These women [were] not motivated by patriotism or political ideals." Éric Alary with Bénédicte Vergez-Chaignon and Gilles Gauvin, *Les Français au quotidien, 1939–1949* (Perrin, 2006), 216.

3. The earliest accounts took the form of articles and public lectures in France and the United States, from 1992. See Paula Schwartz with Kenneth Mouré, "*On vit mal*: Food Shortages and Popular Culture in Occupied France, 1940–44," *Food, Culture and Society* 10, no. 2 (Summer

2007): 262–295; Paula Schwartz, "31 mai 1942: Manifestation de la rue de Buci," "1 août 1942: manifestation de la rue Daguerre," and "Les femmes dans la Résistance," in Association pour l'Enseignement de la Résistance Intérieure, *La Résistance en Ile-de-France* [CD-ROM] (AERI, 2004); Paula Schwartz, "Resistance et différence des sexes: Bilan et perspectives," in *Les Femmes dans la Résistance en France,* ed. Mechtild Gilzmer et al. (Tallandier, 2002), 71–86 (revised version of 1995 *Clio* article); Paula Schwartz and Dominique Veillon, "Ravitaillement, pouvoirs publics et protestations dans Paris occupé," *Mélanges de l'École française de Rome* 112, no. 2 (2000): 645–653; Paula Schwartz, "The Politics of Food and Gender in Occupied Paris," *Modern and Contemporary France* 7, no. 1 (February 1999): 35–45; Paula Schwartz, "La répression des femmes communistes," *Les Cahiers de l'Institut d'Histoire du Temps Présent* 31 (October 1995): 25–37; Paula Schwartz, "Différence des sexes et Résistance: Bilan et perspectives," *Clio: Histoires, femmes et sociétés* 1, no. 1 (Fall 1995): 67–88.

4. Archives pertaining to the Second World War became fully accessible to the public in 2015, with a few exceptions. See Sonia Combe, *Archives interdites: Les peurs françaises face à l'histoire contemporaine* (La Découverte, 2010 [2001, 1994]).

5. For a nuanced account of the evolution of sixty years of Resistance historiography, see Laurent Douzou, *La Résistance, une histoire périlleuse* (Seuil, 2005).

6. Lizzie Collingham, *The Taste of War: World War II and the Battle for Food* (Penguin Press, 2013).

7. APPP, Paris, Fonds "Victimes du Devoir," file no. 93, "Biographie," November 5, 1931. Despite its title, the document is written in the first person by Morbois himself.

8. APPP, Paris, Fonds "Victimes du Devoir," file no. 93, "Biographie," November 5, 1931.

9. APPP, Paris, Fonds "Victimes du Devoir," file no. 92, "Biographie," January 25, 1923. This is a document provided by Vaudrey and written in his own hand.

10. APPP, Paris, Fonds "Victimes du Devoir," files no. 92 and 93.

11. APPP, Paris, Fonds "Victimes du Devoir," file no. 93, Rapport, Martial Perier, Inspection générale, section "Épuration," October 8, 1945.

12. APPP, Paris, Fonds "Victimes du Devoir," file no. 92, Rapport, Martial Perier, Inspection générale, section "Épuration," October 9, 1945.

13. In his thoughtful and subtle article, Jean-Marc Berlière evokes the contradictions and challenges of postwar assessment of police behavior during the Occupation. Jean-Marc Berlière, "L'Épuration de la police parisienne en 1944–1945," *Vingtième Siècle: Revue d'histoire* 49 (Jan.–Mar., 1996): 63–81. Berlière also mentions the deaths of the two policemen who were killed on the rue de Buci, here qualified as an "attack" (*attentat*), 68, 75.

14. Interview with Félix Barthélemy, Paris, October 17, 1985.

15. A marble tablet at the entrance to the police headquarters of the Sixth Arrondissement commemorates Bottine, along with several other policemen from the same district.

16. The plaque reads: "[On behalf of] the officers and police of the 6th arrondissement, [in recognition of] their comrades who gloriously fell for the liberation of Paris, August 19–26, 1944."

17. See the authoritative study by Jean-Marc Berlière, *Poliicers français sous l'Occupation* (Perrin, 2009), and the classic work by Jacques Delarue, *Les Policiers français dans la Résistance* (Confédération nationale des policiers anciens combattants et résistants, 1964).

18. Centre d'histoire sociale du XXè siècle, Fonds André Marty, 2-AM-5A (1941–1951), boîte 13, Témoignage de Madeleine Marzin, Marzin, "Ce que je sais de la manifestation du 31.5.42, rue de Bucci [*sic*]."

19. The *juge d'instruction* is the magistrate in charge of the investigation.

20. Centre d'histoire sociale du XXè siècle, Fonds André Marty, 2-AM-5A (1941–1951), boîte 13, Témoignage de Madeleine Marzin, Marzin, "Ce que je sais de la manifestation du 31.5.42, rue de Bucci [*sic*]"; interview with Houet and Marzin, Paris, May 31, 1992.

21. Dépôt Central d'Archives de la Justice Militaire, Le Blanc (Indre), France, dossier: Jugement no. 214/7555 (Paris, 12 avril 1960), Pièces 34–37, Procès-verbal d'interrogation et de confrontation, Paul Farge, April 28, 1947. Italics mine. Farge's claims of objectivity were undermined by his own record of political bias. In his accusation against Jean Catelas, the PCF deputy whom he sent to the guillotine in September 1941, Farge argued that Catelas's steadfast support of his comrades and his party was incriminating evidence against him.

22. Dépôt Central d'Archives de la Justice Militaire, Le Blanc (Indre), France, dossier: Jugement no. 214/7555 (Paris, 12 avril 1960), Pièces 34–37, Procès-verbal d'interrogation et de confrontation, Paul Farge, April 28, 1947.

23. Dépôt Central d'Archives de la Justice Militaire, Le Blanc (Indre), France, dossier: Jugement no. 214/7555 (Paris, 12 avril 1960), Pièces 34–37, Procès-verbal d'interrogation et de confrontation, Paul Farge, April 28, 1947.

24. Pierre Laval was condemned to death. He was executed by firing squad in October 1945.

25. Yves-Frédéric Jaffré, *Les Tribunaux d'exception, 1940–1962* (Nouvelles Éditions Latines, 1962), 53. (Italics mine.)

26. Interview with Félix Barthélémy, Paris, October 17, 1985. (Italics mine.)

27. Stéphane Courtois, *Le PCF dans la guerre* (Ramsay, 1980). He describes the event is as a "pillage operation by housewives," 255.

28. APPP, press file, *L'Aurore*, May 20, 1970.

29. APPP, press file, *France-Soir*, May 21, 1970.

30. APPP, press file, *France Soir*, May 21, 1970.

31. APPP, press file, *Combat*, May 20, 1970.

32. APPP, press file, *Combat*, May 20, 1970. (Italics mine.)

33. APPP, "Les fournisseurs de papa," *L'Aurore*, May 12, 1970.

34. APPP, "Fauchons Fauchon!," *Le Monde*, June [illegible], 1970. The title of the article is a double play on the word *faucher*, which means "to cut down," as with a sickle. To be *fauché* also means "to be broke."

35. Benny Lévy: "The Fauchon operation had been conceived with the idea of bringing together the leftist ideas of shopkeepers and artisans with those of the G[auche] P[rolétarienne] since it was an operation against a large store. . . . The fact that the store was Fauchon made an even bigger impact because a symbol of rich versus poor was also being attacked." From Michèle Manceaux, *Les maos en France* (Gallimard, 1972), 209, cited in Isabelle Sommier, *La violence politique et son deuil: L'après-68 en France et en Italie* (Presses Universitaires de Rennes, 1998), 132.

36. Interview with Yves Cohen, New York, March 23, 1989.

37. APPP, press file, *Combat*, May 20, 1970.

38. Michel Field with Fabienne Waks, *Jours de manif, années 70* (Les Éditions Textuel/Crayon Noir, 1996), 21–22. Field also alludes to the Fauchon incident in his novel *L'Homme aux pâtes* (Bernard Barrault, 1989), 49–50.

SELECT BIBLIOGRAPHY

ARCHIVES

Archives nationales (AN), Paris and Pierrefitte-sur-Seine, France
Tribunal d'État, section de Paris, 4 W 6, dossier 6, pièces 1–722
Tribunal d'État, section de Paris, 4 W 12
Section spéciale près la Cour d'appel de Paris, Z 4 73
Police, F7 15145, 15156, 15157, 15165, 15900
F / 23/ 4, Services extraordinaires en temps de guerre
F / 60, Secrétariat général du Gouvernement et services du Premier ministre, 1570, 1575
B B18, Recours en justice et grâces
A B XIX, Collection Florien de Rochesnard, 4030, "France 1939–1950"
Ministère de l'Intérieur, F/1/a: 3751, 3761, 3667
Ministère de la Justice, BB/30 : 1709, versements divers ; 1887, dossiers 1, 4, 6
Président du conseil, F60 : 502-506, rapports de préfets; 1575, arrestations; 1591-1694, fiches de personnes
Affaires judiciaires, BB/18 : 7056 Correspondance générale de la division criminelle; 19950395/24, Sous-direction de la législation criminelle, Direction des affaires criminelles et des grâces
Cabinet du Chef de l'État, 2 AG : 449, 524-528 (grâces), 546
Rol-Tanguy (Henri), 672AP/27

Archives de la Préfecture de Police de Paris (APPP), Paris and Pré-St.-Gervais, France
Fonds du Cabinet du Préfet :
  B A/ 1806-1808, Ministère du Ravitaillement
  B A/ 2128, Affaire de la rue de Buci et du Lycée Buffon

B A/ 1752, affaires
B A/ 194W 4 dossier n° 37
B A/ 354W 77 dossier n° 101523
Fonds des Brigades spéciales des Renseignements généraux
    G B 98, Brigades spéciales 2, vues 1-773
    G B 178, Brigades spéciales 1, vues 75-76
Personnel. K B 1-106 : Dossiers d'enquête et de Cour de Justice sur les activités des fonctionnaires de la préfecture de police sous l'Occupation, 75, 77
Personnel. K C : Victimes du devoir et morts pour la France, dossiers individuels 92, 93 194W 4, dossier no. 37

Archives de la Ville de Paris (AVP), Paris, France (includes collection formerly housed in Archives départementales de la Seine, Paris, France)
Cour de justice du département de la Seine, Z/6/878

Archives départementales de la Seine-Saint-Denis, Bobigny, France
Archives du Parti communiste français (APCF), Commission centrale de contrôle politique, archives relatives à la Seconde Guerre mondiale, 261J6/[35], Rapports du préfet de police de Paris au gouvernement, 1942.

Centre d'histoire sociale du XXè siècle (CHS), Paris, France.
Fonds André Marty, 2-AM-5A (1941–1951)

Dépôt central des archives de la justice militaire (DCAJM), Leblanc (Indre), France.
Dossier Farge

Fondazione Feltrinelli (FF), Milan, Italy.
Fonds Angelo Tasca, 1940–1944:
    Resistenza francese, presse clandestine, cartelli 10, 22-35
    Bulletins et rapports hebdomadaires, 152-160

Ministère des Anciens Combattants (AC), Paris, France.
Dossiers of individual resisters

Musée de la Résistance Nationale (MRN), Champigny, France.
Fonds Tollet
Fonds Ouzoulias
Fonds Ricol
Presse clandestine
Archives 2: 1939-1945, PCF I-III, cartons 27, 37, 38, 41, 42, 48, 52, 53, 68, 78

SELECTED INTERVIEWS

Barthélemy, Félix. Paris, October 17, 1985
Borras, Cécile. Paris, April 17, 1986; April 24, 1986
Claudé, Marie-Louise. Paris, December 2, 1987
Cohen, Yves. New York, March 23, 1989
De Gaudemar, Antoine. Paris, June 12, 2004
Dumeix, Josette. Paris, June 5, 1978; August 27, 1988
Houet, Maté. Paris, July 8, 1988; May 31, 1992
Jégouzo, Betty. Paris, September 26, 1985
Lucienne Rolland, Enghein-les-Bains, June 7, 1988; Paris, July 19, 1988
Marzin, Madeleine. Paris, May 31, 1992
Ouzoulias, André. Paris, June 15, 1988
Ricol, Lise. Paris, August 11, 1988; September 12, 1988
Reynal Harrari, Raymonde, Ivry, March 3, 1978
Sézille de Mazancourt, Louise Berthelet. Fleury-Mérogis, August 7, 1988
Tollet, André. Ivry-sur-Seine, May 10, 1978
Van den Branden, Raymonde Berthelet. Fleury- Mérogis, August 7, 1988
Wallé, Georgette. Paris, November 22, 1985

PUBLISHED SOURCES

(See also the published sources cited in the Notes.)

Achard, Paul. *La Queue. Ce qui s'y disait, Ce qu'on y pensait.* Paris: Mille et une nuits, 2011 [1945].

Albertelli, Sebastien, Julien Blanc, and Laurent Douzou. *La lutte clandestine en France.* Paris: Seuil, 2019.

Amouroux, Henri. *La grande histoire des Français sous l'Occupation.* Paris: Laffont, 1998.

Azéma, Jean-Pierre. *Les Communistes français de Munich à Châteaubriant: 1938–1941.* Paris: Les Presses de Sciences Po, 1987.

Azéma, Jean-Pierre. *Les Archives de guerre: 1940-1944.* Paris: Institut national de l'audiovisuel, 1996.

Azéma, Jean-Pierre, and François Bédarida, eds. *La France des années noires,* vol. 1, *De la défaite à Vichy.* Paris: Seuil, 2000.

Bancaud, Alain. *Une Exception ordinaire: La magistrature en France, 1930–1950.* Paris: Gallimard, 2002.

Barthélemy, Joseph. *Ministre de la justice: Vichy 1941–1943: Mémoires.* Paris: Pygmalion, 1989.

Bédarida, François, and Jean-Pierre Azéma, eds. *La France des années noires,* vol. 2, *De l'Occupation à la Libération.* Paris: Seuil, 2000.

Berlière, Jean-Marc. *Policiers français sous l'Occupation.* Paris: Tempus Perrin, 2009.

Berstein, Serge, and Pierre Milza. *Histoire de la France au XXe siècle,* vol. 2, *1930–1958.* Paris: Perrin, 2009.

Bourderon, Roger. *Le PCF à l'épreuve de la guerre, 1940–1943: de la guerre impérialiste à la lutte armée.* Paris: Éditions Syllepse, 2012.

Bourderon, Roger. *Rol-Tanguy, des Brigades internationales à la libération de Paris.* Paris: Tallandier, 2013.

Capdevila, Luc, François Roquet, Fabrice Virgili, and Danièle Voldman. *Hommes et femmes dans la France en guerre (1914–1945).* Paris: Payot, 2003.

Chatel, Nicole, ed. *Des Femmes dans la Résistance.* Paris: Julliard, 1972.

Collingham, Lizzie. *The Taste of War: World War II and the Battle for Food.* London: Allen Lane, 2011.

Combe, Sonia. *Archives interdites. L'histoire confisquée.* Paris: La Découverte, 2001.

Conquéré, Maurice. *Les cinq lycéens de Buffon fusillés par les allemands.* Paris: Lycée Buffon, 1964.

Corday, Pauline. *J'ai vécu dans Paris occupé.* Montreal: Éditions de L'Arbre, 1943.

Courtois, Stéphane, and Marc Lazar. *Histoire du Parti communiste français.* Paris: Presses Universitaires de France, 1995.

Delarue, Jacques. *Les Policiers français dans la Résistance.* Paris: Confédération nationale des policiers anciens combattants et résistants, 1964.

de Pomiane, Édouard. *Cuisine et restrictions.* Paris: 1940.

de Pomiane, Édouard. *Manger... quand même.* Paris: 1941.

Diamond, Hanna. *Women and the Second World War in France, 1939–1948: Choices and Constraints.* London: Longman, 1999.

Doré-Rivé, Isabelle, ed. *Les jours sans: 1939–1949. Alimentation et pénurie en temps de guerre.* Lyon: Libel, 2017.

Douzou, Laurent. "Enquêteur, enquêté: quelle quête et pour qui?" *Interrogations, revue pluridisciplinaire des sciences de l'homme et de la société,* no. 13 (December 2011): 51–69.

Douzou, Laurent. *La Résistance française: une histoire périlleuse: essai d'historiographie.* Paris: Seuil, 2005.

Dutourd, Jean. *Au bon beurre: scènes de la vie sous l'Occupation.* Paris: Gallimard, 1952.

Fajon, Étienne, ed. *Ils aimaient la vie: lettres de fusillés.* Paris: Messidor, 1985.

Farge, Arlette. *Le Goût de l'archive*. Paris: Seuil, 1997.

Favre, Pierre. *La Manifestation*. Paris: Presses de la Fondation nationale des sciences politiques, 1990.

Field, Michel, and Fabienne Waks. *Jours de manif: années 70*. Paris: Les éditions Textuel / Crayon Noir, 1996.

Fillieule, Olivier, and Danielle Tartakowsky. *La Manifestation*. Paris: Presses de Sciences Po, 2013.

Fisher, M. F. K. *How to Cook a Wolf*. New York: North Point Press, 1988.

Fishman, Sarah. *The Battle for Children: World War II, Youth Crime, and Juvenile Justice in Twentieth-Century France*. Cambridge, MA: Harvard University Press, 2002.

Galtier-Boissière, Jean. *Mon Journal pendant l'Occupation*. Paris: Libretto, 2016.

Garçon, Maurice. *Journal 1939–1945*. Paris: Les Belles Lettres, 2015.

Genevée, Frédérick. *Le PCF et la Justice: Des origines aux années cinquante, organisation, conceptions, militants et avocats communistes face aux normes juridiques*. Paris: Presses Universitaires de la faculté de droit de Clermont Ferrand, 2006.

Georges, Monique. *Le Colonel Fabien était mon père*. Paris: Fayard, Mille et une nuits, 2009.

Gildea, Robert. *Fighters in the Shadows: A New History of the French Resistance*. Cambridge, MA: Belknap Press of Harvard University Press, 2015.

Gildea, Robert. *Marianne in Chains: Daily Life in the Heart of France During the German Occupation*. New York: Picador, 2002.

Gilzmer, Mechtild, Christine Levisse-Touzé, and Stefan Martens, eds. *Les Femmes dans la Résistance en France*. Paris: Tallandier, 2003.

Grenard, Fabrice. *La France du marché noir (1940–1949)*. Paris: Payot, 2012.

Guéhenno, Jean. *Journal des années noires, 1940–1944*. Paris: Gallimard, 2002 [1947].

Guillon, Jean-Marie. "Les manifestations de ménagères." In *Les Femmes dans la Résistance en France*, ed. Mechtild Gilzmer, Christine Levisse-Touzé and Stefan Martens, 107–134. Paris: Tallandier, 2003.

Guillon, Jean-Marie. "Les ménagères, du combat quotidien à la Résistance." In *L'engagement et l'émancipation. Ouvrage offert à Jacqueline Sainclivier*, ed. Patrick Harismendy and Luc Capdevila, 279–294. Rennes: Presses Universitaires de Rennes, 2015.

Hamon, Hervé, and Patrick Rotman. *Génération*, vol. 2, *Les années de poudre*. Paris: Seuil, 1988.

Henocq, Michel. *Les Plaques commémoratives des rues de Paris*. Paris: La Documentation française, 1984.

Hillairet, Jacques. *Dictionnaire historique des rues de Paris.* 2 vols. Paris: Les Éditions de Minuit, 1997.

Isorni, Jacques. *Mémoires 1 (1911–1945).* Paris: Éditions Robert Laffont, 1984.

Jackson, Julian. *France: The Dark Years, 1940–1944.* Oxford: Oxford University Press, 2003.

Jaffré, Yves-Frédéric. *Les Tribunaux d'exception, 1940–1962.* Paris: Nouvelles Éditions Latines, 1962.

Jünger, Ernst. *Journaux de guerre II, 1939–1948.* Trans. Henri Plard. Paris: Gallimard, 2008.

Jünger, Ernst. *Second journal parisien, Journal III, 1943–1945.* Trans. Henri Plard. Paris: Christian Bourgois, 1980.

Kedward, H. Roderick. *France and the French: A Modern History.* New York: Overlook, 2006.

Kedward, H. Roderick. *La Vie en Bleu: France and the French Since 1900.* London: Allen Lane, 2005.

Kedward, H. Roderick. *Occupied France: Collaboration and Resistance, 1940–1944.* Hoboken, NJ: Wiley-Blackwell, 1991.

Klarsfeld, Serge. *Le Mémorial de la déportation des Juifs de France.* Paris: Serge and Beate Klarsfeld, 1978.

Koreman, Megan. *The Expectation of Justice: France, 1944–1946.* Durham, NC: Duke University Press, 1999.

Laborie, Pierre, Cécile Vast, and Jean-Marie Guillon, eds. *Penser l'événement, 1940–1945.* Paris: Folio Histoire, 2019.

Lamarre, Hervé [Hervé Villeré]. *L'Affaire de la Section Spéciale I.* Paris: Fayard, 1973.

Lamarre, Hervé. [Hervé Villeré] *L'Affaire de la Section Spéciale II.* Paris: Fayard, 1973.

Lavabre, Marie-Claire. *Le Fil rouge: Sociologie de la mémoire communiste.* Paris: Fondation nationale des sciences politiques, 1994.

Le François, Louis (pseud.) *J'ai faim ... ! Journal d'un Français en France depuis l'Armistice.* New York: Brentano's, 1942.

LeRoy Ladurie, Jacques. *Mémoires, 1902–1945.* Paris: Flammarion/Plon, 1997.

Linet, Roger. *1933–1943: La traversée de la tourmente.* Paris: Éditions Messidor, 1990.

London, Lise. *La Mégère de la rue Daguerre: Souvenirs de résistance.* Paris: Seuil, 1995.

Manceaux, Michèle. *Les Maos en France.* Paris: Gallimard, 1972.

Marcot, François, Bruno Leroux, and Christine Levisse-Touzé. *Dictionnaire historique de la Résistance.* Paris: Laffont, 2006.

Mouré, Kenneth. "Food Rationing and the Black Market in France, 1940–1944." *French History* 24, no. 2 (June 2010): 262–282.

Mouré, Kenneth. "*La Capitale de la Faim*: Black Market Restaurants in Paris, 1940–1944." *French Historical Studies* 38, no. 2 (April 2015): 311–341.

Mouré, Kenneth, and Paula Schwartz. "*On vit mal*: Food Shortages and Popular Culture in Occupied France, 1940–1944." *Food, Culture, and Society* 10, no. 2 (July 2007): 261–295.

Noguères, Henri. *Histoire de la Résistance en France*. 5 vols. Paris: Éditions Robert Laffont, 1967–1981.

Ouzoulias, Albert. *Les fils de la nuit*. Paris: B. Grasset, 1975.

Pennetier, Claude, Jean-Pierre Besse, Thomas Pouty, and Delphine Leneveu, eds. *Les fusillés (1940–1944): Dictionnaire biographique des fusillés et exécutés par condamnation et comme otages ou guillotinés en France pendant l'Occupation*. Ivry-sur-Seine: Les Éditions de l'Atelier, 2015.

Peschanski, Denis, ed. *Vichy 1940–1944: Quaderni e documenti inediti di Angelo Tasca/Archives de guerre d'Angelo Tasca*. Milan: Fondazione Giangiacomo Feltrinelli, 1986.

Peschanski, Denis. « La confrontation radicale. Résistants communistes parisiens vs Brigades spéciales. » In *Les Résistances, miroir des régimes d'oppression*, dir. François Marcot and Didier Musiedlack. *Allemagne, France, Italie*, Besançon: Presses Universitaires de France-Comté, 2006, 335–349.

Pollard, Miranda. *Reign of Virtue: Mobilizing Gender in Vichy France*. Chicago: University of Chicago Press, 1998.

Prévert, Jacques. *Paroles*. Paris: Le Point du Jour, 1946.

Rouquet, François, and Fabrice Virgili. *Les Françaises, les Français et l'Épuration (1940 à nos jours)*. Paris: Gallimard, 2018.

Ruffin, Raymond. *Journal d'un J3*. Paris: Presses de la Cité, 1979.

Ryan, Donna F. "Ordinary Acts and Resistance: Women in Street Demonstrations and Food Riots in Vichy France." *Proceedings of the Annual Meeting of the Western Society for French History* 16 (1989): 400–407.

Sansico, Virginie. *La Justice déshonorée, 1940–1944*. Paris: Tallandier, 2015.

Sauber, Mariana. "Traces fragiles. Les plaques commémoratives dans les rues de Paris." *Annales: Économies, Sociétés, Civilisations* 48, no. 3 (1993): 715–727.

Schwartz, Paula. "Groveling for Lentils: The Culture and Memory of Food Scarcity in Occupied France." In *Food Insecurity: A Matter of Justice, Sovereignty, and Survival*, ed. Molly Anderson and Tamar Mayer. London: Routledge, 2020.

Schwartz, Paula. "The Politics of Food and Gender in Occupied Paris." *Modern and Contemporary France* 7, no. 1 (1999): 35–45.

Schwartz, Paula. "Redefining Resistance: The Activism of Women in Wartime France." In *Behind the Lines: Gender and the Two World Wars,* ed. Margaret Randolph Higonnet et al., 141–153. New Haven: Yale University Press, 1987.

Schwartz, Paula. "La Répression des femmes communistes (1940–1944)." *Les Cahiers de l'Institut d'Histoire du Temps Présent* 31 (1995): 25–37.

Schwartz, Paula. "Résistance et difference des sexes: bilan et perspectives." *Clio: Femmes, Genre, Histoire* 1, no. 1 (1995): 67–88.

Schwartz, Paula. "Résistance et difference des sexes: bilan et perspectives." In *Les Femmes dans la Résistance en France,* ed. Mechtild Gilzmer, Christine Levisse-Touzé, and Stefan Martens, 71–86. Paris: Tallandier, 2003.

Sommier, Isabelle. *La Violence politique et son deuil: L'après 68 en France et en Italie.* Rennes: Presses Universitaires de Rennes, 1998.

Stein, Gertrude. *Wars I Have Seen.* New York: Random House, 1945.

Tartakowsky, Danielle. *Les Manifestations de rue en France, 1918–1968.* Paris: Sorbonne, 1997.

Tartakowsky, Danielle. *Le Pouvoir est dans la rue: Crises politiques et manifestations en France.* Paris: Aubier, 1998.

Taylor, Lynne. *Between Resistance and Collaboration: Popular Protest in Northern France, 1940–1944.* Basingstoke, UK: Macmillan, 1999.

Tillon, Charles. *Les F.T.P.: Témoignage pour server à l'histoire de la Résistance.* Paris: Juilliard, 1962.

Union des Femmes Françaises, ed. *Les Femmes dans la Résistance.* Paris: Rocher, 1977.

Veillon, Dominique. *Vivre et survivre en France, 1939–1947.* Paris: Histoire Payot, 1995.

Veillon, Dominique, and Jean-Marie Flonneau, eds. "Le Temps des restrictions en France (1939–1949)." *Les Cahiers de l'Institut d'histoire du temps présent* 32–33 (May 1996).

Veillon, Dominique, and Paula Schwartz. "Ravitaillement, pouvoirs publics et protestations dans Paris occupé." *Mélanges de l'École française de Rome: Italie et Méditerranée,* no. 112 (2000): 645–653.

Vernay, Laurie. *Lyon des restrictions.* Grenoble: Éditions de terre et de mer, Éditions des 4 Seigneurs, 1982.

Vinen, Richard. *The Unfree French: Life Under the Occupation.* New Haven: Yale University Press, 2006.

von Bueltzingsloewen, Isabelle, ed. *"Morts d'inanition": Famine et exclusions en France sous l'Occupation.* Rennes: Presses Universitaires de Rennes, 2005.

INDEX